BERNARD SUMNER

CONFUSION: JOY DIVISION, ELECTRONIC AND NEW ORDER VERSUS THE WORLD

DAVID NOLAN

Published in 2007 by
INDEPENDENT MUSIC PRESS
Independent Music Press is an imprint of I.M. P. Publishing Limited
This Work is Copyright © I. M. P. Publishing Ltd 2007

Bernard Sumner: Confusion
Joy Division, Electronic And New Order Versus The World
by David Nolan

British Library Cataloguing-in-Publication Data.
A catalogue for this book is available from The British Library.

ISBN 0-9552822-6-8 and 978-0-9552822-6-3

Cover Design by Fresh Lemon.
Edited by Martin Roach.

Printed in the UK.

Independent Music Press
P.O. Box 69,
Church Stretton, Shropshire
SY6 6WZ

Visit us on the web at: www.impbooks.com
and www.myspace.com/independentmusicpress

For a free catalogue, e-mail us at: info@impbooks.com
Fax: 01694 720049

Bernard Sumner

JOY DIVISION, ELECTRONIC AND NEW ORDER VERSUS THE WORLD

by David Nolan

Independent Music Press

About the Author:

David Nolan's first book *I Swear I Was There: The Gig That Changed The World* (Independent Music Press, ISBN 0-9549704-9-7, 2006) uncovered the truth about the Sex Pistols' notorious gig at the Lesser Free Trade Hall in Manchester on June 4, 1976. He's also made over 150 television programmes, including documentaries on the Sex Pistols, The Smiths and Echo And The Bunnymen. He now lectures at Salford University and across the country on writing, directing and broadcasting. One wife, three kids, one cat, one dog. [www.myspace.com/davidnolanwriter]

Praise for *I Swear I Was There: The Gig That Changed The World:*

'Excellent in-depth study, hilarious.' *Uncut*

'Nolan's book has set the record straight.' *BBC Online*

'Nolan constructs the observations and remarks of the crowd with a panoramic blueprint of description that reveals the event in an almost 3D image.' *Entertainment Today*

'Can a book concerning one gig hold the reader's interest from foreword to final chapter? It can [because] Nolan provides a fascinating insight into a gig that really did change the world. 9/10' *Rock Sound*

A fucking great book ... really good!' Peter Hook of New Order

For Kenneth Peter Nolan, my dad.
A very good man, despite his love of jazz.

CONTENTS

ACKNOWLEDGEMENTS

This is not a blow-by-blow account of Bernard Sumner's recording career. It's a book about his life and times, so I have included a discography at the rear to avoid breaking up the narrative. The interviews in this book are my own unless otherwise stated in the rear reference section, again to maintain the flow. With a subject like this, what was crying out to me was a need for some fresh, unheard voices – the *unusual* suspects as well as established players in the tale. Thanks to Tim Ashworth, Andrew Davis, John Berry, Steve Burke, Larry Cassidy, Vin Cassidy, Paul Cons, Elliot Eastwick, Michael Eastwood, Alan Hempsall, Chris Hewitt, Paolo Hewitt, Adriana Leoni, Steve Maguire, Joan Miller, Geoff Moore, James Anthony Pearson, Leroy Richardson, Hillegonda Rietveld, Tom Smetham, Chris Taylor, Jennifer Vaughn, Andrew Wake, Anthony Wilson, Paul Welsh and especially Terry Mason. Everyone gave their time freely – apart from one person who wanted a grand an hour. Thanks also to Rebecca Boulton Negotiations Ltd, Natalie Curtis for guidance and a touch of class and Joy Division Central's Mark Price. Photos, archive pictures and ephemera: Karin Albinsson (karinalbinssonphotography.com), Nat Cassidy, Andrew Davis, Chris Hewitt, Terry Mason, Chris Taylor, Andrew Wake, Paul Welsh and the Local History Library at Salford Museum – they may have pinched the Lowrys, but it's still a great place. You should go. Finally, much appreciation to Martin Roach at Independent Music Press – I'm moving up the ranks of their favourite authors. Slowly.

Explanation

Bernard Sumner and New Order inspire great loyalty
in those who have worked with them. So much so that one person
I wanted to interview for this book felt it only right to check with Peter
Hook, to see if the bass player thought it was okay for them to talk to me.
Hook's response was that it didn't matter about the contents, as Bernard
would never read it.

Bernard Sumner has read this book; it was vital that he be allowed to
respond to some of the issues raised, particularly the very personal ones.

This does not make it an 'authorised' biography – I suspect that Bernard
would rather it didn't exist at all – but at least it makes it a fair one.
And, for once, an accurate one.

To his credit, Bernard took a great deal of time and care offering his
thoughts on the manuscript (these are shown in the text as italics).
As a result, where I had initially made a mistake, I have corrected it. Where
his version differed to someone else's, I've included both. Where Bernard
offers insight into something I could only have guessed at, I have added it
verbatim.

Unofficial biographies often have the sense that the author has the
freedom to write whatever he or she wants, but is hampered by a lack of
insider knowledge. Official ones have the story straight from the horse's
mouth, but sometimes with the suspicion that deals have been struck and
harsher words censored. This is an odd mix of both and is all the better
for it.

Good luck for the future Bernard. Your past has been a fascinating
puzzle to piece together.

David Nolan
Manchester,
Summer 2007

INTRO – LIVE TRANSMISSION

Bold, sharp colours and angles framed by apparently bleak and forbidding backdrops – it's never an easy look to pull off. But that's the job that the northern English pleasure beach resort of Blackpool tries to achieve every day once the summer has gone. The primary visual splashes of laughing day-glo clowns and pink rock stalls fight for attention in front of the harsh grey/brown sludge of the Irish Sea and the tippling rain that seems constant once October comes.

The posters around Blackpool's Empress Ballroom highlight the town's forthcoming delights: Cannon and Ball in 'Home From The Jungle' ... Roy 'Chubby' Brown (stay away if easily offended) ... not to mention the frankly unlikely 'Bradley Walsh And Friends'.

Tonight it's Manchester dance pioneers New Order. The band's huge rig has taken up position at one end of the lavish ballroom and the top tier of lights is scraping the gold leaf paint from the giddy heights of the rococo ceiling. It looks like a rave held inside a giant wedding cake.

Towel roadies are plying their trade on stage as the DJ vibes the crowd with a discreet selection of Haçienda *choons* from back in the day: 808 State's 'Pacific', Grandmaster Flash, Melle Mel and the Furious Five with 'White Lines (Don't Do It)', 'Let The Music Play' by Shannon.

The heaving, largely male crowd nod their heads in approval to the clattering Detroit beats. They're of a type, this audience: thick of neck, cropped of hair and waccy of baccy.

The lights drop and to a spaghetti western intro tape, New Order walk on stage, led by Bernard Sumner from Salford, Greater Manchester. Sumner knows this town – it once provided a refuge for him during the darkest of days, when he had to decide whether it was worth carrying on after the loss of a friend and the apparent end of his short-lived career; dark days from more than a quarter of a century earlier.

A polite lad, the first thing Sumner does is thank the support act, local band and former Factory Records electronic drone and loop merchants Section 25. The band are one of many that Sumner has produced over the years. Later, I ask Section 25 singer Larry Cassidy about the gig and his remark is mistakenly telling. 'It was nice to play with Joy Division again,' he says.

Maybe it wasn't a mistake.

With Sumner are two musicians from Macclesfield in Cheshire, Phil Cunningham and Stephen Morris. Plus one other Salfordian – Peter Hook, who Bernard has known nearly all of his life. Within a month of this Blackpool performance, the relationship between Hook and Sumner – and their musical partnership, which began in the back room of Bernard's grandma's house in 1976 – will be over and done with. Sumner will deal with this crisis in the same way he has handled many difficult things in his life. He will simply not speak of it.

The between-song chat is brief. 'Q', Sumner says. 'Chizz' or maybe even a 'Hissanoowun' if we're lucky. He doesn't say much, this Bernard Sumner, but three songs in and the sprung floor of the Empress Ballroom becomes a bouncy castle.

On stage, the band's leader nearly smiles.

He allows himself a little longer to speak to the audience.

'How times have changed,' says Bernard Sumner ...

CONFUSION ONE: SCUTTLERS & SUEDEHEADS

'The thing is, Mr Nolan,' said Simon from the city register office. 'It's a rather *sensitive* situation.'

I'd been trying to trace the birth records of Bernard Sumner, of Joy Division, New Order, Electronic and then New Order again. Also known as Bernard Dicken, Bernard Albrecht, Bernard Dicken-Albrecht or even Barney Rubble. He's one of the kingpins of post-punk music, a godfather of dance music and someone with an inordinate amount of surnames. When asked about his name changes in the past, his answer was usually an abrupt one: 'Family reasons. I'd rather not go into it,' would be a typical response. In fact, despite being in the public eye for thirty years, very little is known about Bernard Sumner. .

Very little at all.

One thing that is for sure, of course, is that Bernard Sumner was born in Salford. Strange then that the city of Salford's register of births, marriages and deaths had come up with nothing. There was no record of him there at all. Very confusing. I'm advised instead to go across the River Irwell to the city next door – Manchester. The office staff were helpful but refused to give any answers by e-mail. They had to speak to me personally about this *sensitive* situation.

The line went quiet as Simon went to speak to his colleague and then came back to the phone. 'Are you a relative?' he asked on his return. I went into my pre-prepared spiel about being a writer ... looking at the confusions between the Manchester and Salford music scenes ... not being a muck-raker and all the rest.

'It's not that,' interrupted Simon. 'It's just that we want to be sure ... the thing is, you do know that this birth is an *adopted* entry? It's for a child that's been adopted.'

I see.

That *is* a sensitive situation.

Open any music or popular culture book that includes Bernard Sumner – or call up any website – and it will tell you that he was born in Salford. In many cases, it will tell you he was born Bernard Dicken; New Order's very own MySpace will give you that one, for example. It will probably also tell you he went to Salford Grammar School, where a group of pals came together first in friendship and then in music. It will perhaps go into detail about how he went to see the Sex Pistols at the Lesser Free Trade Hall in Manchester on June 4, 1976 and met a young man in the audience called Ian Curtis, how they formed a band originally called Stiff Kittens, then Warsaw ... then Joy Division. There will be tales of suicide, triumph over tragedy, a nightclub called The Haçienda which lodged itself into memory as the most famous club in the world, a massive selling single that lost money every time a copy was sold, a split and then a return.

Trouble is that a lot of these things won't actually be *quite* true.

Not that Bernard has been economical with the truth. More that he seems to have gone out of his way not to correct the misinformation – the *confusion* – that has surrounded his life. Particularly if it involves, as Simon in the register office would put it, a *sensitive* situation. It puts us in a peculiar position. Here's a man who is known and respected around the world, yet no one really knows anything about him.

Until now.

The geographical layouts of Manchester and Salford are another thing that causes outsiders confusion when examining the early life of someone like Bernard Sumner. He is of Salford stock, born in Manchester, but raised back in Salford. Manchester and Salford are two totally separate cities sitting side by side, with only a mucky, twenty yard splash of water to keep them apart.

'With the sheer size of the populations, it's unique for two proper cities to be so close together,' says Tim Ashworth from the Salford Local History Library, surrounded by corporation maps and census reports that chart the city's history. 'It's akin to having Birmingham and Manchester alongside each other. The boundary's always been the River Irwell. Two cities split by a river. Salford's always been more the industrial side, whereas Manchester's more the commercial and retail side of the twin cities.'

So ... Salford did all the work, Manchester took all the credit. This is a theme we will return to.

Salford is older than its sibling neighbour Manchester by twenty five years – it received a charter to hold a market in the year 1230. Manchester took until 1255 to get its marketing act together, but was quicker on the commercial uptake and soon overtook its older brother. Our kid left big brother behind.

Manchester's commercial *nous* and the sheer proximity of the two cities created a historical enmity. In Victorian times, gangs of 'scuttlers' from the two cities – extravagantly dressed youth gangs armed with belts, belt buckles and knives – would carry out violent sorties across the river Irwell, nipping back and forth to tear lumps off each other. 'They used to come over the bridges from Manchester and have a go at the Salford lads,' says Tim Ashworth, 'and the Salford lads used to go over to Manchester. There's always been this rivalry.' This will, again, be a recurring theme in our story.

The three original townships that made up the City of Salford were Pendleton, Salford itself and Broughton. This explains why, although it's a city, Salford has no city centre − another aspect which bamboozles the outsider. As a result of this, Salford has always considered the city centre of Manchester − known to both sides as 'Town' − to be fair game and Salfordians have used it pretty much as they've pleased. Keep an eye on that concept − I *guarantee* it will crop up again.

Historically, Broughton had been the wealthiest part of the district, owned by the Clowes family (pronounced *Clews*) whose name is still carried by at least one street in the area − Great Clowes Street, where the young Bernard would have seen his first films at the Victoria Picture House. By 1870, the Clowes family started to sell off sections of their land and terraced housing was immediately built on the sites. Along with the terraced housing came absentee landlords, slums and eventually that *Coronation Street* look. Lots of people are still under the impression that 'The Street' is set in Manchester. It's not − it's a Salford thing.

Although his family came from Salford, Bernard Sumner was actually born in Crumpsall Hospital, across the River Irwell in what was then called the County Borough of Manchester. Crumpsall Hospital is now called the North Manchester General. Bernard's mother was called Laura Sumner and it's likely that her parents − John Sumner and Laura Senior − took her to Crumpsall across the river to Manchester, because of the special circumstances surrounding Bernard's birth. Laura Sumner's life had not been easy thus far. Physically disabled, with speech difficulties and confined to a wheelchair, she'd always had special needs, long before such a polite, modern term had been coined.

Bernard Sumner: 'My mother suffered from cerebral palsy.'

Now, about to give birth for the first time, her needs would have merited particular, very special medical attention indeed. Despite the understandable concerns surrounding the birth, as well as some considerable obstacles, Bernard was born on January 4, 1956. He'd never know his biological father. He took his mother's maiden name and so, despite the many surnames he would use in the future, his real name is ... Bernard Sumner.

On January 17, nearly two weeks after Bernard's difficult delivery, Mr E. Kearsley, the registrar of births, filled in the child's birth certificate. Laura Sumner's name appears in the section reserved for mother. Sections four and six – the spaces normally used for the name and occupation of the father – have been voided by Mr Kearsley with two firm strokes of his pen. An additional box filled in at a later date by Superintendent Registrar Mr J. Radcliffe adds the simple declaration ... *adopted*. But that would come later.

Bernard's mother Laura lived with her parents at 11 Alfred Street, Lower Broughton. Two up, two down. Front door and the pavement separated only by a single, buffed, red step. There were cobbles on the street – that most Northern of images – and they stayed there till the road was flattened to make way for an industrial estate at the end of the 1970s. Lower Broughton was a bustling, self-contained community, 12,000 strong. Bernard's cousins, the Grimshaws, lived two doors down and were his closest pals. This was tight-fitting, back-to-back housing, overlooked by the enormous chimney of the nearby cloth finishing works. Other employment possibilities were provided by the Broughton Sack Works, a boot and shoe factory and the nearby Corporation yard. Entertainment? That would be the Victoria Picture House round the corner on Great Clowes Street. Hammer horrors on a Friday night, Flash Gordon serials on a Saturday morning. It was a tough area that largely played it straight. At least with its own. If you needed anything by way of a reminder to stay on the straight and narrow, there was always the main tower of Her Majesty's Prison Manchester – better known as Strangeways – just across the river, staring at you across the rooftops and straight through your bedroom window.

After Bernard was born, mum and baby settled back into the tiny house at 11 Alfred Street with Laura's parents. A few months after his arrival, a strange thing happened just the other side of the river. They started making television programmes from a studio within walking distance of Alfred Street. Granada Television, founded by socialist entrepreneur Sydney Bernstein, would soon dominate the nation's television sets with its flagship programme *Coronation Street* – a drama series reflecting life on the very cobbled streets where Bernard lived.

More than twenty years later, Bernard would walk through the doors of Granada himself and appear on one of its programmes, an appearance that would change his life.

By the time Bernard was five, there was a major change in the Sumner household, after Laura married local man, James Dickin, who was also physically challenged and wore leg calipers; he too moved into the tiny Alfred Street house. Bernard was adopted by James and they became a real family, but they were to remain living with John Sumner and Laura Senior. Bernard's school friends recall the major part his grandparents played in his life – many believed that he had actually been brought up by his grandparents. John and Laura Senior certainly oversaw a unique household and their comforting influence was considerable. Grandad John had a collection of war memorabilia that he kept in the back room at Alfred Street. There was a bomb shelter in the yard of the house and Bernard and the Grimshaws also used to play in the underground shelters at the end of the street; reminders of the war that had only ended little more than two decades before. 'When I was a kid, there was loads of talk about the war,' Bernard later recalled. 'It made a really big impression on me.'

Bernard's first school was again within the familiar comfort zone of the nearby streets, St Clement's Church of England School on Lowcock Street, 300 yards away from the Sumner/Dickin household. 'I was rubbish in lessons,' stated Sumner in *The Salford Advertiser* in 2005, 'especially maths. But intelligence is not about passing exams.' Still, a bright kid was Bernard, with a knack for drawing, although encouragement wasn't forthcoming at St Clement's. 'When I was a little kid,' he told Radio Clyde in 1985, 'at primary school, I used to write a lot of poetry. The headmaster told me I'd never get anywhere by doing that sort of thing so I should stop doing it. So I stopped doing it.'

Bernard Sumner: 'The headmaster told me that, "Where you come from, you'll end up working in a factory." I hated some of the teachers. I loved the school as it was/is my only link with that community and my youth. It still stands today.'

What Bernard actually did was what many a bright kid from a working-class home did. He sat the 11-Plus examination, the passport to a 'better' school and a Holy Grail for many families from disadvantaged backgrounds. The school he got into was Salford Grammar, which had a history stretching back to 1914, although there are records of a grammar school in the area going back to the early eighteenth century. The modern Salford Grammar site, built in 1956, was the first choice school in the area that attracted kids from the satellite 'villages' (the second choice being Salford Technical High School). The two schools stood virtually side by side, separated by a much fought over stretch of playing field.

'It was deemed that the grammar school was better,' remembers local lad Terry Mason, whose life would become entwined with Bernard's for the next quarter of a century. 'The people that got the best results were given the choice. Most of them chose the grammar school. We were so poor we didn't know the difference. I wanted to go to the tech high school because the grammar wore green blazers and I didn't fancy that. The tech had a swimming pool. A much better deal.' Broad as a door with a wide smile that distracts from his considerable size, Mason had known of Bernard and another Grammar lad, Peter Hook, as a young child but had temporarily lost touch. 'If Salford Council hadn't decided that it would be a good idea to put a path across the playing field ... that's all they did ... I would have never met them again. Simple as that.'

To be nearer to the new school, Bernard, his mum Laura and James Dickin left the cocoon of Alfred Street and moved to a modern flat on the other side of Great Clowes Street, close to the Broughton Tavern.

Bernard Sumner: 'This was because she wanted a sense of independence.'

Although this was a new home for the Dickins, Bernard would still spend a large amount of time at his grandparent's house. Laura Junior now had access to an electric wheelchair, greatly increasing her mobility and independence.

'She was *very* disabled,' says Terry Mason. 'She was in a powered chair thirty years ago. The NHS wouldn't be giving them out readily. She had problems speaking. She was 'all there' but her body just wasn't doing it for her. If you went round to the flat, his bedroom was the first on the right by the door. You went straight in. You didn't pry. His step-dad had calipers certainly and he had an adapted Mini.'

The 'better' school that Bernard had joined aged 11 wouldn't last for long, at least not in the way he knew it. At the start of term in September 1969, it was decided to merge the technical school with their 'posher' arch enemies across the playing field, Salford Grammar. The new Salford Technical Grammar School existed until the sweeping changes brought by the comprehensive school system in 1973. It merged with Pendleton High School for Girls and is now known as Buile Hill High School.

This new mixed school – rather than simply the grammar – was the real basis of Bernard's future and his musical career. 'I think there were a lot of thick people in Salford in the 1950s and 1960s,' says Terry Mason. 'A lot of people from the grammar school and especially the technical side were thick. It's not the great seat of learning that grammar schools are nowadays.'

The blend of different backgounds and ideas from the two schools would be vital to the mix. At this stage, gangs and cliques were centred on friendships, camaraderie and fashion rather than music. 'That's where I met Barney [Bernard] and Hooky [Peter Hook] ... at Salford Technical

Grammar School,' says former pupil John Berry today. 'I didn't know them before secondary school, but I knew them pretty soon after I started at Salford and started knocking about with them. Barney was called Bernard Dickin then.'

Bernard made no mention of his adoption to his new-found friends. When I showed Bernard's birth certificate to Terry Mason, more than forty years after they first met, he was stunned. 'I never knew ...' he said, short of words. 'You could write a play about this birth certificate.' A precedent was being set here. From here on in, if Bernard felt uncomfortable about something, the shutters would come down. If he didn't want to talk about something ... he didn't talk about it. Ever.

The merging of the two schools made for new tribes, new networks, new allegiances. 'We were all people who'd passed the 11-Plus, but for one reason or another were deemed not suitable to go to Salford Grammar School,' says John Berry. 'The Technical School lads were generally a lot rougher. They were from Kersall, Ordsall, Seedley, Weaste, Broughton ... not the Jewish population [of Salford] like the grammar school. There wasn't that mix of people you got at Salford Grammar. The Technical boys were mainly white, working-class lads.'

Terry Mason points out that there were divisions and hierarchies within the district: 'All of Salford back in those days was generally full of two-up, two-down, near-slum housing. There were perceived differences in areas being better. So, near Regent Road was seen to be slightly better than living near to Ordsall Lane ... Weaste was slightly better than round Langworthy Road. Seedley was 'posh' ... as you moved towards Buile Hill, you were moving into high society as such.'

'We were at the bullying end of the spectrum, rather than the bullied,' says John Berry. 'Not the top end, but the bottom end of the bullying spectrum. Me more than the others. Barney and Hooky were quite good at avoiding the grief. They were quite into robbing ... going down to Islington Mill in Salford and robbing Harrington jackets. Various misdemeanours ... but nothing hardcore criminal.'

> *Bernard Sumner: 'We might have stolen a few things,*
> *but [me and Hooky] were never bullies.'*

Terry Mason: 'I used to be dead hard ... up until I was five or six. The whole school was streetwise.' Bernard – good at art, bad at maths – held one teacher in particular contempt: Mr Barclay, the maths teacher. The 'slipper' (actually a sports shoe) was one of the chosen methods of corporal punishment at the school – and Mr Barclay would slipper Bernard for not doing his maths homework and copying work from the 'swots'.

A gang of lads was forming – based around Bernard, Peter Hook, Terry Mason and John Berry. 'When your 11 and 12, it's a bit more fluid on the peer group front,' observes Berry. 'It solidifies as you get older and we sort of drifted around each other. We weren't the kind of people who'd get expelled. And we certainly weren't consistently bullied. I wasn't bullied. But I did tend to bully. Nothing to be particularly proud of, but it went on.

Things really started to solidify about the time we really seriously got into football and seriously got into fashion. Which may have been around 12 or 13, I'd say. It was when the transition from skinhead to smoothie took place, the battle lines started to get drawn up. It was like a uniform with subtle differences that could be spotted by the cogniscenti.'

Nearly forty years on, Berry – dressed all in black and sporting designer specs – is still able to remember the clothes worn by the Salford gang down to the last, buttoned-down detail. 'A crombie jacket in winter,' he recalls. 'If you were skint or you got no style, you got it from Warren Andrew ... or if you had a bit of style you got it hand-made at Montague Burton. The difference was probably eight or nine quid at Warren Andrew's and seventeen quid at Monty's. Choose your lining, choose your cut. Terry Mason would have an experiment with something that didn't quite fucking work. He was always out there, Terry! When we went to Pips, he was always the guy who had his hair waved, he was the guy who had a little Zoot suit – not a Zoot suit as we would know it today – a bum freezer jacket, soul-style. Parallels [parallel width trousers] starting off at 16-inch ... over the years going up to stupid widths like 30-inch. Fairisle jumpers, patch-work jumpers, Ben Sherman's, black button-downs, platform shoes ... eventually, Oxford bags. All that crap. There was always someone who, instead of going for twelve buttons down here, they'd go for fifteen. Socks were important then, red socks, white socks, diamond pattern socks. Hooped socks? Nah.'

As the 1960s ended, the smoothie 'suedehead' style had taken a grip of Bernard and his gang. It was smarter, easier to manage and frankly safer than the earlier skinhead look. 'Where I lived,' said Sumner in Dave Haslam's *Manchester, England*, 'you had to be a skinhead or you got beaten up, basically.'

Suedehead style involved a grown-out crop haircut, softer brogue and loafer footwear, formal suits and even flares. The music of choice was geared towards glam rock rather than the reggae or bluebeat favoured by skins.

'I don't remember Barney and Hooky setting too many trends,' says John Berry. 'Although Barney always looked good in his gear. He had that sort of face shape and build where he carried it pretty well. He certainly had a scooter. It seemed to be week on week that there was some new nuance appearing on the skinhead/sudehead fashion scene that you had to have. We liked loads of music and used to go to gigs regularly. It felt like once a week or more. I saw Deep Purple ... Fuckin' hated them as a matter of principal, but we went to see them! Bachman Turner Overdrive. Thin Lizzy supporting Slade. The Sweet, T-Rex, Bowie, Roxy.'

By this stage in the early 1970s, Peter Hook's taste in music was greatly limited by the lack of live venues that were geared towards a younger crowd. 'I think the highlight of my musical career,' he says, 'was seeing the Salford Jets funnily enough at [local 'chicken-in-a-basket' venue] The Willows, when they were going through an Alvin Stardust phase, which was quite interesting. The Sweet were big, that's the only group that I can think of apart from [cabaret stalwarts] The Reg Coates Experience. I'm sure music did exist in Manchester, but they were the only ones I knew.'

Bernard Sumner: 'Mmm ... very puzzling.'

John Berry adds: 'As a group, me and Terry – and I'd include Barney and Hooky in that – we had a 'punk' ethos. In that we were anti-this, that and the other ... for the sake of it.'

'Barney was always quite stand-offish, always an outsider,' Berry recalls. 'He had a pretty horrible childhood apparently. He was a bit rootless, somehow. We knew his mum and dad were disabled – he seemed to be brought up by his grandparents ...

Bernard Sumner: 'I wasn't brought up by my grandparents
– they helped my mother, who did the best she could. This was also
complicated by the fact that my grandmother was left
blind after an eye operation that went wrong in the late 1960s.'

... He was never one of the lads, but he was always up for it. There was always weird tales about Barney ... like always wanting things like spitting in your face contests. You'd go to his house and he'd go, 'Do you want summit to eat?' and you'd go, 'Yeah' and he'd give you a cream cake and he'd be sat there looking at you. You'd open it out and there'd be twenty fucking laxative tablets in the cream cake!'

As school life ended and the 'real' world beckoned, the gang expanded. Joining Barney, Hooky, Terry Mason and John Berry were 'Crazy Mike' Thomas, Baz Benson, Dan the Man Lavin, Mini Cropper Cooper, Dek Harrison, Nidder Gresty and Danny Lee and Wroey.

'There wasn't a hierachy as such,' says Terry Mason, a man who will always plump for an exotic turn of phrase when given the option. 'We were more like a number of *federations*. The coming together was all around scooters. Barney had one. With Barney's situation at home, money doesn't seem to have been an object. Barney had a GP200. That was the last couple of years when cool skins – suedeheads – had scooters. After that the licensing changed, so people ended up with fizzies [50cc mopeds]. Barney was always getting good presents off his family. He'd have a chronograph watch, his scooter was newer than anyone else's.

We were cool young lads. To park up on your scooter outside the chippy, you'd find girls coming up and talking to you. That's the whole point of scooters ... it's like being in a band, only you've got a twist grip. Salford precinct was all new then – not like the Dodge City it is now – there was a lot of young people out and about. We used to go to a nighclub called The Cattle Market. Because it used to be ... a cattle market. Traditional territorial club. You knew almost everyone in there. It was safe. But God help anyone from outside.' John Berry remembers the group's other key interests: 'A major part of our 'going out' life was either clubs or bands or footie or the boozer,' he says.

The gang would do what most kids would do at the time, hang around 'Town'. Deansgate, the main drag that shadows the route of the River Irwell, was the key gathering point. There wasn't that much to catch a young lad's attention apart from cafes and an amusingly-named travel agents called Gaytours. Not much, apart from the glittering delights of the Mamelok music store and its jaw-dropping, rotating display of guitars. 'Mamelok had a turntable of guitars in the window. You'd just *stare* ... Fucking *hell*. None of us could play, but you'd go, "That's the one I'd have. I don't want one made of wood, that's an old man's guitar. *That's* the one."' The main jaw-droppers in Mamelok's window were British-made Shergold guitars, some of which were double-necked. The turntable of delights clearly made a major dent on Bernard: Shergold would be his guitar of choice when Joy Division began to break through.

The real world was about to arrive like an unwanted guest for the Salford gang. The decade was almost half-way over, yet little progress seemed to have been made in the twin cities of Manchester and Salford. It didn't feel like the hi-tech 1970s promised on predictive television shows like *Tomorrow's World*. That show's presenters had been foretelling a space-age world since the 1960s, but no jetpacks or meals-in-a-pill had arrived as yet. However, one thing that featured on the programme did seem genuinely futuristic: a group of young Germans playing electronic music on cobbled together 'synthesisers' and drums, played with what appeared to be plugged in knitting needles. Probably more chance of us all getting jet packs than that catching on.

The North West of England was still stuck in its post-war doldrums – bomb sites were still to be seen either side of the River Irwell – with little to show by way of advancement in the twin cities other than high rise blocks built out of necessity rather than design. Bernard would have several brushes with the world of work, but compared to the 'dead end' jobs endured by many of his peers, he would fall very much on his feet. 'I only excel at something I'm interested in,' is Bernard's own self-assessment of his abilities. 'I can't make myself do something I don't like. I can't knuckle under.'

Some of the work he did before joining a band is still to be seen to this day. You'll be surprised how familiar you are with the the things young Bernard Dickin did before he became a musician. His work is easy to find … it's there … up above the streets and houses …

CONFUSION TWO: PAINT THE WHOLE WORLD WITH A RAINBOW

Bernard didn't like school and school was none too keen on him. 'When I was at school,' he later recalled in *Observer Music Monthly*, 'if you were creative, it seemed to puzzle them and even though they taught art and classical music, anything contemporary was ignored. Which of course was what we were interested in, so this resulted in a Do-It-Yourself culture. You were also made to feel useless if you weren't any good at maths – logarithms or algebra. I thought that was a load of bollocks, so I just ignored school and, when it was over, I did what I wanted to do all along.' After leaving Salford Grammar with two O Levels – in Art and English – the teenage Bernard wanted to go to art college, to hone the natural skills he had.

> Bernard Sumner: 'I was accepted at Bolton College of Art
> but as my family could not afford it, I was "spoken to", and had to get
> a job at Salford Town Hall to contribute to the family finances.'

Bernard's entry into local authority administration was his one and only experience of a 'normal' job. 'I worked at Salford Town Hall in the Treasury department, sending out rates bills,' he remembered, speaking on Channel 4's *Star Test*. 'I had to stick letters down, 356 a day. It was incredibly boring. Most of the people there were incredibly boring as well. But it gave me a great shock and it gave me a jolt to go out and do something interesting. You learn off everything.'

Most of the others in the Salford gang got out of school as quickly as possible aged 16. 'I didn't know many people who went to university,' says John Berry. 'They were few and far between. My peer group got jobs, basically.'

Bernard Dickin bided his time and got his next job aged 18, over the river in Manchester. And he got lucky. His second full-time employment was at Stop Frame Films on Peter Street, just off the main city thoroughfare of Deansgate (home to Mamelok's Amazing Rotating Guitar Display). The fascination with the Mamelok display would remain a regular lunchtime appointment.

Peter Street was, and is, steeped in history. It was the site of the Peterloo Massacre where, in 1819, reformist protestors were cut to ribbons by the Manchester and Salford Yeomanry and the Fifteenth Hussars as they went at the crowd with sabres. Eleven were killed and 400 injured.

If you looked out of the window of Stop Frame, you'd see the city's famous Free Trade Hall – said to be the only building in the world named after an *idea*. This is where the rock gods of the day would come to play – David Bowie, Lou Reed, Kiss – it was also the scene of rock's most famous heckle. When Bob Dylan swapped his acoustic for an electric guitar in May 1966, a member of the Manchester audience shouted 'Judas!' at the tousle-haired troubador. 'I don't *belieeeeeve* you,' Dylan replied, in a very Dylan-esque kind of way. The teenage Bernard Dickin was a considerable fan of Dylan, who was still a hip name to drop in 1974.

Stop Frame was part of a bustling cluster of creative firms under the umbrella of Manchester Post Production Services. 'That's where I met Bernard, about 1974,' remembers his work colleague Chris Taylor. 'I finished at college in Liverpool, went for a job at Stop Frame and there was Bernard. He was a little younger than me and [had wanted to go] to Salford Art College. Bernard was the junior – the runner. He did all the odd jobs and errands. Bernard was the youngster as it were – one grade up from tea boy.'

Under one roof at Peter Street was an self-contained artistic community geared towards supplying the film, television and advertising industries. Film editing, sound work and animation all went on at Manchester Post Production. A key client for the companies operating out of Peter Street was Granada Television, situated just a few hundred yards away on Quay Street. The company had done well since it started broadcasting four months after Bernard was born – it now dominated the independent sector, with its mix of soap opera, drama, comedy and current affairs. The company was so productive they had to farm work out to the likes of Manchester Post Production Services. As a result, a steady stream of runners – television's do-anything dogsbodies – would spend their days ferrying film cannisters and quarter-inch sound reels across Deansgate between the two sites.

Within four years, Bernard would walk from Stop Frame to Granada with his guitar in his hand, to make his onscreen debut at Granada's Studio Two as a member of Joy Division.

One of Stop Frame's earliest pieces of work is still one of its most famous: the animated title sequence to children's show *Rainbow*. The programme is consistently voted one of the favourite kids' shows of all-time and its gently sung yet upbeat theme song stays lodged in the head of anyone who hears it: 'Up above the streets and houses, rainbow flying high ...' They also did the cartoon shorts that were to be seen in between the surreal yet slightly suspect antics of Geoffrey, Bungle, Zippy and George, called 'Swallow Street' and 'Cockleshell Bay'. Their work proved so popular that a feature about Stop Frame was published in *TV Times* magazine; Bernard and Chris Taylor can be seen on the team photograph that accompanied the piece, alongside their older and considerably hairier colleagues. Today, Chris Taylor looks back fondly at the Stop Frame years. 'It was a weird and wonderful place,' he says. 'In fact, I'd say it was unique.'

But despite the apparent success and the non-stop supply of work from Granada, Stop Frame went out of business in late 1975. This was heartbreaking news for the young team, starting out in a creative world of work. The firm's leading lights, Brian Cosgrove and Mark Hall, gathered Bernard, Chris Taylor and the other members of staff together and told them they were going to go it alone and there would be jobs for all of them at the new company ... if they could wait for a few months. 'Stupidly we believed it ... and even more stupidly, it happened,' says Taylor.

Although the Stop Frame team had gone their separate ways, they stayed in touch, helping plan the new company. 'We'd meet at each others' houses to get ideas together,' enthuses Taylor, as we chat at his Derbyshire home. 'Ideas that became shows like *Chorlton And The Wheelies* and *Jamie And The Magic Torch*. Bernard would come round to my flat in Didsbury to catalogue a complete library of Letratset we'd taken from Stop Frame and things like that. We kept going until the new company got going.'

Brian Cosgrove and Mark Hall were true to their word and by May 1976, Cosgrove Hall Productions had opened up for business in an old tobacco warehouse in the bohemian south Manchester suburb of Chorlton. The old Stop Frame team was back together again, including Bernard and Chris Taylor. 'I became a director and directed some of the first puppet shows – I did the first series of *Chorlton And The Wheelies,*' says Taylor. 'Bernard became the paint and trace department – doing the animation cells – all on his own. He was the entire department. Bernard was quite a quiet guy, but very friendly and sociable, very well liked. He was Mr Popular – everybody liked Bernard.'

To mark the reunion in Chorlton, a team photo was taken in the small country park to the rear of the building. Amongst the hippies and hairies of the Cosgrove Hall team can be spotted Bernard, resplendent in a striped tank-top.

Bernard Sumner: 'They weren't really hippies and hairies,
they were cool people to work with and good fun.'

The 'hippy' vibe was part and parcel of what Cosgrove Hall was all about. Chris Taylor still walks the walk today, with his hair worn long and his earring firmly in place. The studios can also claim another staff member turned rock star. John Squire of The Stone Roses would also later work at Cosgrove Hall, making props for several productions, including *The Wind In The Willows*. 'Never employ musicians ...' jokes Chris Taylor.

Bernard was never keen on the daily journey from Salford to Cosgrove Hall in Chorlton. The streets where he grew up were disappearing on a daily basis. The times were changing. The houses built on the wealth of the Clowes family had fallen too far into disrepair to be salvaged. Lower Broughton's streets were being cleared. Alfred Street – along with Number 11, his grandparents' home that became his home – would soon follow. A picture taken of the street about this time shows the houses being boarded up one by one, as families are moved out prior to demolition.

Bernard Sumner: 'This was a very distressing time for my grandmother as, by
this time, she lived alone (Grandfather died after a prolonged illness after having
a stroke) and the memory of her house boarded up still haunts me now.'

There's now no trace of Alfred Street on any modern map – like the street, Bernard's Salford childhood was becoming a distant memory. 'I realised that I could never go back to that happiness,' he later told journalist Jon Savage. 'For me, Joy Division was about the death of my community and my childhood.'

'We all seemed to be stuck at the age of 16 or 17, mentally,' says Terry Mason. 'We were all still living at home. We all had junior jobs, enough money to go out at weekends, no responsibilities. You'd give your mam £15 on Friday, the rest was yours. Very nice lifestyle to be honest.' Mason claims that this 'young' mentality that the gang possessed remained for several years to come. They were streetwise, yet naive. They would remain this way up until the death of Joy Division's singer, Ian Curtis.

With money in their pockets, the Salford group's socialising increased, with regular jaunts across the river to drink in the pubs and clubs of Manchester. 'They all had jobs of one sort or another,' recalls John Berry. 'Hooky was working at Manchester Liners – the docks – Barney was at Cosgrove Hall, something to do with the arty side. Straight from school day jobs.' Bernard also had a steady girlfriend – Sue Barlow from nearby Peel Green – who quickly became a regular fixture in their otherwise male-dominated world.

'Hooky had a girlfriend called Maureen,' says Mason, 'who lived off Langworthy Road. No one had even thought about being in a band up until then. Barney's favourite act was Santana, but a working-class oik would never dream of being in a band.' But that's exactly what Bernard did dream of and soon he bought a guitar and a small amp to start learning from scratch.

Boozing, clothes, scooters, music and boozing. As the summer of 1976 approached, the Salford group's desire for fresh, night-time entertainment increased. They were crying out for something new. It lead them to an upstairs theatre on Peter Street, that was just across the road from Bernard's old workplace at Stop Frame. A theatre called the Lesser Free Trade Hall.

'I remember being on holiday in Torquay,' says Peter Hook. 'Me and four friends were sleeping in the car for three weeks – it was hell. I remember getting the *Melody Maker* and [the front cover had] a picture of a group fighting – and it was the Sex Pistols and I thought ... *my God, this is not the normal thing.* It was the day we were coming home and we drove home to Manchester. I used to read the *Manchester Evening News* cover to cover all the time and I spotted a little tiny advert for the Lesser Free Trade Hall for the Sex Pistols plus support. And it was fifty pee. Amazing.'

The Sex Pistols were – on the face of it – a new young band from London. They had only played their first gig in November, as support to Bazooka Joe (featuring Adam Ant) at St Martin's School of Art in London. In fact, guitarist Steve Jones and drummer Paul Cook had been together since the early 1970s in line-ups called The Strand and Swank. The first mention of them is as part of the text for a tee-shirt sold in 1974 at a London clothes store run by Vivienne Westwood and Malcom McLaren. The item of clothing sold at the shop – known as SEX – refers to *Kutie Jones and His Sex Pistols,* a reference to the fact that Steve Jones was then the lead singer. It wasn't until Saturday boy Glen Matlock and teen-about-town John Lydon/Johnny Rotten joined that they became known as simply Sex Pistols. They were making waves in London but outside of the capital they were viewed virtually as a music press fabrication; a band that couldn't play and didn't care.

It would light a spark of recognition within the Salford gang.

Anti-this, anti-that, anti-the-other.

John Berry recalls that the group were getting tired of seeing bands they didn't actually like that much: 'We were always reading the music press and looking for something that didn't quite fit. We were inveterate gig-goers. We had a dabble with Dr Feelgood. That seemed like *fuckin' hell, this is where it's happening!* We were [naive] as far as music was concerned. We had no sense of musical history. We wouldn't know if something had come from [influential 1969 garage rock compilation] *Nuggets* or whatever. We were kids. We didn't know that people would start cutting their hair and binning the flares. We didn't have a clue. We just read the reviews [of the Sex Pistols] in the *NME* ... this lot are *potty*, they can't sing, they can't play, they cause bother wherever they go ... it just seemed to fit with where we come from.'

A great deal of heat has been generated about the events of June 4, 1976, at the Lesser Free Trade Hall, Manchester. It has become part of the Great Manchester Myth: Sex Pistols come to Manchester and half of Manchester forms a band. The other half spend the next thirty years arguing about who was actually there that night. It features as one of the key initial scenes of the film *24 Hour Party People* [the semi-fictionalised account of the rise and fall of Factory Records], has been the subject of at least two documentaries and can cause a punch up to this day. At the risk of spoiling the fun, the truth is, as ever, fairly far from the legend.

The gig had been organised by two students from ten miles up the road at the Bolton Institute of Technology – Pete McNeish and Howard Trafford. They were desperate to bring the Sex Pistols up north after seeing them twice in the space of one weekend in High Wycombe and Welwyn Garden City in February. Not only did they want the Pistols to play, but part of the deal was that Pete and Howard's band – Buzzcocks – would be the warm-up act. They had tried and failed to convince the college authorities in Bolton to let the Pistols play there. So they found an alternative venue.

'We found out we could hire the Lesser Free Trade Hall for about £20 or something,' says McNeish, who by this stage had changed his name to Pete Shelley [Trafford was now Howard Devoto]. 'Just doing the maths, we knew that if we got forty people in, we would be in profit, so it seemed like a good idea.' The Lesser Free Trade Hall was a small seated venue above the main hall, sometimes used by left of centre theatre groups.

After a disastrous try-out gig eight weeks earlier, Buzzcocks conceded they weren't ready to act as support to the Sex Pistols, so Bolton heavy rock covers band Solstice was drafted in. Howard had met their lead singer Geoff Wild during a summer packing stint at a Manchester factory.

Dave 'Zok' Howard, Solstice's keyboard player remembers it as a great gig – until the main act appeared. 'We played and we'd gone down all right. Then this lot [Sex Pistols] came on and they were bloody crap.'

Among the audience that night was Steve Diggle – who would join the Buzzcocks that very night – Smith-to-be Morrissey, TV presenter Tony Wilson, Mark E Smith of The Fall, writer Paul Morley, Manchester punk scene legend Jon the Postman ... and a gang of boozy, twenty-year-old suedeheads from Salford. Records still held in Manchester's Central Library show that Howard and Pete had sold a mighty 28 tickets for the gig. 'In Manchester, you'd play to half-empty halls,' John Lydon said thirty years on. 'But they'd all be there with *notepads.*'

The Salford gang went for a few liveners in Cox's Bar round the back of the venue, before heading up the stairs at the side to the small theatre above the main Free Trade Hall. 'There was acres of space in there that night,' says John Berry. 'There was me, Terry, Barney, Hooky and a guy called Crazy Mike from school. He never got into this stuff – I think it was his first and last dabble with punk. We kept a low profile because of the potential for things to kick off. Having never been to a punk gig before, we didn't know what punk was. We were a little bit wary. It was a case of sinking down in your seat and waiting.'

Paul Welsh, editor of Manchester music fanzine *Penetration* was also there that night. 'The thing I remember the most was sitting in the bar with my friends expecting a band in silver trousers, like Iggy Pop or the New York Dolls. Suddenly, the band came into the bar to buy bottles of lager to take on stage ... ugly bastards in strategically ripped charity shop clothing. The Pistols were the first band to play the sort of music we'd all been playing in our bedrooms on our own guitars for years,' he says. 'They were the catalyst, but I'm sure it could have happened at any time, the scene was like a champagne cork ready to pop.'

What the audience got that night was, in retrospect, really quite straightforward. Four young lads barely free of their teens, playing some Mod cover versions, some Stooges songs and a few originals. Drums, bass, guitar and vocal. The lead singer was confrontational, leaning out into the audience from the lip of the stage, inviting those who didn't like what they heard to fuck off.

'With hindsight,' reflects John Berry, 'Rotten was doing his act. Afterwards, when they'd finished, he was sweet as a nut. Really friendly. He was chatting with the audience. So all the, "*Fuck off you cunts!*" ... it was all a big act.'

It was a short, noisy set. Some of the audience looked at the Pistols and thought *That's fantastic, I want to do that!*; others saw the Pistols and thought *That's shit, I could do better than that!*

'I had my mouth open,' remembers Tony Wilson. 'Swallowing fucking flies. It shows the wonderfulness of the event, the fact that the capacity is only about 150 at the Lesser Free Trade Hall ... seven and a half thousand people claim to have been there.'

Paul Welsh took pictures of the band that night and changed his magazine's content straight away to reflect what had gone on. 'I walked out of that gig on air, I was so blown away by it, it was like a breath of fresh air and they never lived up to that first gig again. However, I do question 'The Gig That Changed The World' idea. I think everything would probably have happened anyway. I was there ... probably the only person nobody's ever mentioned [being there]. My girlfriend and eight other friends were there and I know Pete Shelley and Howard Devoto were there. As for the rest of them ... maybe I was blinded by the show and I didn't notice the others.'

'It was *so* loud,' says John Berry. 'The volume was phenomenal. Whether they were geared up to play the main Free Trade Hall I don't know. But, oh, shit, it was loud.'

To this day, Peter Hook is the most vocal when it comes to the mantra of the Lesser Free Trade Hall and the effect it had on the Manchester scene. 'It was the most shocking thing I've ever seen in my life. We just looked at each other and thought, *My God!* They [the Pistols] looked like they were having such a good time, you just thought ... *God, we could do that ...*'

'They seemed to be getting on with it and having a pretty good time,' remembers Terry Mason. 'We thought, *Why can't we have a go?*' Even those who have no time for punk agree that the Lesser Free Trade Hall was the starting point for an extraordinary string of events in Bernard's life. 'Had it not been for punk rock,' said future guitarist with The Smiths and Electronic collaborator Johnny Marr, in *Magnet* magazine, 'Bernard would have been completely lost and constrained and stifled because of what punk rock was supposed to be like: freeing up people who were really imaginative and genuinely artistic. Bernard is a real punk.'

The Salford suedeheads returned home across the river.

Bernard and Peter Hook had been stopped in their tracks by the Sex Pistols.

The following day, Hook bought a bass guitar from Mazel Radio, a second-hand electricals shop near Piccadilly train station. A flamboyant gesture, especially as he claims he handed over £35 for the instrument. That was an inordinately large amount of money for an office worker to shell out. '£35 may have been an extraordinary amount of money, but it was a lot less than anywhere else,' points out Terry Mason, reflecting just how expensive new guitars were in those days.

Tellingly, Bernard's reaction was more practical. He would finally knuckle down to learning how to play the guitar he already had. If the Sex Pistols could do it, he could do it. They were the same age as him – Johnny Rotten is, in fact, three weeks younger than Bernard – and seemed to be cut from very similar cloth. They weren't flash or pompous, they were young men in a big hurry – in their music obviously, but also in their ambition.

The Sex Pistols *wanted* it.

And so did Bernard.

He, along with Terry Mason, would be the organisers, the ones who would make things happen, if nothing else, because Bernard was the only one among them who had a telephone. June 5, 1976 would be the first day of Bernard's musical career. From that day onwards, painting animation cells for Cosgrove Hall would have to take a back-seat. He would continue working for the company until Joy Division broke through – a little beyond in fact – but it was no longer his priority. Catching the wave that was about to sweep through Manchester was far more important. From this moment onwards, everything would change for Bernard Dickin ...

... including his name.

CONFUSION THREE: 'THEY WERE SHIT'

The Lesser Free Trade Hall performance changed the group dynamic of the Salford gang immediately ... and permanently. Bernard, Peter Hook and Terry Mason wanted to form a band right there and then.

'I think that was probably true for Barney and Hooky,' says John Berry. 'They took to it straight away. Don't think there was any doubt in their minds about having a go. Don't know whether it was the next day ... but pretty damn soon after that.'

Peter Hook concurs: 'I think the people that saw the first Sex Pistols' gig – in the same way that we did – walked out of it, did something and then went and told whoever they knew about it ... and it just came on from there.'

Bear in mind, these were young men, turned twenty. Hardly starry-eyed little bits of kids – indeed, some were slightly older than the Sex Pistols themselves. If they were to do it, they would need to do it straight away, there was no time to waste – there would be competition from other members of the audience at the Sex Pistols' gig. Armed with his newly-acquired – though implausibly expensive – bass guitar, Peter Hook headed for Bernard's grandmother's house on Alfred Street, Lower Broughton, as there wasn't enough room at Bernard's flat.

'I still to this day can't imagine why on earth we thought we could do it,' says Hook. 'I'd never played a musical instrument ... ever. I was twenty one. Bernard had a guitar but he couldn't play it. I can't imagine where we got the idea from that we could do it, or whatever possessed us.'

Bernard had owned a guitar for over a year before seeing the Pistols and was making that grimly slow progress familiar to anyone who's started an instrument from scratch. 'When we first began,' said Sumner, looking back at those first tentative steps for *Jamming* magazine in 1986, 'we were excited by punk and The Stooges. Now, maybe, it's different music ... but it's still the same basic thing.'

'They did what most potential bands do,' says John Berry. 'They got some gear. They found a place to rehearse.' The Alfred Street house was relatively quiet – but more importantly it had one thing Bernard and Peter lacked. Amplification. Peter Hook recalls how they got round this problem in a very punk rock way: 'I remember we didn't have an amp and Bernard wired up his gran's gramophone with four wires connecting my bass guitar and his guitar and we played through that ... just started playing. She went mad when she came home, we'd ruined her gramophone. She went crazy.'

Terry Mason recalls things differently: 'Not quite. They were using Barney's amp with both guitars in. He was sufficiently wise to know that putting bass frequencies though it ... it wouldn't last long. He read up somewhere about valve radios and found one at his gran's. He made Hooky use that.' It was an early example of cracking a problem with deft use of technology that would stand Bernard in very good stead.

Encouraged by the small but relatively lively crowd on June 4, Sex Pistols' manager Malcolm McLaren had agreed to return to the city six weeks later to play again at the Lesser Free Trade Hall. Bernard, Peter Hook and Terry Mason would return to the venue on July 20, to see Buzzcocks and Wythenshawe proto-punks Slaughter And The Dogs supporting the Pistols. Although he didn't know it, Bernard's fortunes would be intertwined with those of the Buzzcocks for the next four years. For now, Pete Shelley and Howard Devoto had a gig to play and to promote; the records show that 121 tickets were sold this time around, with the crowd swelled by a hefty entourage of London punks and journalists bussed up for the occasion by McLaren. The event degenerated into violence as youth culture battle lines were drawn right there in the aisles of the Lesser Free Trade Hall.

Audience member and future Fall leader Mark E Smith told me, 'There was a definite split at that second gig, between the punks – before it was really punk, if you know what I mean – and the rest of the crowd.' Among the 'punks before they were really punks' on July 20 was a young man from Cheshire called Ian Curtis, accompanied by his wife Deborah. They'd missed the June 4 gig and were determined to be there second time around. Curtis was a policeman's son from Hurdsfield – a small community of terraced housing, low-rise flats and bungalows that dithers on the north-east side of Macclesfield. This was a world away from Salford – or at least twelve miles south – but the couple had recently moved to Chadderton near Oldham, a touch closer.

'I always wanted to do something like this [join a band] since I was about 16,' Curtis said in 1979. 'Nothing appealed to me. I listened to The Stones and ... whatever. I got the first two Velvet Undergound LPs. There seemed to be something very real about that. The lyrics were what I was going through at the time. I remember seeing Lou Reed on telly being interviewed. He wasn't the normal singer in a group. There was something more to him that seemed to carry on into the way he lived. Instead of just singing about something, he could actually show it as well.'

In her striking memoir of life with Ian, *Touching From A Distance*, Deborah Curtis recalls the Salford lads talking to Ian at the Lesser Free Trade Hall on July 20. If this meeting happened, then it didn't make an impression on the others. 'I don't even remember if Ian Curtis was there,' says Peter Hook. 'I can't remember if he was there or not.' In the book, Deborah also paints a vivid picture of the man she was married to. Very vivid. Although kind hearted and with an in-built inability to say no to people, she describes in detail his issues with pills and solvents – and his temper. She also describes how she was sometimes shocked about 'how racist Ian could be.' 'The first time we met her,' says Terry Mason thirty years later, 'we were really shocked. Ian was really animated. She was this *wallflower.*'

By the summer of 1976, Curtis had formed a rough musical alliance with Iain Grey, an aspirant guitarist from Wythenshawe. Grey managed to skirt his way around an amazingly wide range of bands on the Manchester scene in the late 1970s, without ever being on the receiving end of an ounce of good fortune himself. The closest he got was with Wild Ram, a forerunner of Ed Banger and the Nosebleeds.

'Yeah, I was in the band with him [Curtis] before he got famous,' says Grey. 'He couldn't sing ... five months later he's on the front cover of the *NME*. And I knocked around with Morrissey for a bit. I got the Midas touch!'

The twin jolts provided by the Lesser Free Trade Hall gigs – and seeing local bands like Buzzcocks and Slaughter actually sharing a stage with the Pistols – energised the Manchester scene. Bands and venues started springing up across the city. Bernard's group were scrambling to keep up. 'There was literally forty, sixty, eighty, a hundred bands. Everybody was forming a band,' says Peter Hook.

It's often assumed that Terry Mason was the drummer with this burgeoning outfit – not so: 'I was too slow on that Saturday morning,' says Mason. 'I should have got the bass. I got a guitar and an amp from the *Manchester Evening News* '£10 And Under' section. Hofner Strat copy, strings caked in rust. By this point, Barney's got nearly two years of guitar, Hooky's got three months. Barney got pissed off because I couldn't do the chords that he could do.'

While Mason struggled with the rudiments of guitar playing, a more pressing issue was the unwillingness of either Bernard, Peter or Terry to chance their arm at singing. 'They tried out a lot of people for the band,' recalls John Berry. 'They tried out guys we were at school with. Certainly none of them could sing. I think they even tried out 'Nidder' Gresty. They tried out Wroey. I don't think at the time Barney or Hooky could have been the frontman. Terry Mason certainly was never ever going to be a frontman. He was put on the drums and he couldn't do it.'

'Who do we know who could be a singer?' recalls Mason. "Nidder' Gresty was brought up ... Wroey was brought up. Nidder Gresty was someone in the AC/DC mould. Nidder would have done anything daft that we wanted him to! He was like John Otway! Wroey was one of Barney's mates – not from school. So was Danny Lee. He could out-Billy Idol Billy Idol. Danny was six foot, blond hair that stuck up and he had the lip. But he wasn't interested. We put up an ad in Virgin Records with Barney's number on. Barney was the only person who had a phone because of his parents' condition. Me and Barney went to meet one bloke at his flat. He had his own songs. He looked like a very thin Mick Hucknall and pulled out this home-made balalaika and strummed these songs to us. And he was wearing a big, giant cushion cover with armholes in it. The same advert brought in Ian Curtis, actually.' 'We were never bothered if they could play or not,' claimed Sumner in *Select* in 1993. 'It was always, "Are they a laugh?"'

Bernard needed help. Fortunately for him, it was available virtually on his doorstep. Buzzcocks were now living and sometimes rehearsing on Lower Broughton Road. 'We had a meeting with Pete Shelley in a pub in Broughton,' says Peter Hook, 'to ask him how we should form a band ... and he told us!' The Buzzcocks' camp would also offer the Salford lads a name for their band – Stiff Kittens. They took it ... not without some reservations ... but never actually used it. Buzzcock Steve Diggle – who teamed up with Shelley and Devoto on the night of June 4 after a quick meeting on the back row – told me he remembers helping Sumner get gig-worthy equipment. 'Barney came with us to this shop, looking for a guitar. They didn't even have a name then.'

'We didn't have a clue what to do,' states Terry Mason. 'Me and Barney used to see Shelley at his flat on Lower Broughton Road. [Buzzcocks drummer] John Maher come out with me looking at drum kits. They were really helpful to start with. They taught us what to do.' Buzzcocks and their manager Richard Boon were savvy enough to realise that if the Manchester scene was to take off, then more bands would be needed, so they actively set out to encourage groups to break through. 'Shelley seemed to be grooming me, Barney and Hooky,' says Terry Mason. 'Richard Boon was grooming Ian [Curtis] and Iain Grey.' Again, Sumner was taking notice.

'Because of the people at the Sex Pistols' gigs,' Mason continues, 'it formed an inner sanctum of a gentleman's club. Everyone who was there at that first gig was a founding member and can never be thrown out. You'd seen your peers at those gigs and they'd help you.'

Although the emerging scene could be a clan within a clique within a clan, Bernard would remember the helping hand offered by Buzzcocks and made a mental note to do the same himself if the chance arose. In the meantime, those members of the Salford gang who'd been to the Lesser Free Trade Hall – with the exception of 'Crazy' Mike – threw their weight fully behind punk rock.

'Me and Bernard went around about ten record shops trying to get 'Anarchy In The UK',' recalls Peter Hook. 'There was only one place that stocked it ... one little tiny shop on Piccadilly approach ... and we went in and we bought that and 'New Rose' [first punk single, by The Damned]. Two records at the same time, ran home and played them ... it was fantastic.'

'Once we started getting involved in punk,' adds Hook, 'we started going to The Squat off Oxford road and we used to go to The Ranch, and then you got to know people and we got to know Paul Morley [*NME* writer] and we got to know Rossi [Mick Rossi, Slaughter And The Dogs] and everybody like that, so next time you went, there was loads of people there [you knew]. Bernard and I couldn't get in any clubs in Manchester, we started going to Pips a couple of times but we had to dress down, had to dress normal. There was only The Ranch that you could get in, dressed as a punk. And the only other club you could get in dressed as you wanted to later was The Haçienda and that was it. It wasn't easy 'cause you got a lot of aggro. It was very shocking, you know, you were actually shocking people and you were upsetting old ladies and it was fantastic. You'd be putting soap in your hair to make it stick up and all that. Me and Bernard used to go to a scout shop and buy those scout shirts and paint swastikas on and put SS badges on and all that crap. God, you wouldn't be allowed anywhere *near* it now. It was funny.'

Bernard Sumner: '"Me and Bernard ..." Eh? I don't think so.'

In two years' time though, the smiles would be wiped fairly comprehensively from their faces, as the Nazi shock aspect of punk would be deemed untouchable virtually overnight, leaving Bernard and Peter out in the cold.

'I think the six weeks between the gigs shaped a lot of things,' says John Berry. 'Bernard started wholeheartedly going to places like The Ranch and The Electric Circus, on a very regular basis. We used to regularly go to

Pips on a Friday, before it was a punk club. That continued for a while.' The group dynamic changed pretty quickly after that [Pistols] gig. 'They fairly quickly got their hair cut, got a pair of tight jeans and got some funky clothes. That marginalised them from their peer group. Very quickly they moved into being in a band and being away from their peers.'

The Ranch. The Electric Circus. Pips. Some explanations are warranted here to lay out some clubland dynamic. Manchester's nightlife has always been an accommodating and broad church. A church that would rarely turn away donations. The Ranch was owned by the late Frank 'Foo Foo' Lamarr – real name Frank Pearson – and clung to the back of his main venue, Foo Foo's Palace on Dale Street. Lamarr was a drag artiste, businessman and old school showbiz charity fund-raiser with the legs of Cyd Charisse and the face of Henry Cooper. It quickly became the meeting point for the city's wannabee punks and musicians.

'It was a small dingy club that held about 200 people,' says Steve Burke, who worked at The Ranch. 'You knocked on the door and a slot came back. The bouncer on the door was [a] six-foot-six gay bloke, really camp and effeminate but he could hold anyone back. It was a nice proportion in there at the time … 150 girls and about 50 lads. It was originally Bowie/Roxy, then the punk thing happened and word started going out about it.'

'Bowie/Roxy' is an expression you'll hear a lot in connection with the Manchester scene. It is shorthand for 'our kind of music' – it doesn't even necessarily have to mean tracks by David Bowie or Roxy Music; it's a vibe rather than a playlist, and The Ranch definitely had the vibe. 'Foo Foo asked me if I wanted to work behind the bar,' continues Steve Burke. 'So I got to know everyone in the club – it was small. Same people all the time … Thursday, Friday, Saturday, Sunday.' Peter Hook: 'Everybody used to meet, go in The Ranch and go *Yeah, I'm a singer in a band* … it was fantastic.'

'You never saw Barney and Hooky that much in The Ranch … it was always Pips for them,' Steve Burke remembers. 'I didn't like Pips. You had to go through the soul room. If you went for a piss, you'd get people trying to trip you up.'

Pips was a regular pre-punk haunt of the Salford gang. A maze-like downstairs club behind Manchester Cathedral with multiple areas featuring different styles of music in each room. You could stand in a certain interconnecting section of Pips and get punk in your left ear and disco in the right, a key experience that would leave a lasting impression. It also meant that the likes of Bernard, hanging out in the Bowie/Roxy room, would indeed have to brave a walk through the soul room to go to the toilet, bringing with it the considerable risk of a beating. It would also be the venue for the first ever gig by Joy Division. True to form, it would be a very violent debut.

As well as serving drinks, Steve Burke sold something else to the *nouveau punks* at The Ranch – his fanzine *Shy Talk*. He'd been to the second Sex Pistols' gig at the Lesser Free Trade Hall and watched as other people present started to form bands. Steve reasoned – somewhat unusually for 1976 – that not being able to sing ruled him out of the city's musical explosion.

'I did nothing, the reason being I'm tone deaf,' says Steve. 'I got told that at school. I never even thought of it. I'd be too embarrassed. Richard Boon then said, "Do a fanzine!" *Sniffin' Glue* [Mark Perry's London fanzine] had been out for a few issues. I was working at 15 – thick! My English, my grammar were not good. But I got a lot of help, Kevin Cummins gave me any photos I wanted, Paul Morley had a couple of pages, I was talking to people like [author] Jon Savage ... although the magazine was shit, those people were saying, *No, no, it's great!* The wife did the first two on the photocopier at work.'

The Sex Pistols returned to Manchester twice in December 1976, playing at The Electric Circus, on the ninth and the nineteenth. The second gig was filmed by Julien Temple and snippets can be seen in the Pistols' movie *The Great Rock And Roll Swindle*. The Electric Circus was a heavy/prog-rock club on the tough estate of Collyhurst, walking distance – albeit a rather tense walking distance – from Manchester city centre.

'I remember going to The Electric Circus to see the Pistols,' says Peter Hook. 'That was when the punk thing had gone off and *everybody* hated punks. I remember all the punters were queuing up down the road and the kids in Collyhurst had broken all these railings off and they were on top of the flats throwing them over like javelins at the punks that were queuing up. Unbelievable, the reaction of normal people against punks. All these punks were quite mild, they were just making a fashion statement really, they weren't heavy or anything. They were ducking javelins and milk bottles and it was absolutely unbelievable. We came out and it was going off in the street and [there's] these kids, just loads of football yobbos waiting for these punks to come out ... [then] this police car drives up, stops and everybody went, "Oh, you've got to help because they're beating us up, they're really hammering us," and the coppers went, "Right, okay .. you get behind the van, follow us ... you run behind the van and we'll take you up out of it, to your cars," [so] the cop van started off and everybody started running behind it and then it just went *rrrrmm* and shot off and left [us] all right in the middle of the street! Oh, it was terrible ... luckily, we'd got the only car parking space that was pretty close and me, Bernard and Terry [Mason] legged it to the car through all the bricks and bottles and everything, got in the car – his car was dented a few times – shot off down the road ... I remember seeing Slaughter And The Dogs being chased [by the kids], "Heeeeey! Piss off!" [as we drove past]. Top time.'

'The Electric Circus was a shithole,' recalls local music scene veteran Chris Hewitt, whose company Tractor Music hired out PAs to the venue. 'All painted black inside. The toilets ... you just pissed against a brick wall with a groove cut into the ground to take it away. It was so horrible, it didn't matter if people threw beer around or were sick all over the place.'

Despite its fearsome reputation, Bernard managed to persuade some of the hippies and hairies from Cosgrove Hall to make the journey into deepest Collyhurst. 'I went to some of those early Warsaw gigs,' says Cosgrove director Chris Taylor. 'I definitely went to The Electric Circus – but I was a hippy, Bob Dylan was my thing. Having said that, Bernard wasn't averse to Dylan either. I liked the energy and the *new-ness* (sic) of it. It was great. But I was a hippy. Sorry. We always knew he had this interest in music, so it was no surprise to anyone when he left to pursue it. No surprise at all.'

The staple fair of The Electric Circus before the summer of 1976 was the likes of The Enid and Motörhead. It was Manchester's CBGB's, for all the wrong and some of the right reasons. 'People might say it was horrible, but at the time it was fantastic,' says Steve Burke. 'It was pitch black – you couldn't see the person next to you. The best part about it was the DJ used to play really heavy dub reggae. Some of the bands were absolute crap. The Damned ... I went to see Motörhead. It wasn't as bad as people said. We walked up there together and we walked back into town together. So there were too many of us to have any bother. It was only little kids throwing a few stones anyway. It was a dirty, scruffy place ... but that added to it.'

It was here that Peter Hook recalls seeing Ian Curtis for the first time. 'We met Ian at The Electric Circus,' Hook states. 'He had a green military jacket on with 'Hate' on the back ... in white letters which I thought was fantastic, 'Hate'... incredible.

I remember the reason that we couldn't get Joy Division together [at first] was that Ian Curtis had a guitarist [Iain Grey] and we had a guitarist and a bass player ... so he couldn't join 'cause you weren't allowed to have two guitars, that was uncool. You had to have one guitar in a punk band

... that was the recipe, you see. So we had wait for his guitarist to leave ... so we joined up.'

As simple as that.

Ian Curtis joined the band with Bernard, Peter Hook and Terry Mason. Initially, Curtis was far from convinced that this might be the band that could take him to where he wanted to be. 'After seeing the Pistols – when we got together was about the 'Anarchy' tour – it took a hell of a long time for us to get everything sorted out,' Curtis recalled some three years later. 'And you could see all these other groups coming up all the time. Barney could play a bit but Hooky had never touched a bass in his life.'

Of all the group, Curtis bonded most quickly and firmly with Terry Mason. 'We were both dreamers,' says Terry today.

> *Bernard Sumner: 'Ugh – Terry dreamer! Ian's best mate!*
> *That's so wrong – leave it in.'*

'There was *something* out there that could change our lives. Me and Ian were the ones who lived our lives though *NME* and *Sounds*. Whereas Barney had not fully bought into it. We wanted something to happen. We both saw punk as that opening.'

Watching from the sidelines, John Berry noticed things were different when Curtis joined. 'It must have changed it when Ian came in. Here's someone who can actually be a frontman. A lot of people didn't rate Ian as a singer. Ian was a shouter who had an attitude. He was very photogenic, he looked good. It was a long time till I thought, "Yeah, they're going somewhere here." Even though they never quite fitted into the punk mode. I really didn't think it was going to happen for a long time ... like most people.'

The Manchester scene was moving at a fierce pace. Buzzcocks became the first punk band to release their own record in January with the *Spiral Scratch* EP. Howard Devoto then uppped and left – making him the first ever post-punk, before most people had even managed to become a punk. Guitarist Pete Shelley stepped up as vocalist and leader and would eventually steer the band to far greater success. If nothing else, this provided a fascinating template: a guitarist really could step into a lead singer's shoes and achieve far more than his predecessor. With Bernard's proximity to the Buzzcocks, this wouldn't have gone unnoticed.

Rehearsals with Ian Curtis were based in Salford, particularly at The Swan pub, also known as the The Clippy's Arms, as it was used by drivers from the bus depot next door. 'My cousin was the secretary of the Salford

Manchester City supporters club,' remembers Terry Mason. 'Not a massive club that – they were based at The Swan and they let us have the function room. We weren't paying a bean. The first songs were Hooky songs. The band was shit – still learning.'

The Salford Arms pub would also be used as a rehearsal venue – even, on one weekend emergency, Cosgrove Hall's studios – as well as premises to the rear of the recently closed-down Rialto Cinema in Broughton.

Some early rehearsals were at The Swan Pub and to the rear of The Rialto Cinema.

'The place behind the Rialto was on Hilton Street at the side of Broughton Baths, next to a dingy night club called Pinkies Place,' says Steve Murray, lead singer of Salford band Fast Cars. 'We rehearsed on the top floor in a small room, [Bernard and Hooky] had a larger room on the middle floor. I think they might have shared it with A Certain Ratio. The fondest memory I have from that place was after rehearsing one night, I went to my car and I tried to start it but nothing was happening. I lifted the bonnet and noticed the problem immediately. The Joy Division boys came out while I still had my head under the bonnet [and] one of them shouted, "What's the problem?" I told them the battery's gone. "No worries, we'll give you a push," they said. "No," I said… "the battery has *gone* … it's been fuckin' nicked, mate!" That's Salford for you …'

'Peter Hook was certainly the most forceful character, a pretty in-your-face Salford lad,' is Steve's assessment today. 'Bernard and Steve Morris were particularly quiet … we couldn't make out whether they were ignorant [rude] or just shy. Ian was the friendliest despite his strange on-stage manner.'

Terry Mason had now assumed a short-lived managerial role and in the run up to the band's first gig, they recruited Tony Tabac as a replacement for their struggling school mate. Like-minded souls were very thin on the ground. 'At the time when we started in Manchester,' said Curtis in 1979, 'there were only three or four other groups of the New Wave type, yet in London there seemed to be a lot more. I think in Manchester a lot of groups expanded and went their own ways.'

Urged on by Curtis, greater focus and direction was needed and a proper manager seemed the obvious answer. Just prior to their first gig, Bernard turned to *Shy Talk* fanzine and its "proprietor" Steve Burke to print an appeal in the next issue. 'I knew Barney and Hooky from before the Pistol's gig,' says Burke. 'When they found out I did the fanzine – I'd done two issues by then – I was the obvious person to come and ask.'

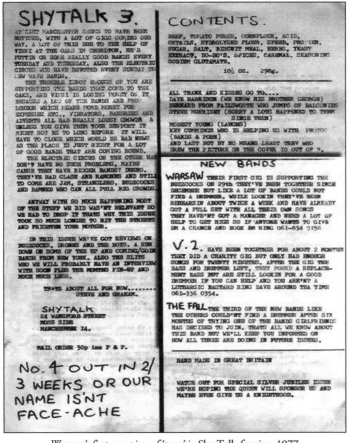

Warsaw's first ever piece of 'press' in Shy Talk *fanzine, 1977.*

The piece in *Shy Talk* describes the band as being together since December but having problems finding a drummer. It also appealed for help in getting the band gigs because they didn't have a manager. 'Give 'em a chance and book 'em,' says the article. It was their first ever 'press' ... and the first time they were to use their new name: Warsaw. 'It's a popular misconception that we were called Stiff Kittens,' said Sumner in Q. 'We were never called Stiff Kittens. At our first concert we changed it to Warsaw.'

The decision to dispense with the somewhat camp name of Stiff Kittens came so late in the day that flyers featuring the 'old' moniker were still being distributed just before that first gig on May 29, 1977, at The Electric Circus, supporting Buzzcocks – obviously – and Newcastle punks Penetration, fronted by the striking Pauline Murray. This would provide them with their second appearance in print, a dry mention in rock weekly *Sounds* that made reference to Bernard looking like a public schoolboy. To start throwing petrol on a fire that would steadfastly refuse to be put out for decades, during the gig a between-song reference was blurted out to Adolph Hitler's deputy, Rudolph Hess. This is usually credited to Curtis, but several eye witnesses now say it was in fact Bernard. Hess's continued imprisonment at Spandau Jail was in all the newspapers at the time and this incident saw the start of a series of Nazi-related problems that would dog Bernard and the band for decades.

Bernard Sumner: 'I was reading a book about Hess called The Loneliest Man In The World, *it's very sad. It obviously affected me in some way, but fuck knows why I blurted that out – read it.'*

Steve Maguire from Stockport saw the band at The Electric Circus aged 14. 'They were so intense, so unlike anything I'd seen or heard before,' says Maguire. 'The strange bass leading the songs ... and the singer scared the shit out of me. Going to Collyhurst never really bothered me, I knocked about in Levenshulme and Gorton as a kid and you didn't see a great deal of trouble at the gigs. Most doormen let teenagers in for an extra quid which was a bastard when tickets were only £1.50. What unnerved me at first was the noise and the darkness ... once I'd seen them I was hooked. I suppose it was just like a football team ... they were *my* band.'

Bernard had also decided that his own name – Dickin – was not really rock and roll enough.

Bernard Sumner: 'The problem with Dickin was that until grammar school, I had been known as Sumner, so on the first day of grammar school at assembly, I was announced as Sumner. At this point my 'friends' from the old school started calling me a bastard because they knew James had adopted me and my real father had buggered off. This is the real reason I felt embarrassed about it.'

Plus, he'd already heard every variation of changing room joke on the subject. It hadn't been easy growing up in Salford with the name Dickin, so he became Bernard Albrecht. To accompany this alteration – the first of many name-changes – Bernard also started to sport a rather unconvincing moustache.

To save further confusion, it's probably best to deal with Bernard's name changes here and now, not least to avoid things getting even more confusing than is strictly necessary over the following chapters. Most of these name changes came about through various stages and levels of embarrassment on Bernard's part. If it wasn't a source of awkwardness to start with, it tended to become one afterwards.

The choice of 'Albrecht' has been attributed to a brand of photocopier that was in use at Bernard's employers at Cosgrove Hall. It's a nice line, but there's no record of any such company. It also happens to be the name of the world's leading brand of precision chuck drill, so there you go. It's also been linked to Albrecht Dürer, the fifteenth century German renaissance painter and art theorist, who was born in Nuremburg in 1471. Dürer's work in print-making and engraving is hugely influential and would be common currency in an artistic environment such as the studios of Cosgrove Hall. His name even had those cool little double dots – *umlauts* – that might come in handy for a future record sleeve design.

With a hefty sigh, Terry Mason offers his explanation. 'Do you really want to know?' he grimaces when asked the question today. 'I've no proof of this, but the Gestapo headquarters in Berlin was on *Prinz Albrecht Strasse*. Perhaps it seemed more punk. He was embarrassed by his name ... Dickin sounded more punk than anything, actually. People had been calling him Barney Rubble as well. He wanted to get away from those names and picked Albrecht because of Nazi chic. That's where I [think] Albrecht comes from.'

> *Bernard Sumner: 'Not true – I actually fell asleep on the sofa at*
> *my mother's house, and when I woke up there was some guy prattling*
> *on the TV about Bertolt Brecht and I thought he had said,*
> *"Bernhardt Albrecht", nothing to do with the Gestapo, I'm afraid.'*

When Bernard dropped the Albrecht tag, he then tweaked his adopted name to Dicken, which has been assumed to be his "real" name ever since. Wrong. Bernard's *real* name is Sumner – Dickin is his adoptive father's name. Dicken is an affectation. One Factory Records' colleague remembers an embarrassing exchange after asking him why his name was spelt with an 'i' on his cheque book, yet with an 'e' elsewhere.

When he opted for a return to his mother's maiden name of Sumner in the 1980s, many newspaper and magazines were, by this stage, baffled. It would be a common occurrence for Bernard to be referred to as Sumner in the text of an article, but Albrecht/Dicken in a photo caption or sub-heading – all on the same page. The paucity of information available on the band's record sleeves – no names, no pack drill to use a military reference – certainly helped push the confusion about Bernard's name even further. 'What we want to do is present music without any of the peripheral rubbish around it,' Sumner said in the early 1980s. 'It doesn't matter who played what solo or what instruments were used or even who we are. If people like the music, that's what's important. That's what they're buying.'

Bernard Sumner: 'I hadn't really wanted my name changing from Sumner in the first place. I had got used to it, you see, I was kind of made to change it.'

Back in 1977, name-changes, 'taches or the removal of 'peripheral' rubbish didn't bring a change in fortunes. Even the band's support system of friends didn't rate them at this stage. 'They were universally panned,' states John Berry. 'They never got a good review. They were shit! In terms of music at the time, they were fucking shit. They couldn't play a note. They didn't know what they were doing. I remember being at one gig at The Squat [an especially grim, semi-derelict venue on Devas Street, near Manchester University]. There was horrific feedback coming off Barney's guitar and the [speaker cabinet]. And he didn't know why. And the people in the audience were going, "Get away from the cab! You're too close to the cab! Get away!" That was the level of it.'

Bernard Sumner: '"Universally panned" means about two reviews out of twenty gigs; at that stage we were a minor band starting out, no one wrote about us.'

When he was interviewed by the BBC in 1979, Ian Curtis agreed that those first Warsaw gigs were grim affairs. 'We changed a lot initially,' said Curtis on *Rock On*. 'When we started, we couldn't really play, to be honest. It was very loose, a fun thing ... "Ooh, look, we're in a group, we're playing ..." It was in about August 1977 when we really started to get out in our own particular way. When we started we got very bad reviews.'

Bernard Sumner: 'Well, we couldn't play very well at first; of course not, we had to start somewhere – daft cunt.'

'I never thought they were anything special,' says *Shy Talk's* Steve Burke. 'Never thought much of them.' They even played on the same bill as a band of 'no fixed personnel' called The Negatives. Paul Morley on guitar, photographer Kevin Cummins on drums and, on this occasion, Steve Burke. 'I had a bass guitar, a sixty foot lead and an 'I Hate Students' tee-shirt,' says Burke. 'It was a mickey-take. I don't think I was plugged in. It was just so Paul Morley could write about how fantastic we were and wind up the London press.' The Negatives were higher up the bill than Warsaw.

The aforementioned Squat gig was a year – almost to the day – after Bernard had seen the Sex Pistols at the Lesser Free Trade Hall on June 4, 1976. Reasonable progress for any band starting from scratch, but pedestrian by the standards of the day and positively static compared to the likes of The Negatives.

Terry Mason: 'We did the Buzzcocks/Penetration gig [at The Electric Circus] then because I was the manager [so] I asked Penetration, "Got any gigs we could do?" and they said, "Aye, pet, come on oop." So we did Newcastle Town Hall on Jubilee Day.' Bernard somehow managed to convince Chris Taylor from Cosgrove Hall to drive him all the way to Newcastle for the gig. 'All the gear was rammed into my Ford Escort van!' says Taylor. 'Pretty reasonable bookings,' suggests Terry Mason, 'for a band that was shit and nobody knew and I didn't have a phone.'

Drummer Tony Tabac came and went, to be replaced by Steve Brotherdale, who also played with another local band, The Panik – they were managed by Rob Gretton, a DJ at yet another Manchester nightspot, the mainstream Rafters (he will resurface later in the tale). Brotherdale then decided to stick with his chief band as they had a single in the offing and Warsaw were only at the demo stage. He would also play with Swinton power-poppers Fast Cars. 'Yes ... "B'Dale" – as he liked to be called back then – was with us for a few months,' says Fast Cars' Steve Murray. We first met him when he was playing for V2. He was always full of stories about who he'd played with. We knew he was the best drummer in the North West ... 'cos he told us again and again and again!'

Brotherdale's departure left the perennial drummer-shaped hole in Warsaw. It would be filled by Steve Morris, another Macclesfield lad who had seen Warsaw's drummer plight highlighted in *Shy Talk*. He'd been to the same school as Curtis – King's School – and had earned rock and roll credentials by being expelled. Even at that stage, Morris was a drummer with a broad talent and taste in music. Terry Mason: 'Steve Morris comes in ... he wasn't like punk drummers, there was more about him. Very knowledgeable. He seemed to know a lot about hippy things. He had quite an esoteric record collection.'

Bernard Sumner. Peter Hook. Ian Curtis. Steve Morris.

To those around the band, it seemed as if the wind changed once the line-up was settled and some early followers fell by the wayside. John Berry: 'I did a bit of running around, I was with them for a few gigs. I drove the van a few times. Went down to the rehearsal rooms with them ... the Rialto in Broughton near the baths. I don't know what point they moved on from the likes of the other guys. Most of the others were still wearing long hair and flares – the uniform. I had no money, I had no job. So I was thinking, "What the fuck am I going to do?" So I decided to go to London ... I might have stayed around and carried on with the roadie-ing with Terry. I was in and out of it for quite a while. I never really thought it was for me. I didn't have the bottle or the background. We were all brought up on superstars. I didn't feel like a superstar. I think the experience of Terry, who tried his level best to do 'this, that and the other' and never got anywhere, put me off.'

Back in Manchester, a pattern was forming. Rafter's. Electric Circus. The Squat and back to Rafters again, where they would once more come under the eye of DJ Rob Gretton. The band pushed on, playing a mix of original material and covers. In December, awash with cash provided by Ian Curtis' bank manager for spurious home improvements, Warsaw recorded a track at Pennine Sound Studios in Oldham, where they'd already made demos in July. The Christmas recordings became the *An Ideal For Living* EP, which surfaced on their own self-financed Enigma label.

There is a tendency to dismiss these tracks – 'Warsaw', 'Leaders Of Men', 'No Love Lost', 'Failures' – as inconsequential. Listening to them today, it's rudimentary stuff, but easily on a par with more lauded contemporary recordings by other bands; Wire in particular come to mind as a comparable sound. *An Ideal For Living*'s first track 'Warsaw' has a opening shouted rally of "*350125 Go!*". Played alongside Wire's '12XU' there's a clear kinship between the intent and execution. The yelled digits just happen to be the same as Rudolph Hess's prisoner number during his detention at Spandau prison in West Berlin. Unsurprisingly, there's Buzzcocks to be found here too. Their *Spiral Scratch* EP had been released in January of the same year, just as Howard Devoto jumped ship, deciding that he'd done what he set out to do. Curtis is unrecognisable as the sing-from-your-boots, lower octave vocalist he'd become in a few months' time, sticking with the disaffected, shouty whine that had proved effective for both Wire's Colin Newman and Devoto. Morris's drums are treated with slapback echo to give them a sci-fi Glitterbeat touch and Hook's bass rumbles along the same lines as JJ Burnel of The Stranglers. 'Leaders Of Men' shows that all those hours spent in the Bowie/Roxy room of Pips weren't entirely wasted, as it bears a strange and strong resemblance to 'Do The Strand' by Roxy Music.

1977 it may have been, but it's still a step ahead of the punk clones fighting over the same three chords elsewhere. If anything, it's Bernard's guitar which lets the enterprise down, as it sounds like it's been recorded against the clock. Still, no reason for these tracks to be brushed aside. They're valid and intense pieces of work. They're just not ... Joy Division. On New Year's Eve, 1977, Warsaw played their final gig, at the Swinging Apple in Liverpool. Four weeks later they would play again – but this time as Joy Division.

A signed copy of the sleeve of Joy Division's first E.P.

CONFUSION FOUR: 1978

On January 25, 1978, the band played their first gig as Joy Division ... at the very place Bernard and Co. had spent many a boozy, pre-punk night: Pips. 'We had some hellish gigs,' remembers Peter Hook. '[That] first gig we did as Joy Division [had] the biggest fight I'd ever seen in my life, that one. It was great, every gig was like a massive release of energy. The Pips thing was like that.'

1978 would see the start of the band's growing relationship – and eventual virtual deification – with the British music press as the saviours of post-punk ideals; their hook-up with Tony Wilson, Factory Records and producer Martin Hannett; their first television appearance; and their first record releases. Bernard got married to Sue Barlow too. Strange year, 1978.

1978 even *looks* funny. It's not as dramatic and bold looking as 1977 – with all its year zero musical connotations. Nor does it have the easy rhetorical possibilities of 1979 – with Margaret Thatcher coming to power on May 4 and bringing with her the casual clichés of the end of post-war 1970s innocence and the beginning of the 'greedy' 1980s. Easy history, nicely digestible – largely nonsense.

1978 was Joy Division's coming of age – yet it's an age that's a world away. Louise Brown, the world's first test tube baby was born in Oldham on the outskirts of Manchester. Nine hundred and fourteen followers of the Reverend Jim Jones killed themselves in Guyana. Sex Pistol Sid Vicious was put on a murder charge in New York after his girlfriend Nancy Spungen was found dead in their Manhattan hotel room. History. These are stories from more than a generation ago. Though their music is timeless to some, this is the context of Joy Division's past. A generation and a half has passed since 1978.

By 1978, punk was a done deal, inconveniently finishing far quicker than anyone could have predicted. The Pistols were over by January; The Damned would split – for the first of several times; The Clash tried and failed to crack America with *Give 'Em Enough Rope;* and kids' shows were booking 'new wave' acts to fill the gaps between telephone toy swaps and custard pie-chucking contests. History would have you believe that the entire music industry panicked when punk appeared on the cultural horizon. Record company executives stood or fell, depending on which side of the punk fence they decided to position themselves. All middle ranking acts that didn't pass the litmus test were cut adrift. Flares were not to be seen after 1976 until The Stone Roses wafted their extra-wide strides through the centre of Manchester well over a decade later. Easy history, nicely digestable – total nonsense. The one true bastion of pop conservatism – and a key indicator of where the industry was really at during this period of confusion – was the British music press, which tried to run a two-tiered system to attract new readers while maintaining their traditionalist core. Crucially, the weeklies took on board a fresh wave of writers that "got it". Sadly for them, "it" had failed to deliver long-term answers and the newcomers were left in a post-punk bind: what do we write about now the very thing we came on board to write about is no longer anything to write about?

'It was the comedown after punk,' says Paolo Hewitt, a staffer at the time on *Melody Maker*. 'People weren't sure where they were going. Everyone was standing around, waiting for the next big thing ... Mod revival, Manchester, The Specials. People were trying to work out what had happenened to punk. They saw Joy Division as the saviours. They're a very talented group that made great records that people respond to heavily. Even all the major acts – Bowie, The Rolling Stones and all that – were unsure of where they were going, it was like a purgatory.'

There would be some novel solutions over the next few years to break the British music scene out of this purgatory. These included blatant attempts to fabricate new 'movements': Powerpop, Oi!, Herbert, Casual, New Psychedelia, a return to 'proper' rock (which put Oldham pub rockers Any Trouble on the front cover of *Melody Maker* with the question 'Is this the best British Band since The Pretenders?') as well as Industrial, New Pop, or indeed 'Anything Scottish'.

But a glance at the music press in 1978 would show that there would be a clear lack of confidence on the cultural markets for the post-punk pound and the new guard would be jostling for space with the old stagers ... and not necessarily winning. Wilko Johnson, Styx, The Rich Kids, Spirit, The Motors, Magazine and Bob Dylan would be a fairly typical 1978 feature and review mix for *New Musical Express*. I haven't just pulled these odd bedfellows out of the air. I have that very June 3, 1978 *NME* right here by my keyboard. The idea that punk 'swept everything away' is simply not true. 'Have a look at the album sales,' advises Paolo Hewitt. 'Those punk albums were going in at number 23 ... and Abba were outselling them ten to one.' Hewitt is suggesting, again, that it's an easy history, nicely digestable – largely nonsense.

Bernard Sumner: 'Punk gave a voice to people and hated mainstream culture.
It wasn't ever about sales – it was about belonging.'

Bets were being hedged across the board. But boy did the music press need something "real" to write about in 1978, now that punk was a busted flush. They needed a band who really did – as Johnny Rotten had put it – "mean it maaaan." If they could *prove* it too, then that really would be ideal. Bernard Sumner once described Joy Division as 'four dumbos from Manchester.' His appraisal was to prove unacceptable to the British music press. So they created their own version instead. Perhaps the pressure of this version would prove too much for the band. 'Nobody else knew where they were going, but Joy Division had a strong image of where they were going and that was very appealing to the press,' adds Paolo Hewitt.

But the name wouldn't help. Warsaw had gone by-the-by, apparently, because of its similarity to that of Warsaw Pakt, a slightly long in the tooth London-based rock act who had a former member of Motörhead on drums. Warsaw Pakt's main claim to fame was the recording, pressing and release of an album called *Needle Time* in 1979 in less than 24 hours. The band hadn't released a single by the time Warsaw became Joy Division but had been on the circuit for a while.

The name Joy Divison was clearly from Curtis, drawn from the 1955 novel *The House of Dolls.* The book tells the story of a teenage girl, Daniella Preleshniuk, and her day-to-day life in a Jewish enclave on the Polish/German border. She is captured and held in a Nazi labour camp, tattooed with a number and the title 'Feld Hure' (field whore) before being transferred to the *Joy Division* of sterilised sex slaves in the House of Dolls. The apparently autobiographical piece is credited to Ka-Tzetnik 1355633 and still divides readers as to its worth as a Holocaust testament or a piece of exploitative trash. If the intention in naming the band Joy Division was to shock, it makes The Cambridge Rapists look subtle. Deborah Curtis remembers her reaction when she first heard the name, as she recalled in *Touching From A Distance*: 'I cringed. It was gruesome and tasteless and I hoped that the majority of people would not know what it meant.'

On its January release, the *An Ideal For Living* EP, recorded at Pennine in December, came with the written proviso that it had been made while 'we were known as Warsaw'. The text suggests that any complaints be forwarded to Terry Mason. The self-funded release – a run of five thousand – also featured a Hitler-youth drummer boy and a gun-toting German soldier in a fold-out poster with the design credited to Bernard Albrecht, whose newly-adopted Germanic surname was now starting to appear a little grim when placed in the context of the sleeve and the new name.

> *Bernard Sumner: 'The climate was very different in those days, it was the time of punk and shock, sticking two fingers up to what we regarded as normal society, and that included some journalists. We knew the name was on dodgy ground and did have reservations about it – but in the end it just felt like it was our name. It's very difficult to explain but we did everything at that time with instinct not intellect and, when you do that, it's very difficult to know when to let intellect intervene and abandon your instinct.'*

Terry Mason is clear on the subject: 'There was *never* any Nazism. We did have some people around the edges who were quite right-wing. One [sold] copies of [right-wing newspaper] *Bulldog* at gigs. But Barney doesn't know the difference between left-wing and right-wing. He was apolitical in the extreme. The only time he bothered voting, he voted Labour because he needed an new exhaust for his motorbike and he figured if he put a bet on Labour and they won, it'd pay for a new exhaust system.'

> *Bernard Sumner: 'If Rob had known anyone was selling right-wing newspapers at our gigs, he would have set the dogs on them.'*

Bernard's apolitical stance is something – when pressed – he has always stuck too. Rigidly: 'We are not interested in politics ... I have never been interested in politics,' he said to *Melody Maker* in May 1981. But he chose to wear a military-style shirt and tie combo for the EP photo shoot. Just for good measure, some Albrecht Dürer-style umlauts were thrown on top of sections of the text too. Defenders will talk of the common-place, Nazi-chic flirtations of the period, of the band aligning themselves with the victims rather than the oppressors, or even of youthful naivete. Again, these were men in their early twenties, not kids affecting a shocking pose. In my opinion, it was stupid then and it's stupid now.

> *Bernard Sumner: 'Yes, I was apolitical in those days – I was 22-23 and more interested in the kind of fun one can have at that age. Not that unusual, I think. The [EP] sleeve was done by me but if you care to take a look at the image of the boy with the rifle aimed at him, it supports Ian's lyrics that are printed below it. The front cover shows "the promise", "the inner", "the reality". History not politics – stupid, yes, but if you can't be stupid when you are 22, when can you be?'*

'Very stupid,' concurs Mason. 'But we had no one else to do the cover ... so Barney said he'd do it because he was a graphic artist.' 'I remember the first single,' says Steve Burke. 'Barney came into Pips and said "Please, please review it in *Shy Talk.*" At the time I was getting records off a lot of people. Never kept hold of them. First *Spiral Scratch*, never kept hold of it. Never been one for keeping stuff.' Both EPs now command fierce prices among collectors.

Despite everything they'd managed to achieve, Bernard and the band were running low on the energy and impetus they'd gained since Curtis joined. Perhaps embarrassed by Joy Division's naked desire to succeed – not to mention their tattooed *feld hure* name – the Manchester music scene seemed to have tired of them. A lot had happened to the punk scene and the wider rock market in the last eighteen months. 'Rock Against Racism', a loose group opposed to apparently dubious comments by the likes of Eric Clapton and David Bowie, had already organised two concerts and launched a fanzine by 1978 and the rules had been clearly laid down by London scene setters: flirting with facism was most definitely out ... it was just *so* 1976.

'By this stage,' says Terry Mason, 'we're probably the most unpopular band in Manchester. We'd gone from being quite liked ... to almost being pariahs.' The Manchester scene had, by now, gone national with astonishing speed. Buzzcocks – a band essentially only a few weeks older than Bernard and Peter's – appeared had already had a hit with 'What Do I Get?' and appeared on *Top of The Pops* with 'I Don't Mind' for the first of many times on April 27; 'Shot By Both Sides' by Howard Devoto's Magazine had charted and Slaughter And The Dogs had recorded their first album. Newer bands like The Distractions and Ed Banger And The Nosebleeds were coming through. But Joy Division seemed aimless and friendless.

Mason strongly believes that what happened next was the most pivotal event in the Joy Division story: the Stiff/Chiswick 'Battle of the Bands' contest at Rafters in April.

'It was *X-Factor* on tour,' he says. 'It was the opportunity for unsigned bands to do nights in front of these clever people from London that would hopefully result in a single. It was near enough our last throw of the dice really. If nothing would have happened that night the band would have disintegrated. Barney would have said "Sod it, we've given it long enough, it's not going anywhere." If nothing would have happened that night, I'm sure that would have been it. This one night becomes this huge focus.'

Bernard Sumner: 'Nonsense, I had no intention of giving up.'

Bumped from the running order of the first night of the competition – and refused entry to the venue – they went for a meal to debate their next move. Curtis in particular was raging. 'We went for an Indian,' recalls Mason, 'to one of Barney's favourites on Great Ducie Street. We saw Ian flip and we saw "Racist Ian" come out. He was there at the top of his voice – before any food had come out – saying how [shouting] he "DIDN'T LIKE FUCKING PAKIS ... I DON'T MIND CHINKS ... CHINKS ARE ALL RIGHT, BUT I CAN'T FUCKIN' STAND PAKIS" ... we said, "Fucking hell, Ian, do that *after* your food comes out."'

Bernard Sumner: 'Yes, I remember this, it was at the Kismet Indian restaurant, £2.50 T-bone steak and curry. They gave you your own table-cloth on the way in and double doors so that you couldn't do a runner on the way out. Ian was not racist, otherwise he would not have been in the restaurant. When he lived in Oldham, he lived next door to a Pakistani family who, apparently, according to Ian, used to throw parcels of shit into his back yard. Understandably, this drove him mad and I think it was these particular Pakistanis he was referring to.'

They decided to try the 'Battle of the Bands' again the following night. Pushed later and later in the running order, drunk on Special Brew and blackcurrant and furious that joke band The Negatives – featuring scenesters like journalist Paul Morley and Buzzcocks' manager Richard Boon – were allowed to play, Joy Division took the stage in a gale of anger and resentment. 'We finally got let on stage, the place is thinning out,' says Mason. 'The people running it didn't want us there. We thought *Fuck it, we'll show 'em.'*

Television presenter Tony Wilson recalls being confronted by Curtis, fresh from the Rafter's stage, and being called a fucking cunt for not putting them on his television music shows *What's On* and *So It Goes.* Wilson was another product of the Salford grammar school system, but cut from a very different cultural cloth than the likes of Bernard and Peter Hook. Wilson went to De La Salle and Cambridge before landing a job at ITN, but instead of London, he'd plumped for life in the regions as a roving on-screener with *Granada Reports,* the North West franchise's tea time magazine show. He became a big fish in a small pond. Wilson also had a passion for music but had recently lost his ground breaking, semi-network *So It Goes* show after pushing the taste envelope once too often. He may have put the Sex Pistols on television for the first time and introduced the likes of The Jam and The Clash to TV screens, but a sweary performance by Iggy Pop had proved to be a prank too far and the show was on hold. With only straight regional reporting to look forward to – council strikes, hospital closures, plus an array of 'and finally' stories – he'd started a club night at Manchester's Russell Club then, subsequently, Factory Records with actor/band manager Alan Erasmus as a diversion. He was convinced that the New Wave bands he'd pinpointed on *So It Goes* were the future and felt he was owed a piece of the action as he'd done so much to create it. 'Tony Wilson,' states Peter Hook, 'was the first middle-class person I ever met.' Middle-class or not, Wilson was looking for talent and felt he'd found it in the angry, raw shape of Joy Division. His response to Curtis was that he would indeed put them on the telly at the next opportunity. 'Some bands are on stage because they want to be,' says Wilson. 'They were on stage because they had no fucking choice.'

Wilson also decided to release some Joy Division songs on his label Factory, which at this stage was based in Alan Erasmus' bedroom on Palatine Road in Didsbury, south Manchester. 'There's no real reason why we should go to a major,' said Sumner in *The Face*. 'The advantage would be that they would hype you, give you money for videos and advertising. But what's the point?'

Terry Mason: 'It's all about confidence. We kept coming up against brick walls and all of a sudden Wilson takes notice. The man who has the veto on music in the North West decides you're good, and you're that good he wants to put a record out by you. All of a sudden your validity is there. The band had been no different in the months going up to the Rafter's gig. But all of a sudden, *the man on the telly, he say yes.* And all of a sudden, all the people now said "they're fantastic," because the man on the telly says so. Wilson says yes and everything falls into place. There'd been that change in the band's live performance ... not about virtuosity, more about confidence. They were ready to move up to that next stage.'

Sometime Rafter's DJ Rob Gretton also saw the band in full, furious flight at the Stiff/Chiswick event. At Bernard's request, he became their manager. 'Quite early on,' says Wilson today, 'Rob and Bernard's egos were like two bulls rutting. Always, always. Always.'

Interest in Joy Division was beginning to pick up. Although second on the bill, a May gig warranted them a cautiously good review in *NME* by former Negative guitarist Paul Morley, who had spotted some issues with 1978 himself in the piece. '1978 isn't so easy [as 1977]. Standards are higher. Shrewd eclecticism is necessary. Technique mandatory. Style an advantage. They [Joy Division] have an ambiguous appeal and with patience they could develop strongly and make some testing, worthwhile, metallic music.'

Top of the bill that night were The Nosebleeds; their new lead singer is described by Morley as 'minor local legend Steve Morrison.' Think you'll find that's minor local legend Steve Morri*ssey*, Paul ...

Shy Talk's Steve Burke could see that Joy Division were changing and slipping away from their punk moorings. 'I don't know whether it was Ian Curtis trying to get his voice round Barney's guitar or the other way around, but it worked between them two. Even though everyone remembers Hooky's bass. I think they were an ordinary punk band. But all of a sudden, something different came out.'

True to his word, Tony Wilson then put Joy Division on television. 'It was probably a corridor job,' recalls Granada Television producer Geoff Moore. '"You've *got* to see this band ..." sort of thing.'

Granada Television started broadcasting just after Bernard was born and was always rightly proud of its unusual regional content and commitment to arts and music. Look in the company's pop music archive and one of the earliest entries you'll find is some silent footage of The Beatles shot in The Cavern. Then you'll move through everything from Jerry Lee Lewis, *The Stones In The Park*, *Shang-a-Lang* with the Bay City Rollers, Marc Bolan's proto-punk teatime show *Marc* and the Sex Pistols on *So It Goes*.

'*So It Goes* started in 1976,' recalls producer Moore. 'I was on *World In Action* and I didn't get out till mid-1977. I was a producer. I used to play in rock bands – didn't we all – I was dead keen on music. I'm a jazz rocker really. Chicago, Blood Sweat And Tears anything like that. I was a bass player. I went straight from *World In Action* to *So It Goes*. They needed a producer, they knew I was interested in music. By then I'd done twenty *World In Action*s and been round the world. I thought it was a good move. It was this odd, late night show. It was presented by Wilson and it came at the right time – 1976 – and got the Pistols on [so] I inherited some bands that they'd already shot. Which was a pain in the arse ... bands like The Stranglers. I hired all the staff for *What's On* afresh ... Margi Clarke [*Letter to Brezhnev*], Ray Teret [Piccadilly Radio DJ], Mike Riddick from BBC Radio Manchester – he was the Terry Wogan of Radio Manchester and Dick Witts [classical musician and member of art rock band The Passage]. *What's On* was 37 half hour shows recorded on a Thursday. Cinema, theatre, TV, live shows. That had grown out of the ten-minute version at the end of *Granada Reports*. It was a good time for regional programmes – Granada was way ahead in the regional offerings. *Granada Reports*, the politics programme was a great show ... there was *Down to Earth* which was a farming show, we did quizzes, we did *Ap Kaa Haak*, an Asian show. It was seen as important to the region and important to the franchise … the regulator would want to know what you were doing for the region. It was seen as a good thing culturally to get bands like Joy Division on … it was seen as part of the service. That isn't the case now. Regional TV isn't looking at new bands – it's an area that doesn't interest them. The old days' commitment to new bands – several a week were regularly shown on *Granada Reports* – was also linked to the public service ethos of the time, showing young talent was what we *ought* to be doing.'

The desire to showcase 'young talent' at tea-time meant that after a round up of the North West's murders, bank robberies and local government argy-bargy, *Granada Reports* would regularly have a 'music outro'. These pre-recorded performances also served another purpose alongside the greater good.

'If you're the producer of the programme,' Moore says, 'you're much more worried about the news coming in than the band. Bands were emergency cover … if you've got an interview with Barry Manilow and he pulls out, then you throw in the Buzzcocks that you recorded the week before. It was kept on a shelf to bail you out of trouble. Standbys. If there was a technical fault you could keep transmitting. I remember once we had to go to the news and there was a technical fault … "Welcome to *Granada Reports*, here is the news. Sorry, we can't bring you the news … here's The Houghton Weavers.'

The pre-recorded footage of the band in Studio Two at Granada Television was broadcast on September 20. This was the same studio where the Sex Pistols had performed on *So It Goes* two years previously. All of the studios at Granada have even numbers. It's been that way since the company began in 1956. Then, the concept of television being made outside of London was considered a joke. The lack of odd numbers gave southern television types the idea that the Mancunian upstarts had twice as many studios than they actually possessed – a *very* Manchester thing to do.

As the piece starts, Curtis stares at the studio floor, hands on hips. Bernard sports shirt, tie, jeans and a wedge haircut. More importantly, he also sports a black, customised Shergold Masquerader – fresh from the rotating turntable of Mamelok's music store on Deansgate. All four members of the band have been placed on podiums. They are introduced by Tony Wilson.

'Seeing as how this is the programme that previously brought you first television appearances from everything from The Beatles to the Buzzcocks,' says Wilson to camera, 'we do like to keep our hand in and keep you informed of the most interesting new sounds in the North West. This – Joy Division – is the most interesting sound we've come across in the last six months. They're a Manchester band, with the exception of the guitarist who comes from Salford. Very important difference that. They're called Joy Division, this number is 'Shadowplay'.'

Bernard makes a last minute adjustment to a guitar effects pedal at his feet and then the band play, as negative image archive footage of motorway traffic is mixed over the top of them via the studio gallery. 'Visually, if you look at it now … it's a real period piece,' says Geoff Moore. 'We couldn't offer them much in terms of lavish sets and lighting. The motorway footage? That was Wilson's idea … I suspect.'

Curtis's arms windmill towards the end of the song in a style familiar to those who'd seen the band live. 'They were inwardly grateful to do it I suspect … being on the telly,' says Geoff Moore. 'But they were hardly going to act like Bruce Forsyth … they were mean and moody. Unlike The Clash, they probably didn't bring their manager in. Joy Division … local band. You didn't get any trouble with bands like that.

Terry Mason: 'How many years had [Manchester soft-rockers] Sad Cafe been dragging their arses around before they got on *Granada Reports*? And we're this bunch of oiks, from the wrong side of town, who are not musos, and we're on there.'

'I think I've become a convert,' says Geoff Moore now. 'I see stuff I never saw before. 'Transmission', 'She's Lost Control'. Really innovative. At the time, I was somewhere else musically. More mainstream. I was a little older than the others. I'm an old Frank Zappa freak. But I think it's really interesting music. Maybe if Wilson hadn't been banging me over the head, I'd have appreciated it a bit more.'

'The power of Wilson is forgotten nowadays,' says Terry Mason. 'He's now this – he believes – elder statesman … but in those days he was the *law*. For people in Manchester and Salford, Granada was Hollywood. We'd got through. We went to the canteen, we thought there'd be *legionnaires* queuing up for their dinner.'

Always in search of a bargain, Wilson and Factory next took the band to Cargo studios in Rochdale in October for their first recordings for the Factory label. Martin Hannett – who already had *Spiral Scratch*, Slaughter and the Dogs' *Cranked Up Really High* and theatre project *The Belt and Braces Roadshow* under his belt – produced the tracks for *A Factory Sample*.

'My theory with Factory,' said Hannett in *NME* in 1980, 'was that it shouldn't have been necessary. I didn't think it would work – it could work much better, but we're too extended. Cash is the main problem.' By

October 1978, Hannett had, in fact, been on the business–end of a bona fide hit. His 'Jilted John' single with Manchester-based student Graham Fellows had just gone to number 4 in the charts.

Bernard Sumner: 'You have to dig a little deeper – to Martin, cash was a problem, because he wanted a Fairlight, which cost the equivalent of about £150,000 in today's money. However, Tony and Rob wanted a nightclub, about £5,000,000 in today's money. We wanted to get out of our council flats, considerably cheaper but apparently more unobtainable.'

John Brierley was the boss of Cargo and remembers the circumstances of Joy Division recording out in the sticks. 'I used to work as a cameraman at Granada at the same time as Tony Wilson was there as one of the presenters. When I left and set up Cargo records, Tony came along one day and said, "I've got this new band and I've got a new record label Factory Records," which didn't have much money, and was I prepared to record this band for the [future] royalties or just get a fee for the day. I said I'd see what the band sounded like.'

'That was very much the Factory way,' says Cargo studio landlord Chris Hewitt, whose dealings with the organisation would stretch into the Haçienda days. 'It was always, "Do us a good deal and we'll see you right!"' Chris Hewitt clearly remembers the band – and their demeanour – as they recorded at Cargo: 'Ian Curtis was a sort of intellectual who'd read quite a few books,' says Hewitt. 'Steve Morris was a proper musician who was into Fairport Convention. The others couldn't really play their instruments. Bernard and Hooky were just the kind of lads who'd talk about pulling birds and having a few pints down Pips disco.'

John Brierley took a listen to the Martin Hannett-produced recordings, to decide which way he should play the deal. 'They recorded 'Digital' and 'Glass' for *A Factory Sample*. And I thought they were awful. I did not like them at all. I decided to take the day's fee for doing the job ... and missed out on all the royalties after. I subsequently got to like Joy Division more. Not particularly New Order though ...'

Bernard Sumner: 'So awful, he didn't mind taking the fee.'

Of the two Cargo tracks, 'Digital' is key, as it is clearly the stepping stone between the old Warsaw sound and Joy Division, as people would recognise them now. Curtis is still a 'shouter', but on 'Digital' he's also got his chin down, singing low and loud. Bernard's guitar is still slightly stuck in New Waves-ville territory but he's not trying quite so hard to dominate. It's Hook's bass that drives the melody. It's ... Joy Division. It's hard not to surmise that this transformation was heavily effected by Martin Hannett. According to those present at the sessions, Bernard was quietly taking it all in.

Tony Wilson: 'To me, the fascinating bit about Bernard is this: lead singers and pop stars are meant to be self-promoters, aren't they? And yet the bit of Bernard that nobody knows is that he became the new Martin Hannett. There's no doubt that Martin created modern music. Martin taught him what he knew ... and Bernard was a great learner. What's really weird about that Cargo session is that Martin helped a bunch of techies in Burnley build the first digital delay machine, he then gets delivery of the machine two days before he went into the studio at Cargo with Joy Division. The machine was called 'Digital' ... it was heaven sent.'

There is a telling photograph of Bernard at Cargo. He's standing next to Martin Hannett as the producer fiddles with some hefty-looking synthesisers. Bernard is quite clearly in awe of both the man and the machines.

> Bernard Sumner: 'Martin, at times, could be a pain in the arse,
> and the look of awe on my face could possibly be the mouthing of the word
> "... off!" as in "fuck off!"'

A little more than a fortnight after the Cargo session, on October 28, Bernard got married to Sue Barlow. Ian and Deborah Curtis were the witnesses to the Salford registry ceremony. In fact, they were also the only guests – no one else from in or around the band was invited. 'I think that was more to do with Sue and Debbie than Bernard,' offers Terry Mason now. 'They were consciously or unconsciously trying to get a girls federation going. I think Sue wanted to get married more than Bernard ... plus Sue's flat was closer to Bernard's work. Sue wanted to be married and I think she told Barney, "You're not going to live here with us not being married."'

> Bernard Sumner: 'Terry really has a very unromantic way of looking at things.'

The foursome went for a meal at the Last Drop Hotel in Bromley Cross, Bolton, a "fancy" restaurant by quaint shops overlooking the West Pennine Moors that was popular with out-of-towners looking to mark that special occasion. Bernard moved away from his family and into Sue's flat at Peel

Green. Within a week, the band were gigging again, at Eric's in Liverpool, The Odeon in Canterbury and at Brunel University, supporting sci-fi Scots The Rezillos. Joy Division went down badly at Brunel and were spat off stage by late-in-the-day punks. It was a clear indicator that the final ties to punk had to be cut. They had to reach out beyond the punks to a different audience.

To get a true sketch of any band on an upward curve, the devil is in the detail. And the best place to find detail is very often in the front row of an audience. The best barometer of that upward pressure can usually be gauged and quantified in the hearts and minds of the teenagers they reach out and touch. Youth – passionate, music-hungry youth – can be knocked sideways by a band. Boys can be far more susceptible to this than girls, I've found. An example would be useful here. Aged 15, Andrew Wake from south Manchester was hit by Joy Division ... and hit hard.

'Joy Division had brought out [the] *An Ideal For Living* EP, which I'd bought and wasn't that enamoured with,' he remembers. 'It was just another Manchester record. *A Factory Sample* then came out. There'd been a massive leap between those tracks and the first EP. And then they came to play in Altrincham, autumn 1978, The Check Inn. On my doorstep. It was a small town disco, sticky dance floor, up the stairs, in the main high street in Altrincham. It was Bob Jefferson from [local record store] Streets Ahead Records that organised it. Bob and his wife ran Streets Ahead ... he was [also] a chiropodist.'

Streets Ahead was on Lloyd Street in Altrincham – a terraced street just away from the town centre. Imagine Coronation Street with a record shop stuck in the middle of it. Local kids could hear a record on John Peel's show during the week, go into Streets Ahead, ask Jefferson to play it again just to confirm it still sounded good, then maybe even *buy* it. Access to Peel's choices was a luxury many kids around the UK could only dream of in 1978. I know. I was one of those kids and I bought 'Teenage Kicks' by The Undertones from Mr and Mrs Jefferson the day after I first heard Peel play it.

'They didn't mind kids loitering in there and playing records,' says Wake. 'I think [the Check Inn gig] came about because of everyone being bored and having nothing to do, so he decided to start putting on gigs and the first one was at The Check Inn. For your pound you got Joy Division, you got Surgical Supports and you got The Bidet Boys. Joy Division were still doing cover versions ... 'Louie Louie' and 'Sister Ray'. The nearest thing they sounded like at The Check Inn was early Banshees. Whereas The Fall just clattered about on stage, Joy Division were different. On stage, they

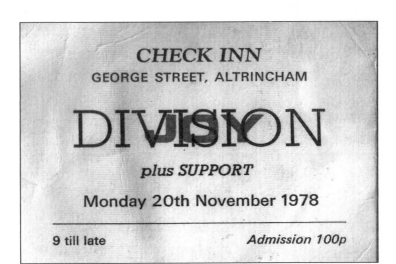

A ticket for the Check Inn gig.

were very different people. None of this announcing of songs, no talking to the audience. It was tight.'

Local journalist Mike Nicholls reviewed the gig for *Record Mirror*, a weekly paper which latched onto the band early. *Record Mirror* is usually forgotten about when remembering the big inkies of the 1970s and 1980s, mainly because of its unashamed pop sensibilities and colour front covers – both of which were considered extremely vulgar at the time. Nicholls notes that the band had dropped their 'denied affinity to Nazism and are instead concentrating on producing some tight, dynamic music with above-average lyrics.' He zeroes in on Bernard's 'Banshee-esque' guitar playing and notes that he has dropped the name Albrecht for Dickin – one of the few times Bernard's adopted name ever appeared in print.

'A band to definitely watch out for,' concludes Nicholls. Audience member Andrew Wake agreed. 'When I next saw them again at Bowdon Vale, something special had happened.'

During the last week of the last month of 1978, Ian Curtis had his first seizure that could be identified as an epileptic fit. Medication to contain the condition began. 'I really do think it was the tablets that killed him,' said Bernard Sumner in *Touching From A Distance*. 'I really do, I know it.'

CONFUSION FIVE: IAN WILSON – A TRIBUTE

Early in 1979, Bernard made good on that apparent mental note he'd made ... to do as you would be done by. Buzzcocks had helped him and Warsaw when they were starting out, so he would help another band on their way up, Crispy Ambulance. A chance meeting with the band's lead singer, Alan Hempsall, would prove vital. It would create a link between Joy Division and Crispy Ambulance that would forge connections well beyond an apparent shared propensity for 'gloomy' music and tie Hempsall into one of the strangest stanza's of Joy Division's story.

'I'd been to see them a couple of times,' says Hempsall. 'I went to see them one Friday night and I was in town the following day in Virgin Records. In walked Bernard. We just got talking and he was really nice. He was like, "What do you do?" Oh, I'm in a band, Crispy Ambulance." "Oh, we saw you about six months ago." He described this gig at the Band On The Wall, probably one of our worst and he thought we were great. That was how it started. This was peculiar to Joy Division. You wouldn't imagine The Fall necessarily offering a helping hand, would you? I hesitate to say it, but Bernard was a sweetie.'

Alongside Bernard's assistance, Joy Division's manager would also prove an inspiration to Crispy Ambulance. 'Gretton was our model. Rob was taciturn and outwardly really quite aggressive,' says Hempsall today, sat at his kitchen table all big bones and lantern-jaw. 'He was also hilarious and quite clever in that he turned round after we'd met Joy Division and said, "Why don't you just put your own record out?" To me that was like, "Why don't you build a rocket and go to the moon?" Don't be silly. He said, "That's what we did with Warsaw... we got a bank loan... we lied to the bank manager." I think one of them went and said it was for a garage extension or something. Next thing you know, they've got a thousand records. So we applied for this bank loan and, bugger me, we got it. So Rob Gretton was there every step of the way. Before we knew where we were, we had a record out and next thing we knew John Peel was playing it ... bless his cottons.'

Helping hands aside, the difference in Joy Division at the start of 1979 was clear in their live performances. Bernard started using a synthesiser on stage which, coupled with Steve Morris' synth drums, cut any final ties with punk.

The band returned to Altrincham to play two gigs in the unusual setting of Bowdon Youth Club in March and May. Bowdon is an almost entirely posh suburb within the slightly more mixed town of Altrincham. Go there today and it's pure *Footballer's Wives* territory. The support acts at Bowdon were local band Staff 9 and Factory act A Certain Ratio who, at that stage, were still using a drum machine.

The band created their own mini Lesser Free Trade Hall experience with the three gigs they played in Altrincham and Bowdon. The Stone Roses' Ian Brown, from just up the road in Timperley, remembers going to see the band at the Youth Club. Brown cites it as the first gig he ever went to and would manage to recount the occasion in a fruity anecdote many years later in Q. 'I was 14 and I went with my friend and his little sister. After the gig, she went and asked Ian Curtis for one of his badges and he said he'd give it to her, but only if he got a blow job in return. She was only 12! I remember thinking, what a disgrace!'

Bernard Sumner: 'So a Nazi, racist and a paedophile! The odds against finding all three traits in one person, let alone an epileptic singer who kills himself, must be phenomenal. This is absolute bollocks – it's just not the sort of thing Ian [Curtis] would have done.'

Joy Division had started to build up a small following – Andrew Wake was one of them. 'I went down before the gig and got all my records signed. I remember Curtis was playing snooker in the back room. They were all really friendly. Bernard was the least talkative of the lot. Between The Check Inn and Bowdon Vale, something serious had changed. The cover versions had gone. You hate using words to describe a band's music but it wasn't just Curtis – it was four people. Steve Morris was a great drummer, Peter Hook's bass lines carried most of the melody ... Bernard's guitar playing was just astounding. If you could play guitar, *everybody* could play that ascending bar chord riff on 'She's Lost Control', but you couldn't *write* it. It was so minimal. They were like washes. You were used to people shouting and playing hell for leather and shouting and screaming ... there was a control to what they did. By the third gig, kids were coming from as far away as Sale! Kids meeting, getting together. Lots of groups came out of that.'

In between the Bowdon gigs, the band went to Strawberry Studios in Stockport to start recording their debut album. The Strawberry building is no great shakes. It still sits just behind the town's market area but was in its pomp during the late 1970s, due to money generated by its owners, local art-rockers 10cc. Joy Division recorded during cheaper 'down time' and by rights the album should have come out on a major – Warner's sub-label Genetic – but this plan was derailed by Rob Gretton's desire to stick with punk ethics and have Joy Division's first album released on an independent: Factory. They had essentially already previously recorded enough material for an album for RCA, but the deal and their view of the recordings had soured. Plus, Wilson had £5,000 of unexpected money, owing to the recent death of his mother.

Peter Hook has described producer Martin Hannett's attitude towards them as 'disgusting' during the sessions. 'He was actually quite frightening,' said Hook in Q in 2006. 'He was a very disturbing character and you didn't really feel like answering back. He was very volatile, throwing tantrums all the time.'

Fellow Salford band Fast Cars were recording at Strawberry Studios at the same time as Joy Division's debut album sessions – to be called *Unknown Pleasures* – were taking place. Fast Cars' Steve Murray recalls the nerves he and the rest of the band felt as they walked into 10cc's domain: 'Recording at Strawberry was a massive thing for us as it was *the* studio in the North West at that time,' he says. 'Our manager, Tim Llewellyn, arranged for us to record with Hannett in the down time after Joy Division had finished. We were really excited about recording, particularly with someone who had such a name as Martin at the time. But we weren't like Joy Division, we were a pop band who could play very well and had a good idea of how we should sound and Hannett tried to change that, but he didn't have the same scope with us as he did with Joy Division, as our songs were well-structured and left no room for him to experiment – they were a producer's dream, providing you could cope with their level of musicianship.' Murray says that Hannett's enthusiasm for the sessions would 'come in waves then fade away' as he snorted cocaine from the studio desk.

Bernard Sumner: 'So tell me, if we were just malleable clay in the hands of an insane, drug-crazed record producer, and the Fast Cars were a real pop band who could play 'very well', how come no one's ever heard of them?'

Listened to today, the reference points for *Unknown Pleasures* are clear: The Doors, Siouxsie And The Banshees and Kraftwerk. Peter Hook can be heard stretching for – and missing – some notes, especially on lead track 'Disorder'. It's no wonder he dislikes the album. But Morris' drums are essentially utilised as a lead instrument and Bernard's reverb-heavy guitar sounds clean and assured, with the need for speed now removed. Curtis has stopped shouting and his vocals are full of light, shade and power. He is believable when the touch is light, and impressive when the time is right for singing from your boots. The Doors can be found on tracks like 'Candidate' and 'I Remember Nothing', the kind of Jim Morrison-esque amble that Echo And The Bunnymen would be honing within the next eighteen months. As for Kraftwerk, along with the sparse, spidery synth lines that would be familiar to anyone with a knowledge of the German band, there is 'Insight', which features the same double-note pulse as 1977's 'Trans-Europe Express' track from the album of the same name. *Tomorrow's World* was right for once: Kraftwerk really were ahead of their time. The song also has that *boowp-boowp* drum synth sound familiar to anyone who has danced like a wedding day drunk to Kelly Marie's 'Feels Like I'm in Love', a number 1 hit the following year. 'She's Lost Control' stars Bernard's oh-so-simple ascending bar chord riff and 'Shadowplay' is the band at their most familiarly *Joy Division* ... sounding like it's been recorded from the bottom of a well. But in a good way. 'Interzone' harks back to the punk days with it's familiar guitar motifs and traditional rock stylings. To accompany Bernard's desire to do away with 'peripheral rubbish', the album artwork lacks even basic information, though he has managed to get another cover design idea away, by spotting up an image from the *Cambridge Encyclopaedia of Astronomy* of the first radio pulsar, PSR1919+21 (originally known as CP1919) discovered in 1967.

Many albums are better produced than *Unknown Pleasures* – there are definitely albums where all the notes are struck more efficiently and in the correct order – but listened to today, it is a post-punk blueprint that's still being rolled out and examined on a regular basis.

Despite the harsh condition's imposed by Martin Hannett's personality during the sessions, Tony Wilson believes that Bernard's second exposure to the producer shaped his future role: 'Messing with those strange boxes and synthesisers, Martin found in Joy Division a group who was entertained as he was by technology. Bernard's role as Hannett's successor is never acknowledged.'

Alongside the rest of the week's releases such as those by Ry Cooder and The Rubinoos, reviews for *Unknown Pleasures* were strong, none more so than Jon Savage's wordy take on the matter in *Melody Maker*: 'Joy Division at least set a course in the present with contrails for the future – perhaps you can't ask for much more. Indeed, *Unknown Pleasures* may very well be one of the best, white, English, debut LPs of the year.' The review is accompanied by a photo of the band looking upwards and beyond, by former Negative nemesis Kevin Cummins.

Sounds was also behind the band with writer Mick Middles highlighting both the album and their live performances. 'A haunting, hypnotic experience of moving, magical music. They could be compared to The Doors or Hawkwind but even those hefty comparisons can't do any justice to Joy Division. They never fail to amaze me with their morbid genius. Sensuous, seductive and deadly. This band cry real tears.'

They'd gone from insiders, to pariahs, to insiders again in just over a year. 'In the very early days before *Unknown Pleasures*, the music press detested us and that was a kind of driving force to go on,' said Sumner in *NME*. 'When *Unknown Pleasures* came out, we were suddenly wonderful. We went from being the most unpopular group to being the most popular. Fucking ridiculous.'

Along with the album reviews came the inevitable press interviews, including one disastrous encounter with Dave McCullough of *Sounds*. The writer – who refers to Bernard only as 'the guitarist' and Hook as 'the bearded bassist' – describes the band and Rob Gretton as giving the impression they suffered from serious mental deficiencies. He tries to engage Curtis but when the replies fall short he becomes angry. 'No amount of undermilling obscurity will convince me that Joy Division's static, murky militancy is real,' states McCullough. 'For, at the moment, the music is too supercilious (like the people) to ring true.'

Encounters like this set a tone for relations with the press. The band clammed up. In the absence of much to say from the group, journalists appeared to fill in the gaps, putting a label of gravity and aloofness on Joy Division that boosted their importance in the eyes of the outside world.

'People tend to get tied down to one particular sound,' Ian Curtis said at the time on BBC Radio Lancashire. I think it's a lot easier for the music papers to do something like that. They like to get you boxed in, THIS group belongs to THIS category. But I'd like to think we don't belong to any category. I'd like to think that the music we play cuts across different things. We never have any intentions of "we want to sound like this or we want to sound like that." Just what comes out at the time.'

In November, the single 'Transmission' was received with open arms by the press. Describing their music as 'the pride and passion of the moment', *Melody Maker's* Chris Bohn nailed his colours to the post-punk mast very clearly. This single was, 'a potent fusion of moral fervour and strident rock and roll and it's the most exciting thing I've heard in a long time. 'Transmission' is fired by coiling, rubber band bass, splendidly set off by a restrained drum beat and the clawing, slicing guitar.' Had it not been for M's 'Moonlight And Muzak', it would have been 'Single of the Week'.

Despite, or maybe even because of an aloof, near-silent image, Joy Division had just about made it.

Peter Hook once described Joy Division as 'beer boys'. The heavyweight muteness was a long way from the reality that those around the band saw. 'I only saw the funny side of Joy Division … I was lucky in that respect,' says Alan Hempsall. 'I was just in on the good times and the japes. Part of the problem was they hated being interviewed … they were once interviewed by *Sounds* and the journalist made certain things up and afterwards that was it. They really hated the whole promoting process.'

The band's gigging schedule was, by this stage, fierce. Everything from the Walthamstow Youth Centre in south east London to the Plan K club in Brussels, supporting American *Naked Lunch* author William S. Burroughs. Plan K was situated at 21 Rue de Manchester and one of the main movers behind the gig was embassy worker Annik Honoré. 'At the time, I was working in London for the Belgium Embassy,' she told film maker James Nice for his *Shadowplayers* documentary. 'I got to know many groups in those days. It was just so easy to ask a group to come to Belgium and play. You didn't need to go through an agency or record company.' Joy Division played twice at Plan K – and Annik and Ian Curtis became lovers.

Back in the UK, a tour with Buzzcocks took the bands across the country's slightly less glamorous Apollos, Top Ranks and Odeons. For some reviewers, Joy Division were surpassing their former mentors. 'Buzzcocks used to be a vital, invigorating band. On Friday night [at London's Rainbow] they displayed no interest whatsoever and subsequently they're no longer interesting,' wrote *Melody Maker*'s Chris Bohn. The paper even made a veiled accusation that Joy Division's sound had been tampered with.' There's no excuse for what they [Buzzcocks] allowed to happen to Joy Division,' Bohn wrote.

There was even a disastrous headlining festival gig at Leigh near Wigan, Greater Manchester, branded 'Top of the Flops' by the local press. What started as a benefit event for a local youth centre on National Coal Board land morphed into a 'Manchester versus Liverpool' affair between Factory Records and their Scouse counterparts, Zoo. A Certain Ratio, The Distractions and Joy Division were among the Manchester contingent, with Echo And The Bunnymen, A Flock of Seagulls and Teardrop Explodes holding up the Merseyside end. 'At the time it was advertised as 'The 1st Leigh Youth Festival',' says organiser Joan Miller. 'The 'Zoo Meets Factory' thing came after the event. It was Tony Wilson and Factory's way of making people believe it was all their idea. They were hired to play, that's all. I remember most of the bands were pubescent and not as great as they later went on to be.

Joy Division were on highly aggressive form that night, with the sound ricochetting around the slag heaps as they battered their way through 'Disorder', 'Leaders of Men' and 'Dead Souls', more than earning their £8 fee. 'Joy Division were great,' says Joan Miller today. 'Ian Curtis was ill that day, vomiting after their set. About 200-250 watched it. Between bands we played 5-a-side soccer with the police.'

The ticket for the 'disastrous' Leigh Music Festival.

'It was a bit of derelict land in between two slag heaps,' recalls Joy Division follower Andrew Wake. 'We got there ... and there was no one there. Big stage. It started at dinner time [midday] in the daylight. Joy Division headlined it. I think they were very pleased at that stage in their careers that they had kids who were willing to follow them around. We missed the bus, so they put us in the back of the van and they took us back into Manchester.

At that time, they were rehearsing at TJ Davison's. Lots of bands used to rehearse there. Sundays we used to go down and hang out. Joy Division were sort of private. But – once – they let us in and we sat quietly in the corner. Bernard was on a synthesiser and was playing the same riff over and over again. Curtis had the mike to his mouth and was humming. He was echoing the melody Bernard was playing on the synth. No verses or anything. Didn't know what it was then but I remembered this little tune. About two months later they were playing it live and it was 'Love Will Tear Us Apart'.

'It was interesting to see the way they were writing,' remembers Wake. 'You could just pop in and watch. Bernard was the creative one. He wasn't afraid to *not* play. Very sparing in what he played. I wouldn't be surprised if it wasn't him that shaped and structured the songs. Who else would let a bass player play all the melody?'

Aforementioned Salford power-pop band Fast Cars also rehearsed there. Stuart Murray, bass player: 'TJ Davidson's was an old warehouse, some of the rooms had huge windows and were very light and airy, but it was pretty damn cold with its brick walls and twenty-foot ceilings. There were some small rooms at the top with no windows at all. There was a tremendous feeling of expectation about the place as bands from all over Manchester rehearsed there, it really was the epicentre of Manchester music. There used to be an old Irish caretaker who was a real character around the place. His catch phrase became immortal ... "That's as far as I know", he always used to say in this thick Dublin accent ... "That's as far as I know."'

Away from rehearsals, things were closing in on Ian Curtis. With a new-born baby arrived in April, he was away from the home he shared with wife Deborah on Barton Street, Macclesfield, for long periods of time. His situation with epilepsy was worsening and his relationship with Honoré was complicating an already difficult situation at home. The band weren't to find out just how intense Ian's life had become until the inquest into his death. 'I certainly didn't know what was happening back at Barton Street when he wasn't with us,' says Terry Mason. 'We saw him at rehearsals and at gigs where he'd have minor episodes or a *grand mal* [seizure]. We didn't know what else should have been done.'

Shortly before his death, Curtis explained how he apparently dragged real situations into his lyric writing. 'It's more to do with personal relations and the way people can cope with certain things,' he said on BBC Lancashire in 1980. 'I tend to be interested in people and how they look at things and the way people can cope with certain problems and how they can adapt and such-like.'

'There was no adult leadership with Joy Division,' says Terry Mason. 'It's like the Vietnam war thing, "What's the difference between the Marine Corps and the Boy Scouts? ... the Boy Scouts have adult leadership." Not Rob Gretton. The nearest to an adult we had was Tony Wilson!'

Tony Wilson told me: 'No. We were all children. Rob is one of the great rock and roll managers of all-time. There's no doubt. Rob invented indie culture in this country. Rob's influence was brilliant.'

Against the backdrop of more UK gigs and a European tour, the band recorded *another* album at Britannia Row Studios, London, in March 1980, again with Martin Hannett. During a rare night at Barton Street in April when the recording had finished, Curtis took an overdose of the barbituate phenobarbitone and left a suicide note, before telling Deborah Curtis what he'd done and being carted off to hospital. The following day, he was press-ganged into a gig at Bury's Derby Hall after an apparently aggressive bedside pep talk by Rob Gretton.

> *Bernard Sumner: 'Ian should not have done the gig, I agree,*
> *but no one knows what Rob said to him in hospital.'*

Sumner and Curtis
at their last ever gig together.

Terry Mason: 'I was personally shocked that we did the gig. Hooky rang me up and told me what had happened to Ian. Ian was all over the show. If it was boxing, the referee wouldn't have let Ian continue.'

'Ian and Rob wanted to do the gig,' said Stephen Morris in *Touching From A Distance*. 'I didn't. I thought that if there was something wrong, doing the gig wouldn't sort it out.'

At that gig, singers from the Factory roster took it in turns to perform with Bernard, Peter Hook and Steven Morris, as an unwell Curtis stood in the wings. The singers were Simon Topping [A Certain Ratio], Larry Cassidy [Section 25] and Alan Hempsall of Crispy Ambulance, who tackled 'Love Will Tear Us Apart' and 'Digital'. Hempsall's *strum und drang* vocal style more than suited the material. 'It was great, just pick your favourite Joy Division songs and away we go,' says Hempsall. Curtis did manage to sing 'Decades' and 'Eternal' – two slow songs – before Topping, Cassidy and Hempsall returned for a mass singalong. This proved too much for the crowd and a single thrown bottle kicked off a mass brawl and glass-throwing session that edged towards a full riot. 'As this was going off,' remembers Hempsall, 'Bernard's sitting in a corner saying ... "I hate violence, it's so temporary." I'll always remember that line.'

Back onstage, Mason and Joy Division roadie Twinny were battling to save the group's gear. 'Hooky grabs me and shoves two empty beer bottles in my hand, drags me out there, to be confronted with this row of people all picking up and throwing empty bottles and pint pots,' recalls Hempsall. Curtis was later found backstage, in tears.

'Basically, we want to play and enjoy what we like playing,' Curtis told the BBC just before his death. 'I think when we stop doing that, that'll be time to pack it in. That'll be the end.'

Curtis managed a few more commitments with the band, including recording a video for 'Love Will Tear Us Apart' at TJ Davidson's rehearsal room and performing live in Manchester, Derby and at Birmingham University on May 2, where they played a new song, 'Ceremony'. On May 17, Curtis was due to go out drinking with Bernard, but cried off, telling him he'd meet him at Manchester Airport on Monday morning instead, to fly off to America for dates due to start in New York.

In the early hours of Sunday morning, Curtis killed himself at Barton Street.

Press clippings about Ian Curtis and his eventual suicide.

'If he was depressed,' says Stephen Morris, 'he kept it from us.'

'There was a lot of disbelief involved really,' said Bernard on Channel 4's *Star Test*. 'It was just very heavy ... "What are we going to do about the future?" That kind of vibe. And, "Oh, my God, what are we going to do? Oh, my God, he's done it."'

Terry Mason, who had taken on an unofficial role as Curtis's emotional minder prior to his death, states that none of them were emotionally mature enough to deal with what happened. 'We were just in shock. We were quite simple naive kids. We didn't know an awful lot about life. I don't think many people did in those days. "Me mate's just killed himself" ... and you can't figure out why he's done it. Everyone had their own private theory. None of us would sit and talk to each other about it.'

At the inquest into Ian Curtis' death, Macclesfield coroner Mr Timothy Dennis listened to a bleak list of circumstances leading up to events at Barton Street. The inquest heard that Curtis had suffered stress over marital problems and depression over epileptic attacks. He'd spent three days in hospital earlier in the year after taking an overdose of tablets. Psychiatric appointments had been made but he'd only kept two of them. The previous year, he'd been found unconscious at home after self-inflicting knife wounds. He was living apart from his wife Deborah and young daughter Natalie. Deborah had asked for a divorce after he'd been seeing a girlfriend. Curtis had been found hanging by a rope attached to a kitchen washing rack and neighbour Kevin Wood and another man had tried to save him after cutting his body down. A letter found by the body said, 'At this very moment, I wish I were dead, I just can't cope any more.'

Deborah Curtis told Mr Dennis that Ian had often talked about taking his own life and always said he was going to die young. Given all the circumstances, Mr Dennis found that Ian Curtis had killed himself. The headline in the *Manchester Evening News* stated, '"I Will Die Young" said hanged singer.'

'I will never be able to cope,' said Bernard in *Melody Maker*, shortly after Curtis' suicide. 'Ian's death will affect me for now, and forever, I will never be able to forget it. Personally, as a friend ... it means so much to me ... regardless of the group ... as a friend.'

The difference that a matter of months made – and Curtis' suicide – in the British music press, was breathtaking. Compare the words of Dave McCullough of *Sounds* in his eulogy, to those of the same writer eight months earlier, when he'd offered the opinion that the band had serious mental deficiencies.

'Ian Curtis was the stuff of enchanted, immutable mystery,' wrote McCullough this time around. 'When I met him, he talked in a whisper and he talked hypnotically and enchantedly about toy-shops. He spun words magically ... he poured pure silver across totally memorable phrases and related scenarios ... his death was poetically beautiful ... that man cared for you, that man died for you.'

Bernard Sumner: 'McCollough was a very confusing journalist
– perhaps there are two with the same surname?'

Terry Mason: 'He didn't die for me ... if anything, he died for Factory. He died because Ian was carrying the rest of us on his shoulders. And the rest of us had became quite numerous by that point. It wasn't just the band, the crew, Rob, Factory, all the other people on Factory ... there's also bloody Rough Trade's distribution, half the independent records shops in the country. He felt he had to stay there, he would have been better elsewhere. Ian had a planet on each shoulder. He had the whole Factory infrastructure on him. Joy Division goes, there's no Factory. A Certain Ratio would never make a record that would break even. Crispy Ambulance did one 10-inch single that no one particularly wanted. Ian's got this situation where he had to keep doing it to keep everyone [else] going. Everyone's given up their day jobs by now. We made our money by Joy Division bringing in money. The record sales weren't enough, we had to keep doing gigs. So he was carrying the band. If he'd turned round in July 1979 and said, "Sorry lads, it's just making me bad," no one would have had any argument with him. But he felt he had to do it. Ian's got all this pressure ... he's got a daughter, he's got a wife, he's got Annik ... and, on top of this, he's certainly physically ill and possibly mentally ill.'

A great deal has been wrung from the death of Ian Curtis since the events of May 19, 1980. Wondering if time has over-dramatised events – or alternately blanched them of personal responsibility – I ask Terry Mason a direct question: 'Did someone not put their hands up and say "Stop, there's a duty of care here, you wouldn't treat a dog like this ..."?'

Terry appears visibly upset and there is a long pause before he answers. 'No. But I don't know how to get over [to you] how young we were for our age. We were streetwise but we didn't know anything about any sort of *illness* ... we knew what epilepsy was, you'd see someone having a fit in the street. It was traditional English black and white TV, someone frothing at the mouth. If we would have signed to a major, would Ian still be alive? We'd have adult leadership, there'd be an A&R department making sure that the golden goose wasn't getting overcooked. He would have had more money. And if we were with a major, would we have moved down south? Ian and Debbie? Clean break. Ian and Annik? Together. Medical and well-being supervision. Did [being on] Factory records kill Ian? What if? What if, after *Unknown Pleasures*, Polydor or whoever came in with a big cheque book and said, "Factory can't take you any further, sign with us, we'll sort things out." Would the band have lasted any longer? Maybe, maybe not. But I certainly think Ian would be alive.'

Tony Wilson: 'No one *ever* got over it. The person who most didn't get over it was Hannet. Hannet was the one still in pieces ten years later.'

In *Melody Maker*, Jon Savage offered strong words of caution to those tempted by notions of idolising Curtis and his death. 'To mythologise and canonise him as a romantic pessimist who dies for his art is to have a corpse in your mouth,' he wrote. What a shame no one listened.

Several weeks after his death, a belated article about Ian Curtis was printed on the 'pop' page of the *Manchester Evening News*. Viewed today, it's impossible not to cringe at what was written. The headline reads: 'IAN WILSON: A TRIBUTE.'

Ian Wilson
—a tribute

SOME of you, and justifiably, are digging into me for my lack of a real tribute to Ian Wilson, the lead vocalist of Joy Division who tragically died a few weeks ago.

I was away at the time and I thought it had been covered. No disrespect was meant, for Ian was, like Joy Division, one of the best things to happen for ages.

He was a great performer and a fine songwriter. He, and the band, made life hard for those who wanted to market them as tomorrow's prepackaged commercial pop offering.

The waxings of the band available — the LP Unknown Pleasures plus single, Transmission — are still in The Indie Chart of Record Business.

If you want more readable words and lots of sense on Ian and Joy Division then I suggest you get hold of the NME for week ending June 14.

'A real tribute to Ian Wilson' extracted from the Manchester Evening News.

'Some of you,' the piece starts, 'and justifiably, are digging into me for my lack of a real tribute to Ian Wilson, the lead vocalist of Joy Division who tragically died a few weeks ago. I was away at the time and thought it had been covered. No disrespect was meant, for Ian was, like Joy Division, one of the best things to happen for ages.'

It seems that the 'pop' page of the *Manchester Evening News* had a lot in common with many others. They didn't know who Ian Curtis actually was. You can look for prior clues to what Curtis did wherever you want. You'll certainly find them if that's what you require. But, perhaps, tarry a second over Curtis's thoughts on Lou Reed, recorded just before he died by his own hand. 'Instead of just singing about something,' Curtis said admiringly of Reed, 'he could actually show it as well.'

Tarry a second.

Then move on.

CONFUSION SIX:
'YOUNG BERNARD COULDN'T HOLD A TUNE IN A BUCKET'

'In a way,' says Tony Wilson today, 'you could see Bernard as the *'put upon'* one. That line that always reverberates in my mind ... 'You take my place in the showdown, I observe with a pitiful eye,' ['Heart And Soul'] from one of those now seemingly prophetic fucking tracks. Yes, we all took Ian's place in the showdown, we all went on to fight the battles – be it with the gangs, be it with the charts or whatever it was with. But the person who really took Ian's place in the showdown was *Bernard*. It is utterly unprecedented.'

Hard on the back of Curtis' death came the second album, *Closer.* Britain's music press had the post-punk moment they had been waiting for: someone who really could prove they *meant* it beyond any question of doubt. You could almost here the preparatory cracking of knuckles and the stretching of arms, as the music writers of the day sat down to their typewriters for their career-enhancing chances to *shine.* Under the circumstances, the critical response was as inevitable as it was unanimous. For *New Musical Express*, Charles Shaar Murray weighed in with a full-page of post-Curtis prose, claiming that *Closer* was 'sufficiently extraordinary to transcend our expectations of what we can get out of a rock album ... as magnificent a memorial (for Joy Division as much as for Curtis) as any post-Presley popular musician could have.' Bernard and the rest of the band got name-checks but, apart from highlighting Morris's drumming, it was all about Curtis.

The editor of *Sounds* handed a review copy of *Closer* to that man again, Dave McCullough. 'Young men in dark silhouettes, some darker than others, looking inwards, looking out, discovering the same horror and describing it with the same dark strokes of gothic rock,' he wrote in the review. 'These are the soul musicians ... if we could look at it from twenty or more years away, maybe we'd know more of what the young men in dark silhouettes have to say. For now, *Closer* is close enough. It will tear you apart. Again.'

Melody Maker – the longest running of the the big weeklies – gave the job to Paolo Hewitt, who actually turned in an eminently sensible piece: 'Paradoxically, given the intense personal revelations of Curtis which run like fire throughout,' Hewitt wrote, 'the actual music is some of the most irresistible dance music we'll hear this year.'

Nearly thirty years on, I contacted Paolo Hewitt to find out more about his thoughts at the time. 'The reason I didn't get all hysterical about the band and about Ian Curtis is this,' he told me. 'What tends to happen when you're a writer – or if you just like music – is that you respond strongly to those bands you can relate to. A lot of the music press people – the Paul Morleys and the Dave McCulloughs – responded strongly to Curtis because he was from a culture of books. They really related strongly to the way he framed his words, that's the culture they knew. Ian Curtis and that whole culture wasn't an issue for me. I just wanted to write as well as I could about whatever I was asked to write about. I never thought about a career.'

Pick up a copy of *Closer* today, you'll notice what a big, awkward album it is – it doesn't do any favours for the casual listener. Heard now – and absolved of the apparent responsibilty of flagging up the clues in Curtis' lyrics as reviewers in 1980 seemed duty-bound to do – it's a surprisingly *proggy* record. A succession of Radiohead albums may have deadened our senses and perhaps our suspicions to all things prog-rock, but that's essentially what can be found inside the tastefully gothic sleeve of Joy Division's final album – a photograph of Italian cemetary statues by Bernard Pierre Wolff. 1970s short, sharp, shock has been left outside and the songs are now as long as they wish to be. On a purely technical level, the playing is tight and convincing, with Morris' drums being fully utilised as essentially a lead instrument from the opening track, 'Atrocity Exhibition'. Structurally, it's clear now to see what's being done – 'Isolation' is a good example – a bass cycle involving four notes, with the guitars/synths/drums changing and building their patterns around it, with Curtis changing his tone on a song-by-song basis, from cry to croon. It just wasn't quite so clear at the time.

Tony Wilson: 'The bizarre thing is, Martin [Hannett] began to experiment. The first place you really hear it is 'Isolation' on *Closer*.' Alongside the mood pieces there are drivers like 'Colony', '24 Hours' and 'A Means To An End', the latter featuring a descending, octave-divided riff that's been given a good home ever since by a variety of bands ... The Bravery, The Automatic and Suede to name but a few. The album ends on two deeply striking tracks: the borderline electro-ballad 'The Eternal' and the Kraftwerk-esque workout 'Decades', which sounds like a lost out-take from *Trans-Europe Express;* you half expect to hear a German accented voice whisper "Meet Iggy Pop and David Bowie" (as Kraftwerk did on

TEE's title track) as the white noise piston sounds huff and puff and the Mellotron chorus rumbles along the tracks into the distance. The overall effect may be more like a Trans-Pennine Express than its more glamorous German counterpart, but it's a stunning departure nonetheless.

As was often the case in the late 1970s/early 1980s, the single to run alongside the album wasn't actually on it. To pull singles from an album was seen as bad form and not in the interests of credibility. However, pushed by the critical momentum behind the band – and the fact that it's a very good pop record featuring a riff practised over and over again at TJ Davidson's – 'Love Will Tear Us Apart' got to number 13 in the UK charts. 'It just shows you,' says Sumner of the period directly following Curtis' death, 'you can get over anything in this world. 'Cos we did.'

Terry Mason says the band and those around them were on a kind of zombie auto-pilot, but that Bernard needed to escape Manchester. 'We just carried on going to the rehearsal room,' says Mason. 'We didn't know what else to do. That's what we did – so that's what we carried on doing. Going though the motions. I think Barney went off to Blackpool with Section 25, they lived at Blackpool and had a boat. We didn't know what to do. Somehow it carries on.'

Section 25 singer Larry Cassidy confirms that Bernard headed for the Lancashire coast to escape the situation in Manchester. 'When Ian died, Bernard came over to Blackpool,' confirms Cassidy. 'He was totally gutted and fucked up – as you would be. You've got a successful band coming in, next thing, the whole things fucking knackered. Plus all the grief and everything. He stayed with Paul [Wiggin – Section 25 guitarist] for a while. That's when our paths crossed, if you will. We'd seen each other at gigs and that but it's work, you're there as a musician to play.'

The press clamour over the album provided the band with a bolt hole – while the critics' gaze was on *Closer,* they were able to fade away as the record took the attentive heat off them as individuals. 'His death was stunning,' said Sumner, when the band finally broke their silence in an article in *Melody Maker.* 'I was very shocked. It is one of those things which is so bad you can't believe it is true, you don't want to believe it is true. The break was a way to sort of comprehend things.'

Nearly thirty years on from Ian Curtis' death, Terry Mason is still trying to comprehend things. Back then, what he did notice was a major shift in the group dynamic and a major change in Bernard. 'I can't drag thoughts out of people's heads,' he says. 'But Barney had the idea that Ian's death was a consequence of being overworked. On paper, the band didn't do an awful lot, the busiest year was fifty gigs, but because the band didn't like to tour, they ended up doing bitty things. They worked ridiculous blocks. Barney had seen what had happened to Ian ... although the circumstances are completely different with Ian's illness. Barney's taken a lot more control over things while everyone thought Rob was running the outfit with a rod of iron. A lot of the time, Rob was scared of bringing up the idea of doing gigs to Barney. One of my roles later on was being the bad guy and getting people to do gigs. Barney knew that Rob was displaying a weakness afterwards. That's how I saw it. And from that point Barney took a lot more control ... if Bernard didn't want to do something, it didn't get done.'

> *Bernard Sumner: 'Well, kind of true, my favourite part of the process was writing the songs and Hooky's was playing the songs. It was important to compromise, which I felt we did. However, the machine always wanted more touring as it meant there was a shorter return on the cash – a quicker process – to get money [later] for The Haçienda and Factory, and I resented this.'*

From the sidelines, others noticed how the support structure around the remaining members changed too: 'If there's one good thing that came out of the whole thing,' says Crispy Ambulance's Alan Hempsall today, 'it's that the band – and Bernard in particular – were really well looked after. The consequences of not looking after people were clear. It just wasn't worth it.'

As rehearsals began and the possibility of continuing was tentatively floated, a variety of solutions were discussed that could lead to some form of return. Tony Wilson: 'Remember, it wasn't clear at the time. I remember thinking, "Do we find a replacement, is there another lead singer somewhere?"'

Alan Hempsall again: 'There were discussions. Conversations took place. Because I'd stood in for Ian that time at Bury, I suppose. Conversations with Rob Gretton and with Bernard. Bernard asked me would I fancy doing some singing with them. How serious the intent was, I don't know. I met up with Bernard in one of our favourite bars in Manchester, about six weeks after Ian died. The conversation turned to what the remaining members would do next and Bernard said that it'd been mentioned that maybe Bernard should have a go, but he said he hated both the idea of singing whilst playing the guitar and also hated the sound of his own voice. He wondered how I'd feel about stepping in. I said I had Crispy Ambulance to think about but would certainly think about it. In retrospect, I can't have come over as sounding terribly keen. I wasn't aware of anyone else being approached, [but] that's not to say that no one else was considered. I kept it to myself for a couple of weeks until one night Gary

Madeley [Crispy Ambulance's drummer] pissed me off by telling me he couldn't play a gig I'd arranged in Birmingham, due to a personal commitment. I was angry as this was our first opportunity to play outside Manchester, so I decided to drop a bombshell. "How about a band with no fuckin' singer then, as I've been asked to sing with Joy Division?!" That got everyone's attention. Still didn't get the gig though! I've never been one for "What if?". Besides, if I'd joined Joy Division there still would've been a "what if?" wouldn't there? Bottom line is, Crispy Ambulance were old school mates and I couldn't just walk out. Joining Joy Division would mean almost certainly I wouldn't have what I have now. Who knows? Maybe I'd be dead by now. It would be irrational to assume I'd be in clover. It just wouldn't have been right. It would have been a betrayal of the band [Crispy Ambulance]. They were my friends, we'd been to school together and I wanted to see how far we could go. I've never dwelled on it or played on it. That would be sad. It's not common knowledge, I think Bernard mentioned it once in an *NME* interview. It's certainly not my style to go around and say, "Ooooh, didn't you know? I could have been New Order's lead singer!" How sad is that? Ultimately, it was very flattering to be asked at all but I'm quite happy with the way things have panned out.'

Bernard Sumner: *'I honestly don't remember asking Alan to join.'*

Crispy Ambulance's Alan Hempsall: 'There were discussions, conversations took place.'

Terry Mason: 'If it happened, it may have been very early on as some knee jerk thing. Rob was bright enough to know that if you gave someone who was the same size and shape [as Ian] a book of lyrics, the band would be panned. Joy Division had to die when Ian died. The only person who was ever mentioned [to Mason's knowledge] was Mal [Stephen Mallinder] out of Cabaret Voltaire. It came out later when Barney was feeling not too happy about singing. That had Hooky feeling insecure because Mal used to play bass. The whole problem was – nowadays you'd have a reality TV show – who do you get to replace Ian? If you did get someone, it'd end up as some bizarre tribute band. Ian wasn't just the singer, Ian wrote everything [the lyrics], who else would be coming up with stuff like that? Certainly no one else in the band.'

'It was Rob's genius,' says Tony Wilson, 'to think ... *look inside the family*.'

On July 29, Bernard, Peter Hook and Steve Morris played their first gig at the Beach Club in Manchester. Helped by a TEAC reel-to-reel tape machine, all three took a turn at singing. An unusual, short-lived venue in the Shudehill area of the city, close to what's now called The Northern Quarter, The Beach Club was a bohemian mix of club, bar, music venue and cinema, often showing films as support to the bands. There's a Buzzcocks connection again, as manager Richard Boon had a hand in the venue. 'Anyone who was anyone went to the Beach Club,' says Alan Hempsall.

'It was just [them] testing to see if they could show their face in public with instruments,' says Terry Mason. 'It was getting back on the horse. Horrible place to do a gig. A wanky, arty set up. It was run by [people] who thought they were so clever. It was shite and tiny.' According to Mason, despite the gig being arranged, it was still by no means certain that they would actually carry on. 'It was a case of, "If it doesn't feel right, you can get back to doing something with the rest of your life." At that point Steve would have been picked up by any band, Hooky probably would have got work, Barney would have carried on hanging out with Section 25, either in the band or producing them.' Larry Cassidy of Section 25 is keen to dispel the notion that Bernard and his guitar could have been welcome in the band. 'Paul [Wiggin] wouldn't have let him in,' he says today. 'Don't be daft, man.'

Bernard Sumner: 'The gig at the Beach Club was right for us. I never considered or was ever asked to join Section 25, although we were mates and I really like them. I never thought about doing anything other than Joy Division or New Order.'

Nine weeks after Curtis' death, no one was expecting a great deal from the remaining members of Joy Division. 'I was shitting myself,' said Sumner of that night, when recalling events in *The Guardian* in 2002. Tony Wilson was there: 'The original New Order was a three-piece, the first gig at The Beach Club was as a three-piece. They played four numbers. They weren't called anything then.'

'The decision to carry on was easy ... the kinship that you had with the group, the roadies and the people around you, meant that even though Ian was gone, the rest of you were still together. It wasn't like your best mate had died and you were on your own. So even though it was awful we just thought, "We're gonna carry on." We did worry about replacing Ian because he was so fantastic and unique, but we still had the music.'

The music press was fascinated by the tentative steps of the new group, surprised yet hopeful that something could be salvaged. 'You don't make an album like *Closer* and fade away,' comments former *Melody Maker* writer Paolo Hewitt. 'If you have drive and ambition – which they obviously had – they wouldn't still be going [years later]. You can adapt and change and move on. I think there was always a sense that this was the start of something new. What that something new was, nobody knew because no one knew what the fuck was going on in music.'

After two more very brief outings in Preston and Blackpool, the three went to America, in part to fulfill obligations that Joy Division were unable to carry out, for obvious reasons. 'The first night there we were staying at the Iroquios Hotel [the traditional booking for British bands] on 45th street,' says Terry Mason, remembering their first ever US trip. 'Tony Wilson does his guide to New York ... here's Broadway, here's Fifth Avenue ... this is the most dangerous tourist place in the world. Wilson's got the band scared. To be hard, Barney did himself a Biro tattoo! Tony tried to scare people that night.'

'The first gig was at Maxwell's Hoboken [in New Jersey],' recalls Tony Wilson now. 'A pub/club in the village across the Hudson from Midtown. People in Hoboken still talk about it. Joy Divison/New Order could always be shit and could be wonderful. New Order in particular can be *really* shit. It was utterly stunning. If you'd known nothing, you would have thought, "God, this is an amazing group, this three-piece group." The whole point was Rob was trying out all three of them. Hooky would sing three of the songs, Barney would sing three of the songs and Steve would sing three of the songs. Very bizarre. The gig after that was Hurrah's [in New York], the club we were originally supposed to play [as Joy Division] near the Lincoln centre. Barney was obviously so nervous about having to be the lead singer, he'd usually drink half a bottle of Pernod before the gig and half after! He drank the whole bottle before the gig and was so out of it. They did 'In A

Lonely Place', the one with the melodica. He was playing the melodica and I could see him thinking, *Hmm. I have to play the guitar now ... hmm. But I've got a melodica in my hand. Hmmm. How do I put the melodica down and pick the plectrum up? Oh fuck it ...* and he starts playing the guitar with the melodica. Just banging it. So the nerves must have been enormous. Incredibly so. Brave of him to do that ...' Terry Mason was now the band's road manager.

Bernard Sumner: 'This is Terry's sixth job. Notice a pattern.'

'I'd lost the role I had as Ian's minder and companion,' Mason says. 'There was no formal set up. We had no agent as such. It's one of those jobs [road manager] that no one gives you training for. I was quite good at making things happen, despite everything. Things would happen and it wasn't as easy as other people have it.' On the US trip, his abilities in this new role were immediately tested. 'We had the equipment stolen,' he says. 'We parked the van outside the hotel. It was fine for a few days, while it was empty. Then we got the equipment in. We looked out one morning and it wasn't there. We did the remaining gigs on rented equipment. We needed a vehicle for the band, but only Barney had a credit card and a licence. He'd only just passed his test and he's got this 19-foot of station wagon with plastic wood trim down the side to drive. When we went up to Boston, he got caught speeding. Everyone else is pissing themselves in the back while this copper is talking down to "*Ber-NARD.*"'

So despite needing a full bottle of Pernod to provide enough French courage to perform, Bernard was emerging as the band's singer in Rob Gretton's inter-band playoffs. 'It wasn't difficult to take over singing,' said Sumner. 'The main problem is to sing and play at the same time ... that is extremely difficult.' Peter Hook speaking in Q: 'My mum used to say, "Young Bernard couldn't hold a tune in a bucket." Every time I'd play her our records, she'd say ... "That's bloody awful."'

Bernard Sumner: 'You should be doing it, Peter.'

As well as pushing Bernard to the fore, Rob Gretton also came up with a name for the post-Joy Division group. It was the perfect opportunity to shed all the Nazi-related issues that had clung to the band for the last three years, a way of making sure there was a clean break from the *feld hures,* the umlauts and the Prinz Albrecht Strasse connotations that had proved so distracting from the music. A perfect opportunity that was utterly ignored.

New Order it was then. Could Bernard – who apparently knew the address of the Gestapo headquarters in Berlin – not know of references to the 'new order of the Third Reich' in Adolf Hitler's *Mein Kampf*?

Bernard Sumner: 'Please see my earlier note about Albrecht.'

Bernard's various defences on this matter have ranged from ignorance to innocence to robust rebuttals. 'It hasn't got Nazi connotations,' he's stated. 'I find it so offensive that people say that, that I will not defend it. The name came from a book that Rob Gretton was reading about Prince Sihanouk of Cambodia.'

Bernard Sumner: 'Rob did suggest the name 'New Order' and it did come from an article Rob was reading in The Observer *about Prince Sihanouk of Cambodia, we didn't know it had Nazi connotations, we'd had enough of that (obviously) and thought it was neutral. I am afraid that is true.'*

Rob Gretton, in a rare interview in 1983 for the long-defunct *Zig Zag* magazine, was just as firm in his defence, turning the question of facism on the interviewer. 'If someone calls you a facist, it tells you more about the person that's calling you it. I'd *never* dream of calling anyone a facist. Why don't they call us communists? We've done Rock Against Racism, CND ... basically we're just mercenary. I've noticed recently, particularly in the *NME*, that they've gone overboard. But I mean *NME*, IPC [*NME*'s parent company, a huge media empire] ... how can capitalist running dogs calls us fascists? What we're doing is ten times more worthwhile and anti-facist than what they're doing. The problem with most journalists is that they realise they're irrelevant.'

Bernard Sumner: 'Rob had very, very socialist – almost communist – ideals.'

Speaking in *The Face* back in 1983, Sumner said: 'You should have seen some of the other names we had on the list – Temple of Venus, that was a good one. It was implying a change, that's all. They use it [the phrase New Order] on [the Disney film] *Tron* but no one calls Walt Disney a Nazi.'

The music press was less than impressed, but because of the bubble of sensitivity that surrounded the band after Curtis' death, they didn't quite go in for the kill. 'I think the whole Joy Division/New Order thing was tiresome,' says Paolo Hewitt. 'The Nazi thing. To do it twice was boring.'

In fact, the name wasn't even terribly original. The British music press were too busy whipping themselves up into a right-on tizz to notice that it had been used before by American Ron Asheton. At the same time as Warsaw were playing their first gig at The Electric Circus, the former Stooge was putting together a band called New Order in Detroit with Jimmy Recca, KJ Knight of the Amboy Dukes and ex-drummer with MC5, Dennis 'Machine Gun' Thompson. Asheton and Thompson later played together in a band called New Race. Imagine the kerfuffle if Bernard and friends had gone for that one.

Meanwhile, the British New Order band 'signed a deal' with Factory – a 50/50 napkin affair which gave them the upper hand in just about every area:

The master tapes of the recordings and any out-takes are to remain the group's property and should be delivered back as soon as possible after each recording. At the end of the term of the rights granted by this agreement, you will have the right to sell off your existing stocks for a period of three months; thereafter you will either destroy all remaining stocks or, at the group's option, they may buy all or part of these stocks at cost from you.

On October 25, New Order played their first gig as a four-piece. The place they chose was a comfort zone – The Squat in Manchester – and again they took Rob Gretton's advice to look inside the family and picked Gillian Gilbert. At the time she was described at Steve Morris's 'friend', a line that would be regularly trotted out for the next few years. In fact, Gilbert was one of an early group of hardcore Joy Division fans and she and Morris had been together as a couple since late 1978.

'I vaguely knew Joy Division,' she said in *NME*. 'I used to rehearse next door to them in Manchester when I was in a punk group [The Inadequates]. I used to go and see them and then I got to know Stephen.' It's also been claimed that Gilbert stood in for Ian Curtis for one Joy Division song after he'd hurt his hand and was unable his guitar part. 'It wasn't a very big bit so as I could play guitar a bit, I played that one number.'

Bernard Sumner: 'No, Gillian stood in for me at Eric's after Rob hit me with a bottle.'

Gilbert's introduction into the band was characteristically low-key. 'Gillian has been a big help and without her not a lot would have been possible. You can only do so much,' Bernard said at the time in *Melody Maker*. 'After he [Curtis] died, we had a bit of a break to think things out, we never doubted that we would go on, and after the break we started to rehearse again.'

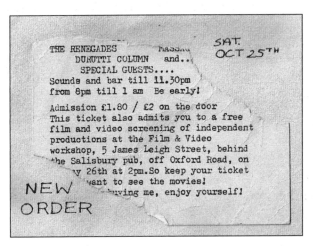

A hastily-scribbled ticket for Gillian's first ever gig with New Order.

The gig at The Squat to unveil New Order proper was another defiantly low-key affair. 'It was an open secret that the guests would be New Order, but it was billed as a Durutti Column gig,' says audience member Andrew Wake, who had continued his allegiance to the remaining members of Joy Division after Curtis' death. 'Sure enough, New Order appeared. Everything was coloured by the fact that Curtis wasn't there, but the music was phenomenal. Bernard was playing the melodica. At that stage, Peter Hook and Bernard were sharing vocals. Obviously, as time went by, Bernard became the singer. It was great to see them back and strong. It was them finding their feet. Half of Manchester were there, though it only held about 200 people. There was a sense of resilience. It wasn't noisy – there was a reverence. I remember that vividly.'

Chris Hewitt, who'd watched the band since their first recordings at Cargo Studios in Rochdale, has his own idiosyncratic take: 'I did the sound at those early gigs. Gillian had stickers on her keyboard to tell her which notes to hit. Bernard used to leave porn on her keyboard, really awful German anal stuff, to make her feel welcome.'

Bernard Sumner: 'That was Terry – he also used to fart
in front of her on-stage fan.'

Alan Hempsall went to the gig at The Squat. It could have been him on stage if he hadn't decided to maintain his allegiance with Crispy Ambulance: 'When I saw them with Gillian – it just felt right. You thought, *this could be interesting*. They'd made a proper break with the past. It was genuinely different. I think they did exactly the right thing, I think Rob Gretton made the point that after Joy Division a total fresh start was needed, a sort of catharsis, any new singer just being plugged in like a lightbulb would have been compared to Ian. I wouldn't have fancied that. So by installing Gillian, it forced the band to totally step outside their comfort zone.'

The comfort exclusion also extended to a collective decision not to play any 'old' songs – that is, Joy Division songs. 'It is difficult not to play Joy Division songs … it is upsetting,' said Sumner in *Melody Maker* in 1981, '[but] it is upsetting to play them after all the work we put into Joy Division with Ian. Without Ian, they are not the same.'

Rehearsals and a further series of gigs would follow. No New Order material was released until March of 1981, then a small flurry of records arrived. Bernard was finding his voice – and he was the first to admit the voice he found initially wasn't quite right. 'For ages it just felt like a square peg in a round hole,' he said in *The Face* in July 83. The single 'Ceremony' – a Joy Division song which reached number 34 in the UK charts – came first, then 'Procession' and 'Everything's Gone Green' in December. The final track was a key indicator of the way forward, with looping, robust synth riffs rather than the spidery, atmospheric washes of the past. Tony Wilson agrees – in an extremely Tony Wilson kind of way.

'The most important song in the modern world is 'Everything's Gone Green',' he says today. 'Everything's Gone Green' is the first time anywhere that people used computers – primitive, early Apple computers with soldering irons and wires coming out of them – linked to these 1970s synthesisers. Historically, music has been melody and rhythm. New York meets Africa. Normally you'd write one thing … a note of melody and then a beat. Suddenly, your inputting melody and rhythm *at the same time*. If you listen to 'Everything's Gone Green' it's the first use of modern digital technology to make … that scrawl, that human marker … with melody and rhythm at the same time. It comes to its apothesis two New Order singles later.'

Just before the most important song in the modern world came out, a debut New Order album was released. As usual the best song didn't feature on it.

Movement was given the number of FAC 50, as part of the obscure but occasionally logical logging system given to Factory associated items. FAC

50 tends to get dealt with very swiftly in the history of New Order – and dealings with the album tend to be done on a negative basis.

From the start, it's unclear what's going on. Opener 'Dreams Never End' with its double-tracked Curtis-esque vocals is a jaunty, ringing starting point. Sumner is not really there but it's a strong template; so strong that The Cure would use it on a regular basis, especially on 'In Between Days' in 1985. Some of the instrumentation on *Movement* – especially the use of drum machines – now sounds a touch more dated than on *Closer*, for example on second track 'Truth'. But on 'Truth' we not only get to hear that much-abused melodica – it clearly survived the Pernod-rage incident in America – we also get to hear Bernard properly as well. Listened to without the preconception that it's Sumner's singing letting the side down, and suddenly it's a perfectly acceptable post-punk vocal performance. In the main, it's the upbeat, uptempo songs that work best; Joy Division improved when they slowed down, whereas New Order put their feet on the gas and things took a turn for the better. A *Closer*-style slowie, 'Doubts Even Here', certainly misses the mark, but overall it's a firm album with a well of ideas and sections that would prove useful to both New Order and other acts. It's better than they think it is. And, if nothing else, it has one tone that would definitely last: the hallmark *kling klang* sound of Peter Hook's bass is briefly heard here on 'Senses'.

Bernard Sumner: 'Making Movement *was a horrible experience.*
Martin was fucked up, we were fucked up and the album was fucked up.
But, very importantly, we never ever considered giving up.'

Terry Mason believes that *Movement* was never going to be given any real chance, no matter how worthwhile its contents were: 'The yardstick was *Closer* and it wasn't a normal yardstick. It was the last album, it was one that had been polished up to a shine by Jon Savage, Paul Morley, all the reviewers. It was *The Holy Album*. So anything coming out after it was always going to be difficult. They just got back into the studio. It seems stupid, but it's what we did.'

As well as Bernard's singing, his lyrics also came under scrutiny.

'We never deal in specifics,' said Sumner about the subjects of his songs. 'If you deal in specific situational lyrics, you freeze the music. They always mean something special ... something personal to me.'

Tony Wilson: 'Interestingly, once every two months I have a row with Peter Saville about Bernard's lyric writing. The first album *Movement* is a bit of a disaster on two counts. One, you can feel – in the sound – the end of the relationship between Martin Hannett and Joy Division/New Order ... they're coming to the close of their creative relationship. Secondly, having the lead singer role thrust on him, he's also being asked to write the lyrics. For *Movement*, he tried to write lyrics like his old lead singer Ian ... and Ian wrote like TS Elliot. Very odd, language rhythm and structures, there's a very TS Elliot quality to Ian's writing. And Bernard tried to write like Ian on *Movement*. It doesn't work.'

Again, Sumner is his own harshest critic: 'On the first one,' he told *NME* in July, 1983, 'I felt so self-conscious because I was coming after Ian, who was such a great writer. I wanted the lyrics I wrote to be good. They were alright but they were not wonderful. After I said "Fuck it!" I started to enjoy writing a lot more.'

Given the events of the last eighteen months, it would have taken a brave critic to slate the album and, as such, reviews were perhaps overly fair. This, and the previous album Bernard had recorded, were both achieved under terribly difficult circumstances. '*Movement* ... that and *Closer* were very depressing albums,' he understated some years later in *Melody Maker*. Still, its simple cover in blue and black was a student bedsit staple that year and the band – especially its surprisingly photogenic new singer – seemed to be on the edge of a commercial breakthrough. 'It is confusing, but having more people like us won't stop us, we must continue ... it doesn't matter so long as we are achieving something, doing something new and not just reproducing ourselves.'

Through the spring and summer of 1981, New Order played across Britain and prepared for gigs in Europe and America. At one gig, there was a reminder that their past would be hard to leave behind. On March 27, the band played Bristol's Trinity Hall. 'It was an old church where they put gigs on,' says audience member Andrew Davis. 'It was a surreal venue, there was a graveyard, and a vicar would come on at the end and thank people for behaving themselves.' The padre's confidence in the audience would, however, be misplaced on this occasion. 'There was something quite sick that happened. About half-way through, someone shouted out, "Hang yourselves ..." Hooky looked like he was going to whack his bass around someone.' Davis remembers very little dancing at the gig, more a sense of curiosity. 'The audience were just standing and staring. It seemed really different. Bernard was playing a melodica. Peter Hook looked really cool but the others looked really uneasy.'

Terry Mason never heard such heckling, but can imagine the situation whereby it would arise, as the band didn't go out of their way to win over audiences. 'The gigs after the release of the first album were short affairs –

forty minute sets and no encores, no matter what. These were quite edgy gigs, especially as the band just wouldn't come back onto the stage, causing some uncomfortable moments with crowds and promoters alike, especially outside of the UK. It's quite possible there may have been some punters who thought that they had paid for a set of 60 to 75 minutes with a guaranteed two song encore minimum – standard fare elsewhere ...'

Bernard Sumner: 'Why should we be the same as everyone else?'

'... and some wags may well have flexed their "wit muscles" to come up with the odd "hang yourselves" ... but it was never as popular as "Gillian Gilbert, Gillian Gilbert, get your tits out for the lads."'

Key American gigs at the end of the year resulted in a series of New York shows at The Ritz, The Ukranian National Home and The Peppermint Lounge. The Ukranian gig was filmed. 'You could see it there onstage at the Ukranian – Bernard finding his voice, *right there*, you can see it in his face,' says Tony Wilson.

There was perhaps another thing that could be seen in Bernard's face: 'I realised what a great party town New York was,' he says. 'We started going to all the clubs, like Danceteria, Hurrah's, The Peppermint Lounge.'

'I literally saw the light when I was in New York with New Order and I went to this club,' Sumner told *Q*. 'Someone had spiked my drink with a tab of acid – let's put it that way – and all of a sudden, all this electronic music – Giorgio Moroder, Afrika Bambaataa – made sense. It was like being blind and someone came along and put these glasses on you that made you see again. That was my conversion to dance music.'

Bernard also realised that in Joy Division, he could just stand at the back and play guitar. Now he was the centre of attention. There was even an incident at L'Ancienne Belgique in Brussels where an audience member was spotted with what appeared to be a gun. 'We never got to find out if it was real or a replica,' says Terry Mason. 'If the band had even thought that they were being threatened, it would have been enough for Barney to pull the tour. The band hadn't seen the guy. Paul, who was working with us as a roadie at the time, jumped off-stage and immobilized him and kept hold of him till a couple of cops came along. Paul was a Kendo blackbelt and just loved the chance to put it into action.'

Being in the spotlight was something that didn't sit well with Bernard: 'I don't really enjoy it when you go into a pub and people start nudging each other. I don't enjoy being recognised at all. But it's a small price to pay. We are very, very lucky to be living this lifestyle. I could never work to a routine. I never have been able to.'

Perhaps what Bernard and the rest of the band needed was a place of their own to hang out. A place of their own. Manager Rob Gretton would provide the idea, Ben Kelly would supply a design and Tony Wilson would tip in with the blarney. What Bernard and the rest of New Order would bring to the table was money – lots of it. FAC 51 would nearly be the breaking of everything they'd worked for.

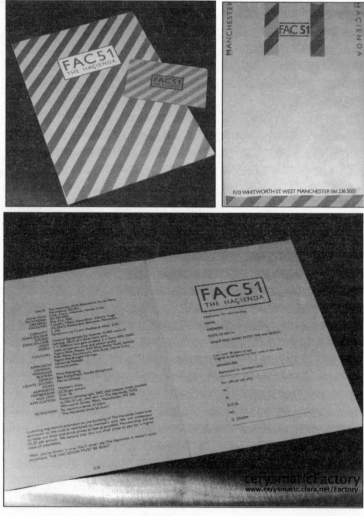

Factory memorabilia: membership card, poster and members' rule book.

CONFUSION SEVEN
– INSIDE / OUTSIDE TENSION

The train line which connects the southern suburbs
of Manchester to 'town' is a relatively straightforward affair. Heading
towards the city centre from my home town of Altrincham used to take
about 25 minutes. Sale ... Dane Road ... Stretford ... I knew the stations off
by heart. Making that journey on a typical Saturday, I'd breathe a sigh of
relief after Old Trafford – that meant the football fans heading for
Manchester United would get off and the train would be drained of nearly
all the tension and testosterone that they would inevitably bring with them.
After that, it was just a few more minutes until you reached the first
outpost of the city, Deansgate station – often still known by its old name of
Knott Mill. As the train pulled out of the station heading for Oxford Road,
a regular thought idled across my mind as I looked out of the window at
the buildings by the side of the line: why would anyone come into the
centre of Manchester to buy a boat? And what's more, how the hell did
you get it home after the purchase had been made? Because off to the left
of the railway line, at street level, that's exactly what happened. At the end
of Whitworth Street West was a showroom – as high as a three storey
house but with no floors to create a single, enormous space – selling boats,
dinghies and yachts.

'Bernard drove me past this yacht warehouse place and said, "That's our
new club,"' recalls Alan Hempsall of Crispy Ambulance. '"Tony wants to
call it The Haçienda ... I think that's a shit name," he said.'

With royalty money from Joy Division's strong selling back catalogue ,
three top 40 hits under their belts and a growing reputation as a live draw,
there was money in the Bank of Factory. Martin Hannett wanted a top of
the line synthesiser. Bernard and the band wanted decent houses. Rob
Gretton wanted a nightclub, a big flouncy discotheque – just like the ones
they'd seen in New York – slap bang in the centre, in the middle of
Manchester. And Rob Gretton got his way.

'The Haçienda?,' says Terry Mason. 'It took 'em ages to find somewhere,
the simpler thing was take over a club and do it that way. I didn't see it till
it was fitting out time. It affected the income of everyone involved, instead
of everyone getting bigger cars and money in the bank, they started to see

95

this club appear – which was fine – but at the start they weren't even allowed to have a bar tab. Rob was the big driver behind it. He wanted it open six nights a week and he wanted the Gay Traitor bar downstairs open at lunchtimes. It was crazy. But this is what Rob wanted.'

'If Rob said, "Cut your arm off", you'd have to have damn good reason not to do it,' says Michael Eastwood, a Joy Division fan who'd graduated to New Order roadie. 'I'd do it. I'd have cut my arm off. Rob was a genius. Rob would do things like, "I'll give you 500 quid to go and push that bloke in the swimming pool." I've seen Rob give people money to smash bars up, that was all part of it. They weren't just here to make money. They were here to make money and have a really good time and have all their mates have a really good time and be really stylish about it. There was a big family thing. They were a formidable bunch to spar with, you didn't want to get into a sparring match with ... but hilarious.

Vicious sence of humour. All of them, Bernard, Hooky, Terry, Rob. Vicious. If they found something out – a weak point – they would exploit it constantly. Mine was the fact that my brother ran a rare record shop, white labels and stuff. So, if I was around and any kind of white labels or merchandising was mentioned, somebody would always make the joke of, "Don't let him near it, it'll be straight down his brother's shop." If you defended someone who was gay ... you'd be labelled as "The Friend of The Gays" for the rest of their life ... ridciculous. Funny.'

There is a wonderfully dumb 1998 American comedy called *Night At The Roxbury*, in which Will Farrell and Chris Kattan accidentally come up with an idea for a happening new venue – a club who's outside was inside. In the movie, a jaded public, aching for something – anything – new, lap it up. The idea itself is not so dumb after all. It was used sixteen years earlier in The Haçienda. As Kelly himself puts it on his website, www.benkellydesign.com:

'*Directional and warning markings created an inside/outside tension — bollards and cats-eyes delineated the dance-floor — a city within a city, of pathways, plazas and bars, which acted as intimate refuge amid the cavernous space.*'

Amid massive local and national publicity, The Haçienda opened its doors on May 21, 1982. Manchester's bright, young, post-punk things had to apply in advance for membership to designer Ben Kelly's groundbreakingly grey club space. To step inside during that opening week – as I did after my membership card finally arrived – was to step inside something that was unlike any other club at the time. If nothing else, because it was really cold.

'It was fucking wrong!' states Terry Mason with customary aplomb. 'That wall at the end where the bar was, should have been the stage. I worked there on the opening night. We were waiting for the arcade machines to arrive ... Ms Pacman and all that ... someone turned round and said,

"Where's the coat hangers ... for the cloakroom?" Slapping of foreheads time. Only club in the world without a cloakroom. What should have been the cloakroom was a video arcade. It was Rob's idea and he carried it on and on.'

In the space of six years, Bernard had progressed from boozing and dancing in the Roxy room at Pips, to having a stake in Manchester's highest profile nightspot. And what's more, it had *inside/outside* tension. It was a club in the sense that you had to be a member to gain entry. In every other respect, it was essentially a gig venue with the atmosphere of an arts centre cafe bar. Its opening would also mark the start of one of the most creatively prolific periods of Bernard Sumner's career.

But The Great Manchester Myth will have you believe that from the word go The Haçienda was a disaster ... a white elephant ... a millstone. The club that no-one wanted to go to. From the start, the Haçienda was a delight, a teasing distraction and the coolest slice of nightlife anywhere. The events it staged were willful and unexpected, the acts on show left of centre and unlike those available elsewhere, the decor and staff a delight. It was stunning. It wasn't just a nightclub.

'The Haçienda works as a myth right from the start,' says dance musician and former Haçienda employee Gonnie Reitveld. 'The place was mythologised by the way it was marketed, a rather mysterious Situationist manifesto that everyone loves to quote ('The Haçienda must be built'). It's enigmatic having a club that's about the love of the music and not a lot else. Plus [you had] the enigma around Factory Records and New Order. And it was like a spaceship from another world ... a European thing or a New York thing. Didn't seem like a Manchester thing – the locals looked on it with suspicion ... it didn't have sticky carpet for God sake! Weird. I didn't think it was weird, [but] then I'm a foreigner.'

Reitveld had already been making experimental music in her native Holland, including early collaborations with Sheffield band Vice Versa – who had recently changed their name to ABC. She was also living with fellow musician Mike Pickering. 'Mike was offered this job as creative director for The Haçienda and me and Mike went over to Manchester, [then] got married in 1982. We were invited to record for Factory Records.' The unit she and Pickering had formed, Quando Quango, would prove to be a vital dance/rock crossroads for Bernard Sumner. In the meantime though, her first job for The Haçienda was cocking up the club's membership system. Now I know whose fault it was I couldn't get in on the opening night.

From the club's very earliest days, key players would arrive and become part of the grey/blue fixtures and fittings. Leroy Richardson began working as a glass collector at the club shortly after it opened. He would eventually run the place and in the process became Factory Records' longest serving employee. 'To go in a club that was full of Rastas and punks and shoe-gazers – and everyone getting on – was quite an eye-opener,' he says. Richardson paints a vivid picture of Manchester nightlife prior to The Haçienda's opening. 'The very first time I went to The Haçienda,' he says, 'Gregory Isaacs was playing. Prior to that, the history of clubs in town was a no-no ... it was often a fight because you weren't getting in. You used to tell the taxi to wait while you went up and tried the door and got knocked back for being black. Excuses such as ... "You're afro's a fire hazard." You'd see some girl with a curly perm walk past and you'd say, "What about her?" and they'd say, "That's different." That's where the fights would come in. The door security wasn't what it is now, it was a big, beer-bellied guy with a tuxedo on. You had places like Rotters that you wouldn't go to. Genevieves in Longsight – which became the International 1 – Cloisters, Rafters and The Piccadilly. They were the four places we went to as clubs. Then there was Placemate 7 and there was also Pips. Pips was no problem getting in. We would more likely be in the punk room than the soul and funk room. Never had a problem there. Placemate 7, never had a problem there. Rafters never a problem. But Cloisters, Genevieves and The Piccadilly ... there was never any rhyme or reason ... I think they had a mental quota and it was "Right, no more are coming in." When I say "no more" ... they meant *no more blacks* are coming in. There were very few black doormen – in fact, I don't think there were any black doormen at that point ... which is weird how everything changes. Rafters was a sure fire hit. They used to put bands on there and I remember seeing Rufus with Chaka Khan there. £2.50 in. Rafters was more like the youth club – but with alcohol – where you met girls. It was like a circuit. Genevieves was always a Wednesday. Cloisters would be the Friday night. Rafters would be your Saturday night. There was very limited transport, very few people had a car. Taxis into town, taxis back. We were all earning ... back then, everyone was working. There was The Reno and The Nile if you wanted a drink later on. Even that wasn't a certain entry. The Russell Club, or The Factory as it became, was a public service vehicles drivers club for the SELNEC bus company – you'd have old black guys in the corner playing dominoes ... and you'd have some punk band on the other side.

The Haçienda was the next step. There was no connection aesthetically, the point was they both put bands on. Each place had its own night and you very rarely deviated from that. It was the same community that moved round it. There was only The Haçienda that broke that for me.'

But despite the overwhelming sense that The Haçienda was unquestionably the place to be, Richardson – fresh from working in the competitive bar culture of Spain – had spotted early doors that the club was not being run along entirely businesslike lines. 'There'd be five meetings about a meeting and who would be at the meeting ... and in the end it wouldn't make any difference because nothing would get done. To me, it was always Factory's club ... and New Order were Factory. New Order, Tony and Rob. They were my bosses. Even surpassing the managers above me. If they asked me to do something ... they're my bosses and if they ask me to do something, I'll do it.'

Those used to certain, stock images of The Haçienda – that goonish, acieed house 'Madchester' look – would be surprised at the club in its early incarnation. After the initial opening flush, things settled down very quickly to a quiet, art house pace. What had seemed so *outré* on the opening night became slightly passé within the space of six months. In the same way that the 1970s club scene in Manchester slotted into a familiar rhythm of the same punters moving in and around the same venues – as described by Leroy Richardson – the 1980s kids treated The Haçienda as yet another stop on the post-punk merry-go-round. First stop on a Thursday was Legends, at the bottom end of Princess Street, close to what's now known as the Gay Village; make-up and New Romantics still ruled the backcombed roost with Billy Idol and Fad Gadget proving to be special favourites; Fridays was still owned by Pips, the Bowie/Roxie room now filled with the sound of The Psychedelic Furs and Bauhaus; Saturday's stop was The Haçienda – if Deville's behind Central Library was full.

The Haçienda DJs only seemed to possess three records: 'The Passenger' by Iggy Pop, The Clash's 'Should I Stay or Should I Go?' and 'Planet Rock' by Afrika Bambaataa – produced by Arthur Baker. Band nights were where it was at, with post-punk and goth offerings such as Malcolm McLaren's protégés Bow Bow Wow and Australians The Birthday Party doing exceptionally well. But a key problem was that The Haçienda always seemed to be open – day and night – whether punters required its services or not. That and the democratic vibe created an 'anything goes' booking system that went way beyond the norm. Gonnie Reitveld: 'The first four years were blissful, naive and irritating at times. It was always a club and always had DJs playing. What can you do with a space like that? What other things can you do? Comedians ... or, at one point, trapeze artists. And at the most extreme there were these two strippers and one of them was doing smoke rings with her fanny. Quite amazing. She did that on stage. I was amazed. How does she do that? She inhaled the smoke and managed to push out smoke rings from her fanny.'

'I virtually lived at The Haçienda,' says New Order roadie Michael Eastwood. 'It was like our youth club. When you worked for Factory you became an honoury member, which let you just walk in the place no matter what was happening ... which we did all the time. We always hung out at the middle level of the cocktail bar, half-way down. That's where we used to sit around drinking chatting – that was Manchester, that little bit there. Never really went upstairs much, never really went downstairs much, just stayed there. The gigs that they were showing. Burning Spear, Gregory Isaacs, The Cramps ... The Cramps, what a night ... all the Fall gigs, absolutely creamy moments in my life.'

'The Haçienda was our playground,' recalls Alan Hempsall. 'We were a Factory band and we got in for free with a pass. We could go anytime we wanted. I saw Klaus Schulze [Tangerine Dream] and Biting Tongues and [Nigerian singer and percussionist] Gaspar Lawal. But it kept New Order awake at night. It gave them nightmares.'

Paul Cons – soon to be The Haçienda promoter – sums up the early days of the club perfectly: 'It seemed like the BBC of nightclubs. It was like a subsidised, creative centre that didn't have to be that successful ... that could explore and experiment. There were no grants, it was all courtesy of New Order. I saw The Haçienda as a great theatre ... I never came at it from a musical angle. I was always much more about the visuals and the theatre and the spectacle of the place. We had people swallowing swords ... and Julian Clary ... and Dollar.'

> *Bernard Sumner: 'It was like The Beatles' Apple,*
> *but we weren't the Beatles or had their money!'*

When I relate Paul Cons' analogy to the likes of Leroy Richardson and Terry Mason, they can only nod in agreement. 'It was a lovely arts venue,' says Mason, 'and in the first few years got the patronage it deserved. One of the most spectacularly awful nights was 'Dome', with the people out of [art rock band] Wire. They'd gone off on some art track. Mike Pickering had booked them and we thought, *no one's going to turn up* ... thirty people turned up, it was awful. The daftest thing? .... breakdancing. Tony Wilson had come back from New York. The future was beat boys and breakdancing. That was the future ... New York's got it, we've got to have it. As luck would have it, there was a breakdancing posse in the Moss [Moss Side]. We had the perfect spinning floors for doing stuff like that. Tony and/or Rob decided this is what we want ... on a Friday night. We had thirteen people come into the club that night. The bouncers were telling people who were coming in not to bother. "Look, you're not going to like it, half a dozen black kids spinning on their heads ... and the music sounds shite." There was a distinct lack of any commercial *nous* in the Greater Factory vicinity. Anyone who'd be stupid enough to say, "The emperor's got no clothes on," was an arsehole and ostracised for it .... What do you fucking know? Well, I know your make your money on a Friday night and you do that by having the bouncers saying, "Come in, it's great!" It was so awful.'

> Bernard Sumner: 'That's one way of looking at it, another way was
> that we were the vanguard of a lot of things but got there a bit too soon.'

New Order's second album, *Power, Corruption And Lies,* in 1983 was certainly ahead of its time and a major upward gear change from its predecessor – with all those nights in The Peppermint Lounge finally sinking in. This is New Order, dance pioneers, almost fully formed and totally recognisable, post-punk yet pre-Acid House. Sumner is now able to let go and even let rip, no more of the schoolboy mumbling of old. His voice is clear and unfettered. Lyrically, Sumner had stopped trying to be Ian Curtis too. 'When we first started, I tried writing serious lyrics and I was just shit at it,' he confessed to *NME*. 'So for the second LP, I just wrote down whatever I felt like. Ironically, the songs on the second LP mean a lot more to me. And because they're less self-conscious, they're more truthful to myself.'

There are feet in the past and in the future here. Opener 'Age Of Consent' has the bass and the syncopated drumming of a prime Joy Division track while 'The Village', 'Ultraviolence' and 'Ecstasy' – ahead of the curve there – have an early, dancey splash of Ibizan sea spray about them. If there's a key, familiar touchstone on *Power, Corruption And Lies*, it's in the shape of Kraftwerk – 'Your Silent Face' uses the forward momentum and synth-run style of 'Europe Endless' from the German band's *Trans Europe Express* album, a familiar reference point since the late 1970s. It builds steadily, contains the requisite amount of mournful melodica and is beautifully sung by Sumner – four words one wouldn't have expected to find in the same sentence at the turn of the decade. One of the album's tracks – the slow-then-quick-then-slow workout '586' – was deemed worthy of further inspection and began to morph into a fresh track: 'Blue Monday'. 'I was going out to a lot of clubs at the time,' said Sumner on

BBC Radio 1. 'Spending a lot of time in New York going to clubs such as The Funhouse and The Paradise Garage, Danceteria, Hurrah's, Peppermint Lounge ... loads of clubs. They were starting to play acoustic music that had been tape looped. I heard this very strong rhythmic music and I thought, *Wow, we could do that with the new electronic sequencers that are coming out now.* 'Blue Monday' was the result.'

Tony Wilson: 'After 'Everything's Gone Green' you get 'Temptation', and that's Martin Hannett's last piece of work with New Order. Then New Order go on their own and what do they do without Martin? They create 'Blue Monday'. A changing moment in history. They had sucked everything out of Martin that they needed.'

Bernard Sumner: 'Martin's last track was 'Everything's Gone Green' – in fact,
he walked out halfway through the mix because Hooky and me
asked him to turn the drums up.'

Larry Cassidy of Section 25 – who Bernard would produce after the breakaway from Hannett – states that Sumner's thinking was quite reasoned and logical. 'Bernard said to me they'd sold more records after they'd stopped using Martin than they had with him. And I thought that was a reasonable justification. They fell out with Martin over cost. Martin was starting to cost too much, so there was a rift then with the band and Martin. Especially if you think, *Fucking hell, I've learnt so much off him ... I'll do it myself. Why not?* They didn't owe him a lifetime's income. The teacher teaches the children, they learn, they grow up and they take over the bloody teacher's job.'

Bernard Sumner: 'It wasn't costs, it was his attitude.
Plus, we weren't children anymore and it was time to leave home.'

'When we wrote 'Blue Monday',' says Sumner, 'There was no electronic dance music around and no one was playing it live apart from Human League [and Cabaret Voltaire, of course] who don't get enough credit for what they do. Really, I kind of saw a gap in the market. I thought if we write an electronic song and play it live, it'll blow people's heads off.'

Even better if the track could blow people's heads off without the band having to do a great deal. There was an on-going live conflict within New Order over the seemingly fake act of coming back on stage for encores. 'We thought we could do one of two things,' said Sumner in Q in 2005. 'Still not do encores, but go off one song early and come back, or get this new technology, a drum machine and sequencer I'd built, to play a song on its own. That way the public would be pleased because they're getting an encore, and we'd be pleased because we're in the dressing room.'

Sumner claims that, one by one, the band then opted back into being on-stage for the new track, for fear of being left out. Famously, 'Blue Monday's floppy disc sleeve by designer Peter Saville was so arch, fancy and expensive, that the band lost money everytime someone was inconsiderate enough to buy a copy. Anything between 2p and 10p per item, depending on which version of this oft-told tale you go for. Given that it went on to become the biggest selling 12-inch single of all-time – the post-punk 'Stairway To Heaven' – this would appear to be madness on a scale even Factory was incapable of. 'It's a good story,' says Terry Mason today. 'Factory have a lot of stories that have you chortling and deflect you away from other stuff that was going on. The first batch will have lost money, but there's always someone who'll do it 10p cheaper … Factory, Joy Division, New Order … it's just a myth business, isn't it? Tony has lots of stories he can roll out, and people like stories. The truth? People can take or leave that. Don't spoil a good story by putting in any truth.'

Bernard Sumner: 'Ask Tony, only he knows the truth behind this legend.'

'Blue Monday' was released six weeks before the first anniversary of The Haçienda. When the first annual figures for the venture came in, they tested Bernard's patience with the project to the limit. 'We were a million pounds down,' states Tony Wilson.

No wonder the expensive 'Blue Monday' cover design was dropped for a more economical version, as the record flew out of the shops and the cash flew into The Haçienda. Unsurprisingly, the band started to take a greater interest in what was going on at the club. Bernard and his wife Sue had a baby to take care of now – young James – so this was serious. Leroy Richardson: 'You'd see the band more and more … coming to management meetings, getting more annoyed – more concerned – about the cash. Them putting more money in and more money in and more money in. It had to come to a stop at some stage. I thought they were getting very little out of it for what they were putting in. I remember very few conversations with the management about cutting costs, or finding things cheaper.'

Bernard Sumner: 'I think this is why we were pushed out on tours of the States so much. It was the only way for us to receive some money.
Our royalties were being wasted on The Haçienda.'

Terry Mason: 'At this stage you will see the fighting between Rob and Barney more and more. He [Bernard] didn't really want The Haçienda – and over the years, as the money got poured into that money pit ... even more so. Towards the end, Barney opted out completely.'

Speaking in *Select* in 1993, Bernard Sumner said: 'I've had some of the best nights of my life there. But I was living in a council flat while we were putting £10,000 a week into The Haçienda. That's wrong.'

Bernard Sumner: 'Yes, that was wrong, it was more than £10,000!'

Chris Hewitt, who'd had dealings with Factory as far back as the early recordings at Cargo Studios, was now a consultant for the club's problematic sound system. At least that's what he thought. His skills were not always put to their best use. 'I'd get called out to The Haçienda on a Friday [or a] Saturday night expecting to deal with a problem with the PA ... and it would be to change a fuse on the till. They'd say "The till isn't working." I'd change the 13-amp fuse, leave a bill for my call-out and go home. Crazy.'

'There was always the issue with the sound,' says Leroy Richardson. 'The acoustic baffling had to be done artistically rather than practically. There was no site maintenance. There was nothing about the upkeep of the building. I was into lateral thinking – Edward de Bono. Something as simple as a fuse on the till could affect things down the line on the ring main which could mean the decks not working. Chris [Hewitt] would have been the only one who might have known about the building. You'd go to the only person you knew who had a screwdriver.'

When the till was actually working, there were growing concerns about what was going into it ... and what was coming out. 'I started keeping a tally of drinks,' continues Richardson. 'Complimentary drinks. That became *de rigeur*. Even if it was Bernard, it had to be written down. Staff drinks were never written down, it was guesswork. When the stock take came, we were thousands and thousands of pounds down. Not that people had stolen it, but there was no evidence of where it had gone. I couldn't understand the set up of the bar when I started. You had a person who would take your order, who then gave that order to another person and somebody else got you your drink – so there were two people to serve each customer. The till was at the front of the bar and the drinks were at the back ... what's to stop someone doing that [hand in the till]? I think it was some American thing Wilson had seen.'

With 'Blue Monday' now a staple in the charts and in the clubs, New Order were certainly generating enough revenue to keep the doors of the struggling Haçienda open. As the song continued its relentless success, New Order appeared on *Top of the Pops*, then the premier UK music show. The programme's producers had allowed them to perform live. As you will have already heard, there is a consensus – even among their most ardent supporters – that the New Order live experience can be a hit and miss affair. They chose that night to miss by a considerable margin and turned in a shockingly poor performance.

'That was a big mistake,' said Stephen Morris in *Future Music* in 1994. 'It was a complete struggle. The crew came round and took every plug to pieces to make sure it was wired up right and stuck "BBC approved" on it.'

Bernard Sumner: 'Maybe it would have made sense to play a rock song live [on Top Of The Pops*] but to do 'Blue Monday' – which was very dependent on production and sonics – was a mistake, bluster over common sense.'*

'I must admit,' stated Sumner at the time, 'that as a member of New Order, it's not my idea not to mime. I believe in miming. Surely the aim of a performance is to attain the best possible performance of that song. Which is the record. I don't advocate playing live. It's some of the other members of New Order that do. But it's a democracy and I'm prepared to go along with the majority.'

You don't have to look far to find the keenest advocate of keeping music live. Peter Hook: 'The reason we don't go on [kid's show] *Razzamataz* and that is that we always play live and they won't let you do it. We don't mime because I think it's ridiculous.'

Despite terrible TV performances, 'Blue Monday' became omniprescent, but the willful and obscure aspects of The Haçienda – the very things that delighted its supporters but baffled its accountants, continued ... and the money – essentially cash generated by New Order for Factory rather than just the club – provided the perfect excuse to carry on fiddling while Rome burned.

It's said that anger can be a great motivational tool. If that's true, then frustration with The Haçienda situation certainly coincided with an enormous creative surge in Bernard. Although it's classed as a group composition, Tony Wilson believes that one man was ultimately responsible for 'Blue Monday' and the track instigated a series of classic songs that all bore the Sumner inprint: 'My memory of New Order in those days is that Steve and Gillian were the techies. The reality is 'Blue Monday' must have been Bernard. Because of what Bernard went on to do in the next six months ... because Bernard went on to do 'Looking From A Hilltop' and 'Cool As Ice' ... and 'Reach For Love', by Marcel King.' The production moniker that connects these pieces is 'Be Music' and has been used by all of New Order as a production alias. But it's Bernard's production efforts and his synth-programming skills that are still revered to this day.

'Looking From A Hilltop' is by Bernard's Blackpool pals, Section 25. Started in 1979 by the Cassidy brothers Vince and Larry, they had recently undergone a radical rethink in their approach after relatively little success with Factory. This much-sampled track – used by The Shamen and The Orb amongst others – is one of their key highlights.

'We've always had a good rapport with Bernard,' says Section 25 drummer Vin Cassidy. 'For me, more so than with Hooky really. I always thought Bernard had a better understanding of where we were coming from. Great ideas, willing to experiment, he was learning as well – 'From The Hip', 'Looking From A Hilltop', Tony's right about him as a producer in that respect.' Tony Wilson: "Looking From A Hilltop' is one of the greatest early techno tracks.'

'Martin produced us to begin with,' says Section 25's Larry Cassidy. 'Then 'Blue Monday' happened and Bernard was producing everything, everywhere, all the time ... he was never home. A marriage can't take that. He worked very hard for a long time and he was learning his studio craft. Technically and in loads of other ways and he got very good at it. Still is.'

'Cool As Ice' by Manchester funkateers 52nd Street was the second of three singles for Factory. It was a club hit here, then went on to dance chart success in US. They were lost in the rush when New Order hit big with 'Blue Monday'.

Marcel King – the man behind 'Reach For Love' was the great lost voice of Manchester music. A decade earlier he had been number 1 in the UK charts with 'Sad Sweet Dreamer' by Sweet Sensation. The all-black vocal group had won TV talent show *New Faces* and the group had 'the new Jackson Five' written all over them. After a failed follow-up and an attempt at representing Britain in the preliminary rounds of the Eurovison Song Contest, King had fallen on tougher times.

Bernard Sumner: 'Marcel had unfortunately developed a bad heroin habit and the sessions with him went from being sublime to sheer hell, but I liked him a lot when he was nice and we share the same birth-date.'

'Marcel King, 'Reach For Love' ...' marvels Tony Wilson, '... one of the great singers of all-time. Any other label in the world would have had a hit with it ... again, that's Bernard. That little collection of records he did in 1983 are wonderful. That genius side of him goes unreported.' A favourite among Factory followers, the single proved to be a final day in the sun for King. Sadly, he died of a brain hemorrhage in 1995.

'No one knew they were Bernard,' states Wilson. It said Be Music and DoJo Productions. Donald Johnson [of A Certain Ratio] was helping him, but it was Bernard's way of saying *I did this* – instead of saying 'Produced by Bernard Sumner'; to this day people don't know.'

Bernard Sumner, the self-taught techie, had taken what he'd learned from Martin Hannett – starting from those early Cargo sessions – and put it on a world stage. 'You can't ignore technology,' he said to *Jamming* magazine, of his life-long fascination that can be traced back to his gran's house, fiddling with the speakers to get a sound out of Peter Hook's bass. 'And more importantly, you've still got to play these things. It doesn't matter if you play a Fairlight or a saw. It's the tune that matters. A strong melody was always the most important thing and always will be. However easy it is to play, you have still got to produce that melody. That's the art.'

Terry Mason: 'The thing with having somone from New Order doing your record is, you had access to their toys. A lot of New Order was about them having access to technology. If they wanted a DMX drum machine, they were in a position to get it. They had a technolgy advantage over other people. We had Emulators [samplers], we owned one. We had a spare as well.'

Bernard's production work for Gonnie Reitveld's Quando Quango would not only provide some great records, but also help put in place links between the dance and rock communities that were gradually moving closer together. The meeting point was a QQ b-side that Bernard had a hand in called 'Triangle'. The track also featured Johnny Marr, guitarist with another Manchester band who were annoying *Top of the Pops*' producers with their own idiosyncratic performances: The Smiths.

'Bernard was actually lying on the floor when I first met him,' recalled Johnny Marr in Q. 'He'd been up all night. Things don't change much. I remember at the time he was surprised that I had a knowledge of New York dance music and I was surprised that he knew about early Rolling Stones singles and Neil Young album tracks.'

Johnny Marr's stock was well and truly on the up. He and musical partner Steven Morrissey had the British music press at their beck and call since forming the band in 1982. In the same way that Joy Division had filled the post-punk void, The Smiths had satisfied the need for a group to be carried shoulder high by journalists left bereft after the loss of Joy Division. Along with Morrissey – sat a few rows back from Bernard at that Sex Pistols' gig at the Lesser Free Trade Hall gig in 1976 – he had formed The Smiths as a song-writing unit with designs far beyond Manchester and its tight-knit, catty scene. And he wasn't about to let the groups clingy fans stop him from getting involved with the likes of Quando Quango. But those outside the scene were still wary of dance and rock sharing the same headspace.

'When we did the stuff with Johnny Marr, we needed a funk guitarist and Johnny could do Bo Diddley,' says Quando Quango's Gonnie Reitveld. 'He was like, "Don't tell anyone, 'cos The Smiths' fans will be really disgusted if they found out that their guitarist was playing like this." I think that split between rock and dance is quite artificial. The fan base can be quite divided and quite conservative. The musicians tend to cross genres a lot more. In the dance world, producers use different names to produce different genres, so they don't confuse the fan base. In the heads of the fans, they are in very different worlds, but it actually comes out of the same studios. When I was in Chicago in 1992 with Vince Lawrence – a black producer – using his studio for dance tracks for the black market ... on the other side of the loft space was a rehearsal room for his girlfriend. She was white, she had blue hair and she had an all-girl punk band. The two of them lived under the same roof, worked more or less in the same space and on one side was gospel-y house music and R&B and on the other was punk rock. These are people who live together, sleep together, eat together, are in the same space and communicate with each other. So I think the split between rock and dance is probably more historic. One of the first successful DJ nights at The Haçienda was an indie night – all records by guitar bands. People like to think there is a huge divide.'

'Synthesisers were das verboten in The Smiths,' pointed out Sumner in *Music 365*. 'It was a guitar band. When Johnny started to work with me, we got all those computers and stuff in the studio and he was like, "Wow, what can this do? Let me have a look at that!" It's only natural.'

In fact, Morrissey had clearly stated that the day a synth appeared on a Smiths record would be the same day that he didn't. With Quando Quango, the creative gloves were off. 'I remember Bernard spending a lot of time faffing around with synthesisers,' says Reitveld. 'I [also] spent a lot of time with Bernard doing that. I had this bass line and this rhythm and this chord structure but Bernard wanted to put some triggered, sequenced extra bits on it – arpeggio. He was just, "Go on, Gonnie, put your hands on the keyboard." We just recorded it and never did a re-take. Sounds a bit mad because of that but that's what's right about it. Mad energy. Bernard was very interested in new music technology – he read all those [technology] magazines with great interest and he always wanted to try out technology and see what he could do ... bit of a mad scientist seeing how far he could push it. He was quite inspiring in that way and would give me advice about what kind of equipment to buy. Bernard hated playing live and preferred to mess about in the studio. Bernard was sick often, mostly before gigs. He was terrified of going on stage. Maybe that's why he started doing production work and ended up with Electronic.'

Bernard Sumner: 'Not true.'

Back at The Haçienda, New Order were top dogs. The run of post-'Blue Monday' success, their constant appearances in the music press and their erratic yet memorable TV appearances meant they were suddenly very famous indeed and even having their own club wasn't enough to help someone like Bernard keep a low profile. As former glass collector Leroy Richardson moved up The Haçienda ladder – becoming a bar manager – his other responsibilities increased. As well as being deeply street-wise, the small matter of Leroy's abilities in full-contact karate were something that also made him stand out. 'Rob asked me to go out on the gigs with New Order, driving. They put me through my test and bought me a car on Christmas Eve, like a Christmas present. Rob used to get me to go to the gigs, especially the festivals, because of the liggers who came and tried to influence Bernard – drugs and all this. I used to get hold of them [New Order] and say, "Come on, we've got to go." Look after them ... say to Bernard, "We've got to go at ten past," ... then at ten past I'd get him. It was never fans, it was people who were always at The Haçienda who were friends ... but I thought they were taking the piss and taking advantage ... at least I gave something back – doing a good job. You're taking the piss, you're taking advantage because you know his nature. He's a very astute person and he's nobody's fool. I thinks it's more that he was a bit too polite for his position. I've seen him go off on one at a gig through something not being right. But too polite to say to these people "Leave me alone," he's enjoying himself but we've got to get away otherwise it won't happen. I wouldn't say he was easily led – I'd say he was too polite.'

Away from the club, New Order's travels were paying greater and greater dividends as fact-finding missions. Gonnie Reitveld: 'We played Paradise Garage as support for New Order in 1983. Mike [Pickering] and I, plus Simon Topping [A Certain Ratio] who was then living in NYC to learn

Latin percussion. Paradise Garage was an amazing warehouse like-space without alcohol. I'd never been to anything like it. There were two spaces, one for lounging and one just for dancing, with the best sound system I've ever heard in a club; you could have a conversation on the dance floor and still feel the sound stroke the hairs on your arms. This place was a major inspiration of where to go with the club as a dance space where the DJ inspires the crowd.'

Reitveld believes The Haçienda had a lot to learn from the likes of The Paradise Garage – it put the problems with the Manchester club into sharp relief. 'The sound came from all directions at The Haç,' she says. 'Not very good fun. But I think the really interesting thing about The Haçienda – especially those first four years – was that it was an experimental space that was organised by people who loved music, for people who loved music. In a rather idealist way, not a money-grabbing enterprise. But a cultural institution. One of the sad things is that no one thought of asking for support from any arts funds or cultural fund. Because Factory and New Order are the kind of people not to give in to anything ... in pursuit of what they want to do.'

It would take a major sea-change to alter The Haçienda fortunes – akin to turning round a tanker. A half-empty tanker staffed by sulky goths at that. And it would happen by accident rather than design. For the time being, the club would tread water as a gig and arts space, dodging financial success with dogged persistance but achieving creative goals at every turn. Leroy Richardson: 'A lot of people who were there [working] would make an effort with the way they dressed – like the two goth twins who used to go collecting glasses in six-inch stilettos ... two glasses at a time. *Eventually* the glasses would get collected. But it gave it the *image*. The Haçienda was more about the people who worked there more than anything else. It then became about the people who went there ... and the music ... and the place itself kind of gelled.'

And when The Haçienda gelled – when the music and the times and the drugs and the decor and the sound system and the clothes came into alignment – another thing arrived at the club's doors on Whitworth Street West. Considerably more *inside/outside* tension than Bernard, New Order or designer Ben Kelly could ever have imagined.

CONFUSION EIGHT:
A WIZARD WHEEZE

Terry Mason, school friend of Bernard Sumner and Peter Hook, guitarist-turned-drummer of Stiff Kittens, minder-cum-confidant of Ian Curtis and the road crew chief of New Order, found that his responsibilities had expanded a touch after a sudden change in the group dynamic. 'At this point,' states Mason over a mixed grill in a Salford pub, 'Rob Gretton had gone mad. I'm not sure what was on his certificate when he was sectioned, but he was taken off in a straight jacket ... he'd turned manic.'

Coincidentally, a sense of mania would seep elsewhere too. It would spread through the group and mark a souring of Bernard's relationship with Tony Wilson, a collapse of his trust issues with the press and the end of his marriage. Given that these were relationships already strained at the best of times, it was a dark period all round. Just to press the point home, New Order released a new album. It was called *Low-life* and it was given the Factory catalogue number of FAC 100.

Low-life is a push towards a more easy-access New Order – it's even got a photograph of a member of the band [Morris] on the cover. Just like normal bands do. It's an open attempt – without being blatant – to be liked; an album you'd offer to someone impressed by the thrust of 'Blue Monday' and it plays like the soundtrack to a raucous night out in Manchester, with New Order as your tour guides and party organisers. It opens with a traditional technique – a wrong-footing. First track, 'Love Vigilantes' is a rare stab at a linear story song, whereby Sumner tells a tale of woe as he returns home from battle, just slightly behind a letter to his loved one telling her he is dead. With its stuttering melodica and 4/4 drums, it comes across as a slightly folksy change of tone, but the Country and North-Western tone doesn't last long. The spurs are soon slipped off and left at the saloon and the disco vibe kicks in. 'The Perfect Kiss' is an extended dash to the dancefloor with double handclaps and hedonistic lyrics that would suit Pete Burns and Dead Or Alive down to the ground. 'Sunrise' is a clattering rock song that seems to see the band repaying a previous compliment to The Cure – Sumner even seems to drop his Salford accent for a more fey, southern, Robert Smith-style twang. There are modish textures reminiscent of Mike Oldfield's *Tubular Bells* and synth glamour pusses Japan in the instrumental 'Elegia'. 'Sooner Than You Think' is a big city driving song, perfect for cruising down the Princess Parkway, the dual carriageway that connects Factory's offices in Didsbury to The Haçienda. 'Sub-culture' continues the party once you've got passed through the Haçienda doors and 'Face Up' is a synth whoop-fest that will see you through till chucking out time at 2a.m. There may be a feeling of coming down from a party like *Low-life*, but any post-celebration downer is definitely worthwhile after being shown such a good time.

'The Perfect Kiss' and 'Sub-culture' were both released as singles – and only reached a disappointing 46 and 63 in the UK charts respectively. This was perhaps more a reflection of an on-going post-punk suspicion of album tracks as singles, rather than a genuine representation of how good the tracks actually were.

'I don't think we get anything like the recognition we deserve ... we are much better than people give us credit for. We are very underrated,' Sumner said in *The Face* of *Low-life*'s release. 'Sometimes we make pure dance music and if some people have decided to ignore dance music then that's their problem, not ours. We can't be blamed for people's narrow-mindedness. But a lot of our music isn't what you would consider dance floor anyway.'

FAC 100 may have been a triumph, but some other nearby numbers in the catalogue would prove more painful. FAC 99 was a dental bill for work done on Rob Gretton's teeth. FAC 98 would also be the cause of discomfort in the New Order camp – the latest eccentric installation at The Haçienda, a hairdressing salon called 'Swing'. And one of the crimpers had caught Bernard Sumner's eye. 'Sarah?' says Terry Mason. 'She was part of the Swing gang who ran the hairdressing out of the dressing rooms of The Haçienda. It was run by Mark Berry and she was part of that extended gang.'

Sarah Dalton shared a house in Didsbury, south Manchester, with New Order roadie Michael Eastwood and was going out with a lighting operator at The Haçienda. A small, yet striking, figure, if nothing else she had a singular nickname: 'She was known as 'The Vision',' says Eastwood. 'She was an Edie Sedgwick-type figure, flouncing round the place. Some would say beautiful. A waif ... thin ... small ... petite ... great sense of humour. It was pretty obvious Bernard had his eye on her. Every time I saw Bernard, he would quiz me incessantly about Sarah. For a while, she wasn't the slightest bit interested. One night she just clicked and said, "I'm thinking of going and seeing Bernard." I said, "Do you know what you're getting yourself into?" And she said, "Yes."'

Alfred Street, Lower Broughton: Bernard's home up to the age of 11.
Photo courtesy of Salford Local History Museum

Young Scuttlers – Bernard Dickin and Peter Hook at Salford Grammar circa 1969.
Photo courtesy of Salford Local History Museum

Bernard aged 15 on a 'Family Fun Day' in Heaton Park, Manchester.
Photo courtesy of Terry Mason

At the newly formed Cosgrove Hall in
Chorlton, pictured top right next to
director Chris Taylor
Photo courtesy of Chris Taylor

Working as a paint and trace artist at Stop Frame

Photo courtesy of Chris Taylor

Braving the hecklers at Bristol's Trinity Hall in 1981.
Photo courtesy of Andrew Davis

With producer Martin Hannett at Cargo Studios, Rochdale.
Photo courtesy of Chris Hewitt/Ozit Morpheus Records

Backstage at The Tropicana, Los Angeles, 1981.
Photo courtesy of Terry Mason

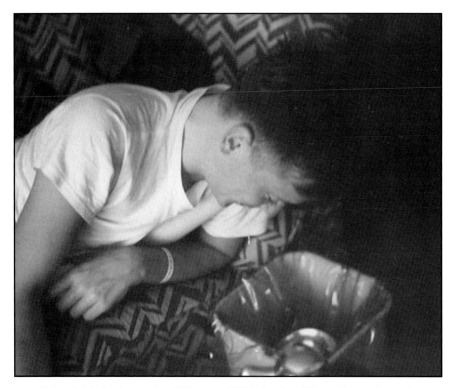

Being 'sick' backstage in 1981 tour of USA, bottle of Pernod not pictured.

Photo courtesy of Terry Mason

The deification of Ian Curtis – a ghostly image of Joy Division's singer from a mural erected in Manchester's Castlefield district to acknowledge local artists.

Photograph of an original work, painted by Matt Aindow

Electronic: Johnny Marr, Karl Bartos, Bernard
Sumner.

Photo courtesy of Rex Features

With Section 25, backstage at Blackpool's Empress Ballroom.
L-R: Roger Wikeley, Vin Cassidy, Bernard, Larry Cassidy and Ian
Butterworth

Photo courtesy of Nat Cassidy

New Order versus the kids at Oakwood School, Salford, February 2005.

Photo courtesy of Manchester Evening News/Salford Advertiser

Bernard's family history means he has a special connection with Oakwood's pupils.

Photo courtesy of Manchester Evening News/Salford Advertiser

Bernard Sumner with New Order, 2006.

Photo courtesy of Karin Albinsson

Sumner's persistence paid off and the pair became close. So close in fact, that Bernard decided to fly her out to join him on New Order's 1985 tour of America. 'That was a complete shock to me and to most people ... that someone as tight as him would pay to bring Sarah out!' jokes Terry Mason. 'That actually did cause a hell of a lot of shit. Once I got told, I could then re-arrange flights and make sure he had different rooms, the numbers changed for travelling about. She came and that caused ... hmmm, you can imagine. We went out there, in the run up to Christmas, and Tony Wilson played a wizard wheeze ...'

Today, tucking into a light bite and a glass of lunchtime vino, Tony Wilson is repentant, yet as ever simultaneously protests his innocence. 'Bernard always blames me for his divorce,' he says.

Terry Mason takes up the story: 'Barney had gone off on tour, bye bye to [wife] Sue at the door, knowing he was going to bring Sarah on tour in the meantime, but he wasn't going to bring her until after the first few gigs. The band had had a bit of a run in with [pop weekly] *Smash Hits* ... Tony thought it would be a wizard wheeze to have *Smash Hits* come over to the LA shows and hang out with us for a few days. And didn't bother to tell anyone.'

'I got a phone call from *Smash Hits*,' continues Wilson. '"Can we come and interview the band?" They're in Santa Barbara. "Fine, fine, see you there." I get there and the gig's over and and I get to the Best Western [hotel] about midnight ... and there's a *great* party in progress. That's the great thing about the rock and roll business – you all meet up in some foreign city somewhere and become what Martin Hannett used to describe as "an active service unit."'

Terry Mason: 'We did a show in a beautiful theatre in Santa Barbara, this reporter's watching what's going on and she noted it down ... how people were ushered about.' Tony Wilson: 'One in the morning, I see this photographer and journalist from *Smash Hits*. I'd forgotten all about them. Two weeks later *Smash Hits* comes out and there's a photograph of these two girls, 7 o'clock in the morning, running out with Bernard's underpants in their hands ... and because I forgot to warn him about *Smash Hits,* I get the blame. But then, I get the blame for everything.'

'That then caused a bit of a kerfuffle really,' recalls Terry Mason, understating the situation somewhat. 'Sue went completely mad at him. But he also had the prospect that Sarah would have seen this – and she was coming out to join him on tour. Then Sarah comes out [for the] gig at the University of Pennsylvania. He goes to meet her and they go back to the hotel ... must have been a few words said. Afterwards, Barney's come out with "I'm never talking to any journalist ever again." That's when the war opened up on another front. That there was when the war between Barney and Wilson opens up. After that, you couldn't tell if the war was with Wilson ... or with Rob. It may have been [around] this time when Barney says ... "That's it with Factory. See how funny Wilson finds that.'"

Bernard's marriage to Sue Barlow was over, cutting a connection with the original Salford group dating back to the early 1970s. The change was felt within the New Order camp. 'Professionally, you had to start blanking people,' says Mason. 'When they split up, it would have been difficult for her [Sue] to speak to me and Hooky because she would have known we knew what was going on ... maybe she felt there should have been some loyalty.'

Sarah Dalton is now Sarah Sumner. 'She did it by being with him all the time and sticking to him like glue,' says her former housemate Michael Eastwood. 'If that's what you've got to do to keep hold of a man ...'

Bernard Sumner: 'We stuck to each other like glue and still do!'

Although it caused some uncomfortable moments, no one questioned Bernard's relationship with Sarah. By the same token, the days of questioning whether Bernard was up to the job of fronting the band were also gone. He'd found his own way through the self-consciousness and the criticisms and by the time of the 1985 tour was coming out of his shell as a performer – with or without the aid of Pernod. He even looked the part, with a much-copied haircut. Walk into any hairdressers in Manchester at the time and ask for a 'Barney' and you'd be provided with a lookalike do: super-short up the back and sides, longer on top, preferably with blond streaks.

He looked like a pop star – and Tony Wilson believes that Bernard's on-stage persona came to the fore at this time and that it's a persona that works on two levels. But then again, Tony Wilson believes everything works on *at least* two levels. 'Aaah, the post-modernism of Barney's stage performances,' says Wilson. 'He does those moves like he's farting or something, that are utterly awful. He's saying, "Look ... I know that you know, that I know, that you know, that I know that I look like an idiot." There's this whole series of layers. He looks an idiot. But because it's layered, it makes it a quite wonderful piece of art. I remember a gig at Meadowlands Arena, 28,000 people with the Sugarcubes, PiL and New Order. Bernard spent the first ten minutes taking the piss out of Johnny Rotten. There was a full page piece in the *NME* about it saying New Order were wonderful. They were utterly appalling. So appalling they were great. Only New Order could play a bad gig and get a good review for being so bad. As they came off-stage, I said to Tom Atencio, their American manager ... "Fucking *appalling*." He goes, "Appalling?" He got hold of me ... and shouts, "He *stood up*, didn't he? For fuck's sake!" I didn't realise, the previous night in Miami, Bernard had sat on the back of the drum riser for the *entire* set. The fact that he actually stood up – as far as Tom was concerned – was something of an achievement!'

Bernard's live reputation has always been tinged by inconsistency, but quality control was made more difficult by New Order's uncompromising stance that, despite the technology, they wouldn't just go through the motions. 'Every night they went on stage, they played a different set,' says roadie-turned-technician, Michael Eastwood. 'They would write the set just before they went on stage. Nobody does that. Don't just have a set list and bang it out every night, not one other band has ever been able to do that. In 1989 in America on the *Technique* tour, they had 37 tunes that they could do any night, which is fucking amazing. From a technical point of view it was really difficult because of the way you had to load samplers and all that. It was really fucking difficult. They'd walk on stage and, as they walked on, you'd get handed a set list. Nobody does that.'

'Barney's funny,' adds Wilson. 'There was a whole gig once where he kept saying, "Hello Kilkenny ... Kilkenny, you're the best." We weren't in Kilkenny at all. Bernard can be very annoying. He knows he's being annoying and does it to wind everybody up. God bless him.'

He was having his moments off-stage too. Sumner was – according to those around him – flexing his muscles, at a time when the band's manager Rob Gretton was at a low ebb. 'This was after Rob had been sectioned,' says Terry Mason. 'Rob was going about with prescriptions ... some injections. He was shaking and a right old state. The drugs were so bad we were worried that the Americans wouldn't be allowed to make up the prescription. We had to go into Canada to have it done. The results of him going mad ... he had something to control that, stop him being a jack in a box. And, of course, like most of these things, you have to counter-balance it, so he needed another drug to counter the depression and bring him up.'

To some observers, it appeared that Sumner had now realised the power he had: if he didn't want to do something, the solution was a simple one. He didn't do it. Tony Wilson: 'A typical story would be we were a bit late for a gig and at Chicago airport Bernard goes, "S'cuse me, how many seats has that plane got?" Small intercity plane with 35 seats. Barney's rule was nothing less than fifty seats. So everybody else gets on the flight, Bernard has to be re-routed through Boston. So Bernard makes everyone's life a misery ... part of the fun, I suppose.'

Bernard Sumner: 'Again, there is a little more to this story. I had just been released from a three-day stay in hospital, I had vomited continuously for 24 hours because of lacerations in my stomach and I was nervous of flying on a small plane. Anyway, it was only me that was inconvenienced.'

'Barney's got complete control of Rob by the late 1980s,' says Mason. 'Once Rob was sectioned, he'd lost the war with Barney." One of Rob's big things was that he could never admit he was wrong. He'd made some ... questionable calls. The tax situation with New Order. The taxman wants his cut when you earn it, not when you receive it ... the fact that it's gone into The Haçienda this month ...'

Bernard Sumner: 'The situation with the taxman was dire, but it was not because of The Haçienda. We had sold a lot of Joy Division and early New Order records in the States – Rough Trade America had gone bust without paying us ...'

Mason recalls on incident shortly after Sumner's run-in with Tony Wilson and *Smash Hits* that he says demonstrates Bernard's new-found bullishness. 'We did this gig,' says Mason. 'As is the law in America, after the show there's a meet-and-greet. The local PR come into the dressing room and Barney's there ... thunder and lightning in his face. "You've got to meet some of these people, just say hello to this guy whose shop's sold all these records." We get an agreement that this guys comes in, just shakes hands, that's it. This guy comes in, says something and the next minute, Barney's hitting him. That was a great night ...'

Bernard Sumner: 'The guy walked in and ordered me to "sign these records." He was arrogant.'

Diplomatic incidents notwithstanding, Bernard also widened his production output, proving no job was too tricky. Two years earlier, New Order had played a gig in Macclesfield supported by Tony Wilson's latest attempt to find a new Joy Division: Happy Mondays. The task to sort out their second release fell to Sumner and he's widely credited as having jolted what potential the band had into the open.

'Here's this man who learned everything off Martin Hannett,' says Tony Wilson. 'He became the ultimate modern music producer – doesn't let anyone know about it. Then we bring him in to do the Happy Mondays. You'd think he'd use what he does and use computers. Bernard comes in to do the single, he looks at the situation, looks at the Mondays and says, "Right ... do it live." So he recorded 'Freaky Dancin'' almost live in Strawberry Studios ... and it's the first great Mondays single. That's an example of the boy's genius. When he was asked to produce something that wasn't right for his skills, he threw his skills away.'

It's not the only thing he threw away. Sumner recalls how, during the sessions, the Mondays dived into the studio bin to retrieve some discarded Chinese takeaway that he and an engineer had finished with. The incident would be recreated down to the last noodle in the film *24 Hour Party People*.

Bernard Sumner: 'The Mondays were utterly, unbelievably lovely lunatics and I wanted to capture that rawness before they changed. They didn't change.'

Clearly, demand for New Order product was high. Not just from the public, but from Factory and, by default, The Haçienda. Hard on the heels of *Low-life* came *Brotherhood* in 1986 and *Substance* in 1987.

Brotherhood sounds dated. Not because of the songs or the synth textures, but because of the running order. It's designed to be listened to on two sides of vinyl. Side one is the 'Strum-along-a-Bernard' guitar section, side two is 'Plug the keyboards in and let's get programming'. The idea is rendered redundant though, when it's listened to on CD. This desire to please both sides of their fan base – the guitar fans and the danceheads – would continue for some time. Of the 'strummalongs', the double-tracked opener 'Paradise' is the strongest, with 'Weirdo' and 'Broken Promise' bordering on variations on the same theme. 'As It Is When It Was' allows Sumner the chance to slow down the acoustic rhythm and it's very close to being a lighter-in-the-air moment. The familiarity and bounce of 'Bizarre Love Triangle', which opens up the dance account, belies the fact that it only reached number 56 in the UK charts. It feels like a big old hit to start side two with, although it plainly wasn't. 'All Day Long' is the by-now traditional Kraftwerk moment with its big, Christmas-y synth runs while 'State Of The Nation' rounds off the album with another single – and another less than storming chart performance as it only just reached the Top 30. *Substance* came soon after. A collection of singles, remixes and non-album tracks from 'Ceremony' onwards, it can lay claim to being the best New Order retrospective/collection. With 'Blue Monday', 'Everything's Gone Green' and 'Confusion' on there too, it may even have a look in as New Order's best album.

New Order's poor run of singles success was finally reversed with 'True Faith', a number 4 hit in August. After 'Blue Monday', it's probably the ultimate New Order song. All the boxes were ticked this time: clattering percussion, a swoonsome tune, *kling klang* bass lines, an obscurist, happy slapping video and baffling lyrics about small boys and morning suns. 'It's about drug dependency,' Sumner told Q magazine in 1999. 'I don't take smack but when I wrote that song I tried to imagine what it's like to be a smackhead and nothing else matters to you except that day's hit.' The drug inference was explicit in the initial version of the song, with a line about the aforementioned young boys growing up together and "taking drugs with me." 'Stephen Hague, our producer, made us change it because he said it wouldn't be a hit if we kept that line in. He was right.'

The same year as the release of 'True Faith' would also mark the initial departure of Terry Mason from the New Order camp. Spotting a wind-down in the band's level of activity after the recent flurry, he decided to depart, believing that he'd done his bit. 'I was [on the] pay-roll and when Rob went mad, I was running it. They stopped doing shit gigs and had an American agency. I left at the Wembley gig, Christmas 1987. I left the country on Christmas day ... went chasing the love of my life to California. I went the long way. Went to Australia and New Zealand with The Pogues, just as they had a hit with 'Fairy Tale Of New York'. The band were going to have six months off anyway, so I was going to see what happened. Sometimes you just need a break. I had enough money, I had a work permit.'

So, it's with a heavy heart that we say goodbye to Terry Mason. He's been good company along the way so far in this tale of *Confusion*. From those Salford school-days, through early incarnations of Stiff Kittens and Warsaw, via the rise of Joy Division, the fall of Ian Curtis, the resurrection of his schoolmates as musicians in New Order and the initial days of the Haçienda. Then, gone for good. Only – as ever – thing's just aren't as simple as that, as there's life in Terry Mason yet. 'I came back and did some UK gigs with them freelance as a production manager. Then I did the 1989 tour. And then I got sacked ...'

Back at The Haçienda, there were serious changes afoot. Bolstered by the delayed success in America of 'Blue Monday' – thanks to a remix by Michael Jackson producer Quincy Jones – the club's doors were miraculously still open by 1988. Rest assured, there were no 'sleeves that are so expensive we'll lose money on every copy' wheezes this time round. Good job too, as the the song was a US Top 5 hit. The timing was, for once, impeccable, because then Acid House came along and positively jammed the doors of The Haçienda open. The possibilty of snatching success for the club had been building since 1985/86. First the positively outré concept of actually *promoting* The Haçienda had been instigated. Promoter Paul Cons began his involvement with the club as a Vidal Sassoon model for a fashion show in 1984. 'It was the first time I'd ever been there actually,' he says. 'Out of that experience, during the miners' strike, we were looking for a venue for an event, 'Lesbians And Gays Support the Miners'. It featured Pete Shelley [Buzzcocks], The Redskins and Trevor and Simon from kids' TV. So we did it at The Haç. I was one of the few people to get a job out of the miners' strike. Promotions were often aimed at targetted audiences. Fairly basic stuff but quite a departure for the deliberately obtuse Haçienda. Buses were laid on to ferry [people] to student nights. There were gay nights, funk nights ...

That was part of the shift from it being about bands to being about club nights. The Haçienda was so different, people who were used to a grungier venue were a bit thrown when The Haçienda first opened. It was like some space ship that had landed from some completely different culture. Which is maybe why it took a few years for people to work it out.

I came in at the same time as Paul Mason, who'd been brought in from Rock City in Nottingham. He'd had a very successful student night at Rock City, so the idea was to do one at The Haçienda, which was called The Temperance Club on Thursday night. And that was marketed ... which they'd never really done before. When they started, there'd very much been the attitude of *anti*-marketing; The Factory idea of 'you put something on and it either works or it doesn't'. After losing lots of money, they realised they did actually have to tell people what was on and market it. That was one of the big changes. New Order seemed to have quite a big income. A lot of Mancunian bands tend to leave Manchester and take their money with them. New Order decided to re-invest in Manchester. Also, from their travels to New York and Europe, there were influences brought in. There was a conscious decision to make it more accessible and to actually go out there and market it and connect with what was going on in Manchester.

I started off as a leafleter, handing out flyers. I started a gay night in 1985, which I imaginatively called Gay Monday. It was a disaster because it was at a time when the gay village was segregated. The Haçienda was seen as a very strange place full of weird people. We were trying to play Hi-NRG. I started a student night with [DJ] Dave Haslam, then Zumbar in 1987, then whole rave thing kicked off in 1988.'

The 'whole rave thing' was powered by an old drug in new clothing. MDMA (3,4 methylenedioxy-methamphetamine) had been patented in

Germany as early as 1914, languishing unused for decades as it had been synthesised as a by-product during research into methods of reducing bleeding. It resurged slightly during the 1950s, as the possibility of military use was investigated, using the substance as a form of truth drug. Variations on the formula have variously been tried as an anti-depressant, an aid to slimming and a tool in psychotherapy. Therapists found its "cleansing" properties highly useful and it became known as 'Adam' – in the true Biblical sense – as it was felt the drug could return subjects to a state before guilt or unworthiness took hold of an individual. During the early 1980s, the true recreational possibilities of the drug kicked in as it picked up the nicknames of "Empathy" and "Ecstasy". It arrived in Manchester via the party island of Ibiza – the Mancs have always loved a fortnight in Spain and now they were bringing back considerably more than a lobster tan and a straw donkey.

The choice of records – plus the drugs – added to the previously unpleasant acoustics of The Haçienda suddenly seemed to lock into a highly workable formation. Gonnie Reitveld could see that the time may not have been right in 1982, but it was becoming very right five years later. 'A lot of different things happened there, that were quite experimental. Because of that it gave you space to do things differently and re-think what a disco and a gig space was all about. It was quite a privilege to have been there and to have been involved. When it became successful, it was almost like that space had been waiting for that moment. House music became synonymous with The Haçienda. The two of them combined became a success. Think of how that music developed – Chicago, also warehouse spaces. The sound of that music and the sensibility of that music, the post-industrial, embracing information through technology. Industrial spaces became re-used for a better use and the sonic space in that music suited a space like The Haçienda really well. A lot of echo and noise ... it all seemed to make sense.'

By a series of architectural, musical and chemical coincidences, The Haçienda was coming good. The last of the post-punks and goths held up their hands and surrendered. Rock and roll learned to dance. Tony Wilson, for one, was delighted: 'Manchester is the only city in the world where no one ever differentiates between rock and dance. Ever. The two things are the very essences of rock and roll ... never a problem.'

Confidence became so high, in fact, that it was decided to expand into a new venture: Dry bar. Tony Wilson again: 'That was Bernard's idea actually. What a brilliant name for a bar ... Dry. When we had our first month of actually making money at The Haçienda – after six years of losing money – we thought we were so clever we'd open a bar, modelled on some LA bars we liked. We had a meeting and everybody else ... Factory board members, New Order board members, no one gave a shit where it was. But two people did. Me and Bernard. I wanted it to be in Oldham Street [at the top end of the city centre, now known as the Northern Quarter] because I thought that part of Manchester was ripe for regeneration. Bernard, stupid bastard, wanted us to build the Dry bar on Oxford Road. Imagine putting a *bar* on Oxford Road where all those students would pass by and *buy drinks* ... absolutely disgusting. So I won the debate, we were in Oldham Street. The Northern Quarter finally took off 20 years later ... after we'd lost another few million. Typical. Bernard was right, I was wrong. The rest is history.'

Despite this apparent instance of losing money, it's very difficult to squeeze a bad word out of Sumner on the subject of Tony Wilson: '[People say] Tony's a money grabbing arsehole breadhead,' he said in *NME* in 1993. 'And he isn't that at all. He's not the ogre that certain articles have been insinuating. He's just not the world's best businessman, that's all.'

The conflict over Dry was typical of the dynamic by now. There were factions within cliques, but there seemed to be one constant: Bernard Sumner was out on his own. 'Rob would come up with ideas,' says New Order stage technician Michael Eastwood. 'Steve would go along with the group decision, Hooky would side with Rob, especially if it had humour involved! Bernard would be the lone dissenter.'

Across town, The Haçienda was now party central in Manchester and New Order were the party chairmen – and chairwoman. 'The Acid House era was incredible,' said Sumner in *Q*. 'The Haç must have been the wildest place on the planet. I remember being on the balcony watching 2,000 people and every one of them was off their tits on E. It was almost worth losing all that money to see that. Almost.'

At the height of all this hedonism came the album *Technique*, which many feel is New Order's definitive word on the subject of Madchester, ecstasy, The Haçienda and the end of the 1980s. Although popular with fans, the dance tracks are in the minority and the whole exercise does feel a touch *1983*. The dance modes work best and feel appropriate to the times; less so the guitar pop; there's still a sense of playing safe by holding court to both camps: guitar and dance. An out-and-out dance album perhaps would have felt more unrepentant. 'Fine Time' starts off the dance-floor fillers, with so many pieces of synth tricky-ness, it sounds like a keyboard demonstration setting. It's so eager to please it borders on Stock, Aitken Waterman territory – although as a number 11 hit it must have pushed the right buttons. 'All The Way', 'Love Less' and 'Run' are all strummers with varying degrees of light or heavy touch – 'Round & Round', 'Vanishing Point' and unsurprisingly 'Mr Disco' are all designed for 'largeing' it across the dance floor of The Haçienda.

Technique is seen as a classic New Order album, but at the time, not everyone was convinced. 'However hi-tech New Order have become,' wrote Mark Cooper in Q, 'that dance rock fusion sounds increasingly dated, out of time, as if they were relying on dance floor sounds that have been upstaged and have yet to fully incorporate the latest styles from their very own Haçienda.' Perhaps what *Technique* lacks when listened to today, is a real representative sense of the heady excesses of the time. Maybe you had to be there.

Bernard Sumner: 'What about 'Fine Time'?'

When the album was toured in America, New Order were at their technological and performing peak – but the rot was beginning to take a hold of the band's internal relations.

'I went over and did some shows on that tour – and that was quite an eye opener,' says Michael Eastwood, who by now was heavily involved in the massively complex series of samples and sequencers that were an integral part of New Order's live show. 'Even then, Bernard wasn't really travelling with the rest of the band. They were getting limos and he would get his own with Sarah. He wasn't enjoying it. He gets really fractious ... he doesn't enjoy it at all. I can remember Terry saying to him, "What's your problem? You work about an hour a day, you get limo-d around the place, you get all the drinks, whatever you want, you just have to turn up and do an hour, what's your problem?" Mason was back as a freelance and his upfront attitude – a remnant from those Salford schooldays when he was top dog – perhaps marked him down as a man whose days back in the New Order camp were going to be short-lived.

Bernard Sumner: 'The problem was that there was no soul in what we were doing, we were just fishermen with a large net, catching money and then giving it away. Plus, I had fears about my health.'

It's been widely reported that Bernard's excesses had by this stage taken him to the physical limits. It's been repeatedly claimed he was hospitalised in America in 1989 after a 'Pernod and champagne binge' damaged his stomach. Those who were there tell a different tale.

'We had the debacle in Chicago,' recalls Terry Mason. 'Barney and Sarah stay up all night. Time to move the next day, Barney's not moving. No one can get him to move. We're in Detroit. He won't move out of his bedroom.'

In Detroit, as the crew were setting up the show, there was no concern that Sumner hadn't been spotted yet. 'At this point, Bernard wasn't even coming to the sound checks. The first I knew was Hooky's roadie Jane Roberts [who] said, "Dressing room, now!" They were popping champagne corks ... here have some, drinking slammers the lot. They knew the gig was cancelled, so if you drank as much of the rider as possible, then the promoter can't take it back!'

'America's a lot different from the UK,' explains Terry Mason. 'Especially when you've got a sold out concert – 18,000 people – you're likely to have your arse sued. You can't play those games over there, you need to see a doctor. Reshedule it, not a problem. But if you became ill in Illinois, you can't just call a doctor, you have to have paramedics. So we have paramedics into his room. It's obvious he's not ill, but he has to be carried out on a gurney and taken to hospital. They can't find anything wrong with him. The whole LA office kicks in, they were trawling through to find [another] doctor. The only thing they could think of was a bad stomach – not enough. So he has to have tests for ulcers, including all the cameras down his throat and up his arse. So just not getting out of bed has caused all this.'

An anonymous, mischievous fax was sent by the crew at the Detroit venue to Bernard's hospital in Chicago. It read: '*Dear Ulcer. Sorry to hear about the Bernard ...*'

> Bernard Sumner: '*By his own admission, Terry wasn't in Chicago when I got ill. What happened was that Sarah and I were in the car on the way to the Metro Club in Chicago – we had a night off. I started coughing uncontrollably in the car and told the driver to turn around. We went back to the hotel and I started vomiting – this continued for 6-8 hours at which point a doctor was called and I was transferred to the hospital, which handily enough was opposite the hotel. I had lesions on my stomach lining, they were unsure of what had caused it (years later, I was diagnosed with a stomach disorder caused by a bug called hellicobacter priori) but almost certainly drink didn't help, even though I had not been out night before. The gig was rescheduled.*

Mason claims that the Chicago event marked a power shift in the New Order camp that remains to this day. Bernard was in charge and the villain of the piece was Rob Gretton. 'The tour was making him ill,' says Mason. '"Rob, you're making him ill ..."' After that it was E [ecstasy] ... Bernard can't have spicy food, no alcohol, but the doctor didn't say he couldn't have E ... clearly an oversight on the doctor's part!'

This marked the beginning of the end of Mason and Sumner's relationship. The final straw was an apparent disagreement over drugs several weeks down the line on the same 1989 tour. Mason claims he was accused by a tour guest of necking a stash of E's that should have been shared out, something he strongly denies. 'Barney gets himself into a mad fit and decides that's it, I'm sacked. I was sacked that night but no one tells me till the end of the tour... but I'm told not to be anywhere near Barney. Typical Barney, he doesn't remember what people have done for him. Because of his "ulcer" earlier on that tour, it was determined that he could only have E ... his only consolation. So for me to be taking E out of baby Bernard's mouth ... well!'

> Bernard Sumner: 'Yes, I did sack Terry, but I did it to his face,
> which is obviously why he is so bitter ... someone had to
> call time on him eventually, that was me and I told him.'

It would, of course, be nice and neat for the whole matter to end here. Mason exits stage left, only to confide in the attentive, muck-raking biographer more than fifteen years later. But life is rarely so straightforward and there is a twist in the tale that, to his credit, Terry Mason offers up. 'In 1990, I was working with The Mighty Lemon Drops, a band who wanted to do gigs, do signings, were happy to get on a tour bus at the end of the night ... strange fuckers! I also had a Pete Murphy [ex-Bahaus] tour. A year's work and my daughter was due in February.'

Mason and his partner had put aside enough for a fixed fee birth in an American hospital and were happy that things were going to plan. Until the plan went wrong. 'I got the call from Kansas, went back to Phoenix and she'd gone into labour,' says Mason, shuddering at the memory. 'After two epidurals and a c-section, the baby turned blue and went into special care. Really big bill. Then the Pete Murphy tour fell through. Desperate times. The [hospital] bill was *THIS* big and it was down to the last cotton bud. When you go *a la carte* in America, it's very expensive. I went to Rob and the band ... and I'm very grateful ... they paid for it. Rob always said there'd be money at the end of the day. I was very grateful. And that was it.'

Exit Mason stage left. The friendship between him and Bernard, which began after their two schools merged in Salford all those years ago, was over. One good thing did come out of the whole sad affair though: Sian Mason – the little baby girl born in such dramatic circumstances in America – is now a healthy, happy teenager.

Terry Mason.

CONFUSION NINE:
ELECTRONIC – A WAR BETWEEN
ROB AND BERNARD

When asked how he first met Johnny Marr, Bernard Sumner once claimed that, 'We met in a rugby scrum and he was on the opposite team ... and Neil Tennant was the referee.' In fact, it was Manchester dance collective Quando Quango that brought Sumner and Marr together – with surprising longevity – as Electronic. With or without Pet Shop Boy Tennant, they were a constant presence through the 1990s, produced three very well-received albums and a brace of crisp singles.

But there are other, less run of the mill aspects to the whole Electronic experiment. The band also formed part of a bizarre televised experiment into the effects of anti-depressent drugs on creativity and 'aggression directed at the self.' It was also – according to some of those around Sumner – a fantastic opportunity to stoke up the levels of conflict between Bernard and Rob Gretton. 'When Bernard started doing Electronic,' states Tony Wilson, 'he announces before a big New Order gig in Orange County that he was going to do a solo project. That was a real shock to everybody. He begins to work with Johnny Marr and decides that Rob isn't going to manage him. This was the biggest kick in the teeth to Rob at the time. Bernard knew that ... that's why he did it. There really was a war between Rob and Bernard.'

Electronic also had a further effect, according to Tony Wilson. Never one to use hyperbole when splendid overstatement will do just as nicely, Wilson says this about the coming together of Bernard Sumner and Johnny Marr: 'It led to one of the great disasters in Manchester,' he says. It seems an awful lot to pile at the door of a musical collaboration between Sumner and Marr – what could they have done that was so detrimental to Manchester? All in good time ...

The Smiths, after a virtually uninterrupted run of critical acclaim and the kind of momentum that only the most devoted fanbase can provide – twin pillars of support even stronger than those experienced by Joy Division – had collapsed in 1987. It appeared to be one of rock music's more sad and messy splits and one that would require a High Court judge to solve the Gordian knot of its finances. Marr may have left The Smiths, but his position seemed to have remained largely unchanged: that of the supportive sideman, aiding and abetting strong musical personalities. His work on Bryan Ferry's solo album, *Bete Noire*, had come swiftly after The Smiths' split, including the cool-as-cotton single, 'The Right Stuff'. Marr was also to be seen next to Chrissie Hynde as a Pretender on the single 'Windows Of The World', assisting on two albums with Kirsty MacColl, playing with Talking Heads on the *Naked* album and had an on-going collaboration with Matt Johnson of The The to occupy his time. Versatile, ever-dependable Johnny Marr, said many. But why doesn't he just join a group? ...... said others. A great deal had happened – especially in Manchester – since The Smiths had split, and the company Marr kept struck some cynics as being slightly middle of the road.

'With The Smiths, I felt stuck in this nostalgic, black and white *Coronation Street*-type place,' says Marr. 'All my mates were turning on to the local Acid House scene, and Electronic was my route into that. It felt great to be part of something new.'

'We decided it was a good thing to work together,' said Sumner to Jeff Jolley on Rational Alternative Digital, 'because I wasn't particularly enjoying working on my own at the time. So we got together and did the first album. I was a bit fed up with the politics you get in a group, where everyone has his own place of work within the group ... and I wanted to do something where you could vary the chemistry. So basically, Electronic is me and Johnny, and we vary the chemistry by bringing guest artists in.'

Bernard Sumner: 'It started during Republic. *The problem in [this album period] was this: Hooky didn't respect Gillian, Gillian thought Hooky was a sexist pig and Steve was in a fix because he was Gillian's boyfriend but also in the group. I had decided to try and devote myself more to just vocals and the group would jam together more. However, because of this mutual lack of respect, it was tough going. I would be in a room writing the vocals and get to a bit of music that I thought was weak, I would ask the others to work on it and nothing would get done. I would then ask Stephen Hague to ask them and still nothing would get done. So then the only option left would be to write the piece myself. When I did this, I would then be accused by Hooky of taking over the show, this was very difficult for me to swallow as he'd been outside the studio sun-bathing while I'd been working – true. I did have problems with Rob, we fell out for two years. I can't even remember what about now.'*

At first, the guests were the Pet Shop Boys. Neil Tennant and Chris Lowe's electronic project had started off with the bold gesture of a number 1 single with 'West End Girls' at the tail end of 1985. They seemed like ideal candidates for one hit wonder status: a not-very-pretty synth duo with a 'posh' rap style. But there was more to them than the single initially revealed and although their eyes were on the disco dancefloor, a reasonable portion of their hearts was still in earlier, more straightforward musical times – Tennant's voice still sounds remarkably like that of 1970s singer/songwriter Al Stewart and there was a tug towards the 1960s and even show tunes from the 1950s. Tennant's oft-misquoted description of Electronic as being a 'Blind Faith for the 1990s' baffled Bernard just as much as younger listeners, but left wiser heads nodding in amusement. Alluding to Electronic's 'supergroup' make-up, Tennant was harking back to 1969 and the blues royalty that made up Blind Faith – Eric Clapton and Ginger Baker of Cream, Steve Winwood of Traffic and the Spencer Davis Group and Ric Grech of Family. Since punk had essentially outlawed the use of the *word* supergroup – let alone the formation of one – the comment showed former pop journalist Tennant, ex-assistant editor of *Smash Hits*, at his most mischievous.

'That's just the disease of people having to draw analogies between old groups and new groups,' commented Marr in Q when the supergroup label stuck. 'Fair enough, it's a reference point for people, but it's inevitably inaccurate. It's unfortunate.' 'It's a healthy thing,' said Sumner in the same magazine, about the idea of high profile collaborations. 'As long as it's not a mutual wank-off, cash-in indulgence, like Rod Stewart and Tina Turner.'

Electronic was, to say the least, a slow burner. Described initially by Marr and Sumner as 'weekend work', the first single, 'Getting Away With It', was released in December 1989, eighteen months ahead of an album. The time taken paid off. The single, released on Factory, went to number 12 in the UK charts and broke the US Top 40. It's a 1980s single – just – but it felt very 1990s. Sumner and Tennant's voices work perfectly together, each trying to understate the other.

'I don't have the type of voice that can do that acrobatic stuff,' said Tennant. 'So it's not an option for me. Years ago in an interview I was asked, "Why do singers like you and Bernard Sumner sing in such a deadpan way?" I think it's because that's all we can do.' 'We were real Pet Shop Boys fans,' said Johnny Marr in Q. 'And when they came up to Manchester to record with us, we all sat in the room – I think we were all pretty nervous – and we had the equipment on one side and we were all on the other. Then Neil said, "Well, I've got this chord sequence," and he'd go over to the synthesizer and play it. Then I'd go, "I've got this bass line," and wander over and play it, then come and sit down again. It was like some musical quiz show.' According to Sumner, the other thing they did on the Pet Shop Boys' arrival was to show them the "delights" of Manchester and The Haçienda.

Aiming high, Electronic made their live debut on a massive scale, as guests of amped-up electro-poppers Depeche Mode. The Dodger Stadium, Los Angeles is an impressive way to open your live account, which is exactly what Electronic did on August 4 and 5, 1990. The Pet Shop Boys appeared for two numbers, a relatively stress free way for the duo to make their US debut too. Lyrics were still being scribbled just prior to showtime and Sumner is believed to have spent the rest of the build up chucking up backstage.

> *Bernard Sumner: 'I did throw up, but not with nerves,*
> *I'd had a heavy night the night before.'*

'Electronic were very interesting,' says New Order technician Michael Eastwood, who also did live work with Bernard and Johnny's band. 'They'd done a few early gigs where they basically did live vocals with a bit of guitar over the top of tapes. The rest of the band was miming. Johnny's stuff was on tape and he played some live stuff over the top of it and Bernard's vocals were live. They decided to rectify that because I'm sure they both hated doing it. The early gigs were due to circumstance ... we've got to promote this, but we haven't got time to programme it up. I know Bernard hated it ...

> *Bernard Sumner: 'We just didn't have time to set up a rig capable of*
> *what we wanted to do. We hadn't even finished half the songs yet.'*

... whether it was a moral sense of cheating people, or if it was a case of being seen to be doing it, I don't know. Electronic decided to put it right and they built the best system I've ever worked with, a load of samplers and sequencers connected to a mixing desk. It was an amazing feat of engineering. Hats off to them for doing that.'

In between 'Getting Away With It' and Electronic's eponymous debut album, was the small matter of a number 1 single for New Order, or more precisely, *ENGLANDneworder*. The 'least worst' football song of all-time came at a difficult period for New Order, a low point in the band's relationships. 'It was at a time when we all hated each other,' states Peter Hook. The band had gone in three distinct directions. Bernard was doing Electronic, Peter Hook was mid-Revenge, (his unloved, leather-clad side band) and Steve Morris and Gillian Gilbert were The Other Two. In fact, the England track, 'World In Motion', was originally a section of soundtrack work that Morris and Gilbert had done for TV projects they were involved in. One such project was for Manchester-based rag trade drama *Making Out*, which starred the confrontational Welsh comedian and actor Keith Allen, who would fill a key gap in the project: none of New Order had the remotest desire to write a football song.

Bernard Sumner: 'It wasn't the lack of desire, just that we did not know how to approach the lyrics. We were excited about doing the song.'

'None of the rest of them were interested,' says Tony Wilson. 'So it fell to me to put the whole thing together. I set about finding someone who could do lyrics about football. I spent a month and a half ringing up witty, literate people who I thought might be right and then Barney rings up one day and says, "I've got Keith Allen."' Allen would write the majority of the lyric, with Bernard contributing one verse and Tony Wilson coming up with the three syllable 'En-ger-land' chant. Despite an initial wheeze to call the song 'E For England', and the Football Association's bafflement over the chorus references to 'Love' having got the 'World In Motion', the song provided New Order with their only number 1, albeit through the back door.

Even though they'd just had a chart-topping single, New Order were in bad shape. These were up and down days. And just as the debut Electronic album was about to hit the shops, a name from the past came back to remind Bernard of former days when he wasn't quite the master of his own destiny. On April 18, his former producer and mentor Martin Hannett was found dead. His lifestyle had become too much and the producer of Joy Division, New Order and Jilted John had died of a heart failure. Sumner did not go to Hannett's funeral, something that did not escape the notice of other mourners. 'After Martin died,' says Larry Cassidy of Section 25, 'I went to the funeral. Wilson was there, Hooky was there. I sat next to Hooky in the church and I says, "Where's Bernard?" Hooky says, "He doesn't like funerals." Who does? I thought Bernard should have turned up. Wouldn't you think he'd have that much respect for Martin that he'd go to his funeral?'

Bernard Sumner: 'I had good reason to hate funerals after watching my family die, one after the other, and then Ian. I'd had enough by then.'

Amends of sorts would be made in August 1991 at Manchester's Heaton Park, when a two-day music event was held in honour of Hannett.

Buzzcocks, Happy Mondays and Revenge played at the event – and so did Electronic. The park – one of the biggest municipal green spaces in Europe – was a favourite play place for Bernard as a youngster, as the photo printed in this book clearly shows.

When the Electronic album was finally released, it came as a surprise to many, as it wasn't quite the New Order/Smiths/Pet Shop Boys genetic splicing that many had expected. Johnny Marr has a co-credit on every song alongside Sumner, with Tennant contributing to two tracks and Chris Lowe one.

The stakes are high for Bernard from the off – opening track 'Idiot Country' kicks in with a ridicule-risking Manc rap that Sumner just about gets away with. The Kraftwerk vibe is present as ever on this first track, with electrobeats reminiscent of 1983's *Tour de France*. After that initial surprise, the album settles down with housey keyboard stabs on 'Reality', backed by Marr's 'Bom Chikka Wah-Wah' guitar fills. When the acoustic guitar starts on 'Tighten Up', it feels how we'd imagined The Smiths versus New Order would be: you could almost sing The Smiths' 'Bigmouth Strikes Again' over sections of it without being too wide of the mark. 'Patience Of A Saint' is essentially the Pet Shop Boys with Bernard as a guest singer – Marr neither Boms, Chikkas nor Wah-Wahs on this one. 'Gangster' suffers slightly from its modish keyboard settings – they are so dated you can practically pinpoint the hour they were recorded in – and 'Soviet' is, with the best will in the world, a two-minute instrumental filler. But 'Get The Message' gets things back in shape – Marr returns to the room and so does his wah-wah pedal – and as the album's second single it snatched a deserved Top Ten placing. Rather than some peculiar experiment, the Electronic album is a great pop record.

'We were aware of the pressure to not make a doodly, improvisational, jazz odyssey-type record,' said Sumner in Q in 1999. 'We wanted the challenge of making a commercial album. We could have made a shit avant-garde record and, when people criticised it, said, "Well, it's avant-garde, mate, what did you expect?" It's very hard to come up with a good set of chords and a decent melody.' The aforementioned pairing of chords and melody pushed the album to number 2 in the UK charts and number 1 in the independent listings.

In 1992, Bernard's mother Laura died. His beloved grandmother Laura Senior would follow her within the year. Having already lost his adopted dad and his grandfather, Bernard was now on his own – of the unique family he'd been part of at 11 Alfred Street, he alone remained. He had never made any direct reference to the disability which was so pronounced in his family. Only *once* – in an interview carried out just a month after Laura Senior passed away – did he even hint at his family background. 'It sounds like a bloody tragedy,' he told *Select* magazine, still raw from the deaths of the two Lauras. 'But there's always been a lot of physical illness in my family, so it was kind of a relief. It's liberating ... sort of.'

What with everything else going on, it's no wonder the next New Order album was slow in coming. So slow that the band managed to sit out the demise of Factory Records. Receivership almost came as a relief. Gang wars on the steps of The Haçienda, ill-advised property investment with new, hi-swank offices close to the BBC, no new talent to fill in the gaping hole left by the grumpily, slow-moving New Order and the quickly busted flush of Happy Mondays. No surprises here. Still, at least Factory had assets. They had back catalogue. No, they didn't, because everything, especially the music, belonged to the bands – all part of the Factory manifesto. As Wilson puts it: 'On the day we finally wanted to sell out, we wouldn't be able to. How can you sell out when you've nothing to sell?' [Tony Wilson, *24 Hour Party People - What The Sleevenotes Never Tell You.*]

'When they went down,' said Sumner in *NME* when the Factory ideal finally ended, 'they had the Mondays, who made money and New Order, who were going to make money ... and Electronic who, although Tony denies it, made Factory a lot of money. Those three bands should have made Factory financially secure ...'

Recorded in the midst of half a million pounds worth of bad feeling, New Order's post-Factory album, *Republic*, was their most cosmopolitan album to date. It even looks cosmopolitan with its split screen cover and sub-heading proclaiming it as 'A New Order Release'. The design was apparently intended for Gillian and Stephen's Other Two project, but was co-opted to New Order instead. Released on CentreDate/London Records – that went down well in Manchester – *Republic* is the New Order dance album that they'd always seemed capable of yet never previously delivered. Single 'Regret' kicks it off and features Sumner's best guitar riff since 'She's Lost Control'. As well as being a number 4 hit in the UK, 'Regret' topped the US modern rock and hot dance charts. A perfectly straightforward promo video was shot, but an alternative version set on a beach – 'live by satellite from Los Angeles' – and filmed for the BBC's *Top of the Pops* is far better known, as it features Baywatch star David Hasselhoff. The Hoff is never actually in shot with the band, suggesting his bits were perhaps inserts, maybe ...?

Bernard Sumner: 'David Hasselhoff was there, he even wanted to sing vocals (the vocals were live), he wasn't in the same shot because it was a live broadcast and he was some distance away from the band and couldn't move from his camera position.'

One thing that is amusingly in shot though is a g-stringed, orange-peeled arse, wobbling away right next to Gillian Gilbert as she half-heartedly prods at her sand-locked keyboard.

'World (Price of Love)' – another single and another Top 20 UK hit – kept the sophistication levels high with smooth backing vocals and breathy samples. 'Spooky' is the Kraftwerk moment and 'Young Offender', 'Liar' and 'Chemical' all keep up the BPMs. 'Times Change' has the slower lope and Anglo rap of 'West End Girls', but it's still designed for dancing. You wait for a strummalong song to arrive and it never does. There's even a chill-out instrumental, 'Avalanche', at the end to help the party come down. Producer Stephen Hague gets co-writer credits but he should also get a medal: to pull an album this good out of a band apparently at its lowest ebb is truly heroic.

Touring the album proved too much for Bernard Sumner and Peter Hook. The two Salford Grammar lads, who had been through so much together, decided they could no longer bear to share the same space. Indeed, they decided they could no longer work together. The fact that this decision was reached in New York with several US dates still to play made the whole affair even more dispiriting. 'There are tales of the US tour in 1993,' says former road chief Terry Mason, 'where Barney went about with a cardboard sign on a string round his neck with "Fuck off, don't talk to me," written on it. No one did.'

A lesson had been learned with Bernard's 'stomach ulcer' no-show in 1989. The remaining dates were silently carried out. To Bernard, with so much going for him with Electronic, the split was a blessed relief. Peter Hook felt otherwise. 'I was devastated,' he said nearly a decade later in *The Guardian*. 'It was a bloody tragedy. We'd never sounded better.' On Sunday, August 29, 1993, New Order fulfilled their final commitment, the Reading Festival. The last song they performed was 'Blue Monday' – how does it feel to treat me like you do? Bad enough for them not to play together for six years. A lexicon of euphemisms would be brought into play to avoid using the 's' word. But split is the word most people use when you do something with virtually the same group of people for more than fifteen years, then you stop doing it. Still, it wasn't all bad news in 1993. Stephen Morris and Gillian Gilbert got married.

Keeping to the original premise of chopping and changing who they worked with, the next collaborator brought in for the second Electronic album was Karl Bartos, former 'drummer' with Kraftwerk, the band that continued to be the main influence in Bernard's musical life. It's been said that with their electronic influence on everything from hip hop to the New Romantics, Kraftwerk can lay claim – pound for pound – to having more sway on the course of popular music than The Beatles. Sumner cites his meeting with Bartos as one of the highlights of his life.

As well as Marr and Bartos, there was another collaborator on the second Electronic album: Fluoxetine Hydrochloride. Not only did Bernard agree to take the drug – better known under its trade name of Prozac – as a way of clearing his lyric writing block, he also took part in a TV programme that was looking at the drug's use. For such a notoriously low-key person, it was a strange decision. 'I regret it,' he said when later asked by Q why he agreed to take part in the show, 'but not bitterly.' *Prozac Diary* was produced, directed and presented by psychologist Oliver James for BBC2's *Late Show.* James had previously shown a sure touch when it came to crossing psychology and music, working on *Sex With Paula* with the late Paula Yates and *Room 113* for Channel 4 youth show Network 7, a series of probing pop culture interviews that included a memorable run-in with Van Halen's David Lee Roth (in the interview, James managed to get the singer to admit his childhood behaviour had caused his parents to split up and that they'd tied him up like a dog). By comparision, Sumner got off lightly. In the programme, he admitted that fifteen months into the recording of the second Electronic album, he still hadn't written any lyrics. 'I get extremely frustrated, go to bed, wake up the next day extremely frustrated, scratch my head for five hours, get depressed about it and then get annoyed with myself, then get so angry that I'll start writing,' said Sumner. 'It's like breaking a horse every time I do it.'

> Bernard Sumner: '*The reason for this block had nothing to do with Prozac. It's just that I had decided to write straight for the first time in many years and it was a bit of a shock to the system.*'

Bernard is seen working on 'A New Religion', the b-side of 'Forbidden City' with Johnny Marr and Karl Bartos, as well as sitting at his study, struggling to get lyrics down, tongue practically poking from the corner of his mouth. Sumner's level of self-criticism is classed by James as a symptom of mild depression, which is itself deemed in the programme as 'aggression directed at the self.' 'I've always got this voice,' Sumner tells James. 'I've always got this other person going: "You can't say that, you can't do that."'

The solution was to put Sumner on Prozac, just before he went on a family skiing holiday. On his return – either as a result of the Prozac or maybe the skiing – Sumner's writer's block has cleared. 'Normally, if I'm writing lyrics, it's like squeezing the last bit of toothpaste out of a toothpaste tube ... now the flow of words is good. I actually enjoyed it. I'm less inward-looking, more observational, about how the world looks, rather than how I look to me. I don't feel sad for no reason.'

Sumner is no 'reality TV' natural and there's no pleasure watching him being questioned by James. Despite this strange interlude, he still felt there was merit in the experiment. 'It was interesting taking Prozac because I don't really suffer from depression, but I can be melancholic. It was interesting being a different person for seven months. It really agreed with me. I still think it's a very, very interesting drug.'

In terms of the album that came as a result of the experiment, the words may have been squeezed out a little quicker, but the casual observer would be hard pushed to have noticed a radical lyrical departure on *Raise The Pressure*. It's still a great album, though, and probably the purest collaborative expression of Electronic's two key members – it may even be Marr's best post-Smiths work. There are guitars – lots of them – on the aforementioned opening track 'Forbidden City'. They strum, tinkle, reverse feedback and chime their way across an open-topped tune that's hard to dislike. Lots of people did like it – it was a number 14 hit. By second track, 'For You' – another Top 20 hit – Marr is confident enough in the album to pull the most Smiths-esque set of riffs and chord changes ever, out of the bag. It's a delightful song that anyone could cover right down to the last 'la la la'. 'Dark Angel', 'Freefall' and especially 'Until The End Of Time' sound, on the surface, as if Bartos has wrestled control back from Sumner and Marr – not so, said Johnny in *Total Guitar*. 'Oddly, out of all of us, Karl was the one who tended to lean towards the traditional. He's really into his 1960s pop – The Small Faces, The Kinks, stuff like that. So it was a bit strange, the way things turned out.' If that's the case then we've misjudged Karl Bartos, because simple songs like 'One Day' – straight-ahead guitar pop with syncopated, shimmying backing vocals – would be welcome anywhere. 'I spent two years in Manchester hanging out with Johnny Marr,' said Bartos. '*Raise The Pressure* brought all the guitar culture back to me.' In fact, Bartos lodged with Marr at the guitarist's home close to Bowdon on the Cheshire border, the suburb where Joy Division formed all those years ago.

'We were trying to get a balance of guitar and technology, but to keep it sounding contemporary,' continues Johnny Marr. 'When I listen to it now, it sounds a bit dense – full of ideas and hooks ... but, y'know, give it time and I think everyone will see it as a really strong pop album, which is pretty much what we were trying to do.'

As well as a German house-guest, Marr had something else to occupy him: the ongoing legal wrangle between himself, Morrissey and ex-colleagues Andy Rourke and Mike Joyce, which had reached the High Court. The bass player and drummer had taken action against their former band-mates. As songwriters, Morrissey and Marr were entitled to the royalties from the songs they wrote. Despite the fact they'd played on all The Smiths' records and played them live for five years, Rourke and Joyce were only entitled to 10 per cent for performing. Morrissey and Marr contested this, saying the others were always aware of the 10 per cent agreement.

Rourke dropped his action at the eleventh hour, leaving Mike Joyce to continue the fight alone. 'It's just such a surreal unnatural situation,' said Joyce. 'Because when I was banging my mum's settee at home, before I got my first drum kit, wanting to be in a band ... not in your wildest dreams – not in your worst nightmare – do you think you're going to be in the High Court in London.' Although complimentary to Johnny Marr, Judge John Weeks famously described Morrissey as 'devious, truculent and unreliable.' The case was described as 'a million pound win' for Joyce.

Despite all the legal wrangles, Marr maintained a hefty work rate outside of Electronic, including production work for a young band called Marion from Cheshire. Marion's intertwining connections to the scene that pre-dated them were considerable. Based in Macclesfield, *Melody Maker* had dubbed them a 'Joy Division for the 1990s.' Morrissey was a voluble early supporter and The Smiths' manager and Marr's mentor, Joe Moss, was their talisman. Marr produced their second album, *The Program* – it's not as good as their lauded and excellent debut but that's probably not his fault. More importantly, it brought Marion guitarist Phil Cunningham into the fold, first as a touring guitarist with Electronic and eventually as a replacement for Gillian Gilbert in New Order.

Despite having the final hours of The Haçienda to contend with, Bernard did manage to knuckle down to a third Electronic album. *Twisted Tenderness* has a set of interesting collaborations to its name – all relatively low key compared to the two previous outings – but it's the most *Johnny Marr* of the three albums. Pushed out in just a few months, as opposed to the long term tinkerings of *Electronic* and *Raise The Pressure*, it also marks a real turnaround in the accepted demarcation of responsibilities within the band. Marr took the opportunity to try his hand at singing and helped out with lyric writing. Bernard, to his credit, was persuaded to play guitar on the album. It shouldn't be such a big deal for a man who'd been a professional guitarist for twenty years, but if you're sharing a studio with the most celebrated player of your generation, fairly intimidating.

Twisted Tenderness starts off with a track that supplies all the major food groups: 'Make It Happen' has guitar wig outs, a trancey breakdown for a chorus and a verse that sounds oddly like Pink's 'Get The Party Started'. It's a hefty seven-and-a-half-minutes long, but it doesn't outstay its welcome. 'Haze' weighs in with a stadium-sized chorus and Johnny Marr singing – his voice is similar to Chris Difford of Squeeze and he and Bernard perform an octave harmony that's reminiscent of Difford's vocal pairing with Glenn Tilbrook.

'I learned a lot about singing from Bernard,' Marr told *Magnet*'s Matthew Fritch in 2003 – not something Sumner's vocal detractors ever thought they'd hear someone say. 'It's the approach: leave your insecurities and neuroses at the door 'cause we've got a job to do. Be subjective when you write a song and when you're getting your melodies together, be as emotional as you like, but then when you're doing the thing, just drop the shit and do the job.'

The single, 'Vivid', honks along like a slowed down Marion track and 'Can't Find My Way Home' serves two purposes: it's Sumner's first recorded cover version and it's an elaborate in-joke, as it's a Steve Winwood song as recorded by Blind Faith. This was, after all, Electronic's last chance to be a Blind Faith for the 1990s, as predicted by Neil Tennant in 1989. It's probably the weakest track, but the temptation to include it must have been irresistible. The title track is the first opportunity for a dance groove to hit home, with its housey keyboard stabs and synth-treated vocals, and a chorus that sticks like a half-sucked lolly. Cher could have covered it and had a monstrous hit. 'Like No Other' is a rock out with Sumner's snappiest lyrics to date and 'Prodigal Son' has an Eastern Vibe and fuzztone vocal that recalls Ian Brown. Final track 'When She's Gone' is all breathy girl backing vocals and when it's done ... so are Electronic. No filler instrumentals, no dated tones and modes, just track after track that hit home and stayed home. It's a great album that stands on its own two feet, aside from anything else that was happening in Manchester and the wider scene at the time.

'One thing you can say about me and Johnny is that we're long-term musicians,' Sumner told Jeff Jolley. 'For us to write along with a movement would be a stupid thing to do, because when the movement is over, we'd be over with it. I think we've always done our own thing – Johnny and The Smiths and me and New Order ... Joy Division made a point of not being like anyone else around at the time.'

Critically, Electronic managed to bow out with heads held high. No make-weight, contractual obligation last album for them. '*Twisted Tenderness* is pop-rock of swaggering calibre,' said Andrew Collins in Q. 'They do, it seems, make 'em like this anymore.'

Electronic was clearly Johnny Marr's best post-Smiths work – and he knew it. 'We were together every single day,' he told Undercover.com of his working relationship with Bernard. 'More than anyone else I have ever been involved with. I think this idea that we were a project and would get together every couple of years and make a record is false. In fact, we were together every single day. When we took a break from working and being in the studio and writing these beats and these melodies, we would get on a boat and go sailing together. I have never been closer to anyone than I was with Bernard.'

As well as the aforementioned trio of well-received albums and a brace of crisp singles, we also have Johnny Marr's assessment of Bernard Sumner to add to the picture we've built up so far. And here's a startling fact: his collboration with Bernard lasted twice as long as his tenure with Morrissey. 'Complicated and simple at the same time,' is Marr's summary. 'Simple in the best possible sense. Almost Zen-like detachment. Great guy with a real sense of what's important in life. He deserves everything that's come to him because he put the work in.'

After three albums, Electronic simply stopped. Their stock was still high – final single 'Vivid' easily made the Top 20 – but there were major rumblings of activity from outside the group. The split, if we can call it that, must go down in history as one of rock's least bitter. 'Electronic is one of the rare examples of a band that split up with no acrimony whatsoever,' said Johnny Marr in *Magnet*. 'We were too smart and our friendship was too important to let that happen.'

In fact, there might be life in Electronic yet – Marr stated in 2006 that he still wanted to record more material with Bernard, with a particular eye on a soundtrack collaboration. 'That'd be something that we should really investigate because, to me, that would be artistically valid and that's where I'd be right now in terms of the intrigue of working with Bernard,' he says. 'We've done the modern pop thing and I'd like to do something that was artistically not obvious.'

So, commercial and critical success, integrity and friendship intact, a back catalogue to be proud of and a chance to add to it in the future; it's all good. Just one key question remains unanswered: why did Electronic – according to Tony Wilson – lead to 'one of the great disasters for Manchester'? Wilson describes the rot setting in with the very formation of the band. 'Bernard says to Johnny Marr, "We need a manager,"' says Wilson. 'So Johnny's manager, Marcus Russell, manages Electronic. Three years later, Noel Gallagher [is] in Dry bar and Noel says to Bernard, "We need a manager for Oasis." Bernard says, "My manager's quite good ..." So it ended up with all this Oasis money flowing through an office just off Marylebone Road [in London] as opposed to Manchester. The history of Manchester is the the history of 10CC money, Buzzcocks money ... Manchester money flowing through this city. Then you've got Oasis money – the last big band from this city. The money goes through London. That's because of Barney's war with Rob.'

CONFUSION TEN: POST-MODERN SLEAZE

Practitioners in the art of the nocturnal economies tend to
gravitate towards each other. Neither needs interest or interference from
the normal world – there's nothing here for the straights, they're tucked up
in bed where they belong. So it's no surprise that places of entertainment
have always attracted those of a criminal persuasion. Post-war Manchester
saw the rise of glamourous nightspots like the Cromford Club in the 1950s
– swanky yet with an undercurrent of criminal glamour. In the 1960s came
the rise of the semi-mythical Quality Street Gang, an apparently loose
configuration of local crime faces. In fact, the organisation was so laid-back
in its structure that some senior detectives even doubted its actual existence.
The QS loved the centre of Manchester – 'Town' was their playground.
And their Rat Pack–esque city centre lifestyle would continue through the
1970s and into the 1980s without any of their number actually being
convicted of gang activity.

By the early 1980s, a second generation of criminals began to emerge,
with three main centres of operation: Cheetham Hill, to the north of
Manchester city centre; Moss Side to the south; and Salford across the
Irwell to the west. All were in swaggering distance of the entertainment
centres and all had their vested interests, styles and motifs. Cheetham Hill –
The Hillbillies – were armed robbers of military precision and ploughed
the proceeds into drug dealing. The Moss Side gangs were run on
American lines, sporting colours and guns with an eye on how cool they
looked. Salford gangs liked to cross the river into Manchester because –
rightly or wrongly – they believed that if caught, they would be treated
more leniently by Manchester judges than on their own turf. Modern-day
scuttlers? Maybe, but in place of the knife and the swinging belts favoured
by the Victorian street gangs, came the machete and the semi-automatic.
Instead of dodging across the city bridges on foot, they favoured the
mountain bike and the Golf Gti. The rise and success of the gangs mirrored
the rise and the success of that other symbol of local ingenuity: The
Haçienda. As time went by, it would become very difficult to disentangle
the two.

Leroy Richardson – who'd started as a part-time glass collector and was
now working as a manger at The Haçienda – noticed a major change at the
club. The post-punk days were over. Slowly, a different kind of clubber was

emerging and they wanted more than to merely mooch around a half-empty dancefloor to Iggy Pop. 'There was nothing overnight,' Richardson told me as we sat in his latest club in the mid-afternoon. Tall and wide, with dreads and an open face, Richardson is friendly in the extreme and very good company. If you met him in a club, you'd want to be his friend rather than cause trouble. That's the skill, I suppose. 'A lot of people forget the Go Go period ... Trouble Funk. That made it a steady progression. When I think about it, it's gone from Spear of Destiny ... to Acid House. Boom! But Grandmaster Flash was always a sure fire hit. That's when I started thinking ... something's happening here. To have Grandmaster Flash on ... and a 70 per cent white audience ... that's how the audience was changing. Everything was getting a bit more fluid, it wasn't like rock and roll and teddy boys and skinheads, it was all merging. White boys dancing – particularly with ecstasy – it was just great to see. No hassle, no trouble. It was a natural progression when I think about it ... but *not* thinking about it ... it happened overnight.'

New characters in the story began to gravitate towards the club, including DJ Elliot Eastwick, who would go on to find a curious infamy in being the person who played the last ever record at The Haçienda. 'I grew up in Poynton on the outskirts of Manchester – technically Cheshire,' he says today. 'I got a job at The Haçienda when I was 16, collecting glasses. I was a big fan of Joy Division/New Order, as were a lot of people of my age group and my generation who lived in Altrincham, Sale, Poynton – those kind of provincial, surrounding areas of Greater Manchester. Most New Order fans seemed to come from those kind of places. I'd been to other clubs and they were all right. Going to a club is about being with your mates, it's not about what the club looks like ... you don't even notice. That was the first place I went to that was like a dream-like thing. I don't even remember who I was with. I just remember thinking, *Wow, they've got plastic curtains that you have to walk through to get in.* It looked 'New Order-y' and it looked 'Factory-y'. It is cool and well designed and stark. So to go get a job there was like working on a big film set.

I liked House music a lot which was why I wanted to work at The Haçienda. Acid House had just blown up – 1987 – so I went and got a job at the club. It was only really when Acid House came along that I realised New Order had been doing that, or their version of it, a number of years before.'

Starting – as was The Haçienda fashion – as a £1.75-an-hour glass collector, Eastwick noticed the different ways that the members of New

Order used the club. 'You'd see Hooky all the time. He'd be there during the day. Pacing around, stressing about the sound system. All the cleaners would be in the club – they had this crack team of cleaners. I remember thinking, *Fucking hell, even the cleaners are cool in here.* They're all young and bring their tapes in and have the best equipment. Hooky'd talk to the cleaners and know all their names. Steve, you'd see a reasonable amount at night. New Order all stood in the same place, which was by the door by the main bar where there was a little corner where you couldn't be seen. You didn't see that much of Bernard. When he came into the club, it was alway a bit ... *Bernard's here so everyone on your best behaviour.* With Bernard, it was remember to keep asking him every five minutes if he wants a drink. I don't think he commanded it. Later on, he went in The Haçienda an *awful* lot.'

Just before his seventeenth birthday, Eastwick manged to get on to the decks and started DJ-ing at the The Haçienda: 'I remember putting the first few records on ... the DJ booth was incredibly futuristic, like the rest of the club. Probably because New Order would spend hundreds of thousands of pounds on the latest synthesiser that would record about eight seconds of samples. That went through into the club ... "What, they've got *three* turntables? Is one *spare?* Do you put *cakes* on it or what?" New Order must have been to New York and seen booths with three turntables. They had a reel-to-reel in case you'd done any of your own edits. The mixer was *this big*, [a] tank thing, like a studio mixing desk. It's like someone handing you the keys to a cockpit and going ... "I'm going for a brew, off you go." The turntables were sprung ... it was like they were on *water.* As soon as you put your hand on the turntable, they'd bob around. You try to line the record up and the thing would be going everywhere like it was *alive.* Everything was so expensive, so you had to be really gentle. I remember the first half hour of the set being really appalling. The volume was all weird, the whole sound system went through limiters and compressors. That's pretty standard in most clubs now, they spend shit loads of money on the technology. The Haçienda did that before *anybody.* The problem was just the building. Even by the mid-1990s, they had the best sound system in there ... and it still sounded a bit crap. The design of the building was ultimately the downfall of the sound quality. But there was a metre square in the centre of the dance floor where it sounded great. You'd always see the same guy – black guy, very sweaty, incredible dancer – he'd always be in that metre square every week. You'd think ... *he's the guy with the ears.*'

In July 1989, the outside world was rapped on the forehead and informed as to what was going on in Whitworth Stret, with the UK's first high profile ecstasy-related death. The victim was a 16-year-old girl, Claire Leighton. Ten years after Leighton's death, Bernard Sumner was asked to sum up his views on drugs. After condemning cocaine and heroin, he offered these words on MDMA in Q: 'Taking ecstasy's like Russian roulette, except you've got 99,000 bullets that are empty ... and one that's loaded.'

> *Bernard Sumner: 'What happened to Claire was an absolute tragedy,*
> *but I don't think it was the fault of the club. She didn't buy the drug in the club or*
> *take it in the club. I think she was the victim of the general culture at that time;*
> *people were taking E's in pubs and at football matches. However, we were devastated*
> *that she was taken ill in our club and felt very much for her parents.'*

'We were always really concerned that it can't just be left to happen,' says Leroy Richardson. 'The ideal thing was, have it before you come in and not try and buy it in the club.' Reporters flowed into the city, looking for the ecstasy angle. In the process, they missed the bubbling gang crisis – which was spilling over into and around many clubs, The Haçienda included.

The kids, in Manchester and Salford at least, were most definitely not alright. Youth and its attitudes were changing. Respect for your olders and betters was being eroded. Across town, there was one of the biggest single gestures of underclass defiance the city had ever seen: on April 1, 1990, during a Sunday chapel service lead by the Rev. Noel Proctor, prisoners at Her Majesty's Prison Manchester – better known as Strangeways – took control of the service, the wing and then the entire jail. For 25 days the prisoners, led by the devastatingly passionate and articulate Liverpudlian Paul Taylor, delivered a giant-sized, televised fuck you to the prison system, the Home Office and the world, from the roof of the Strangeways rotunda. The rioters created an unprecedented media hoopla – entrepreneurial Salford types even knocked up their own 'I Escaped From Strangeways' tee shirts and sold them to the sightseers. People noticed that Manchester was changing – it was dangerous and certain elements *genuinely* didn't give a shit. These elements chose to play out their ambitions and plans under the bright lights of Manchester's nocturnal economy.

From the north, west and south of the city, the gangs swaggered into 'Town'. Drugs and armed robbery were their business – and business, as they say, was good. With money in their pockets – but no intention of spending it – they demanded the right to enter premises without the constraints of queues and the hassle of entry fees. Then they wanted service

– pronto, regardless of who else was waiting and how long they'd been there. If the men on the doors were too intimidated – or friendly – to do anything about it, then all the better.

Salford gangs moved in on Konspiracy – the club where Pips used to be; black gangs zeroed in on The Gallery, formerly a serious-minded music venue near the Free Trade Hall; The Hacienda, being the biggest and shiniest of all the clubs, was the obvious next target. Security needed beefing up, but finding lads with the front to keep the door secure from this level of intimidation was going to cost; according to Tony Wilson, £375,000 a year was being paid for security at The Haçienda amid the peak of the gang troubles. In other clubs, the latest trainers or ski top was the thing to be seen in; at The Haçienda, the gangsters and the door staff were both sporting bullet-proof vests.

But like any war between superpowers, escalation was inevitable and when a member of staff was threatened with a gun, it was decided to make a protest about the way the gangs were using and abusing the club. They went on strike and closed the doors.

'The Haçienda is closing its doors as of today,' announced Tony Wilson at a press conference held on the club's dancefloor in January, 1991. 'It is with the greatest reluctance that, for the moment, we are turning the lights out on what is, for us, a most important place. We are forced into taking this drastic action in order to protect our employees, our members and all our clients. We are quite simply sick and tired of dealing with instances of personal violence. We hope, we must *believe* we can re-open the Haçienda in a better climate. But until we are able to run the club in a safe manner and in a way that the owners believe will guarantee the role of the Haçienda at the heart of the city's youth community, it is with great sadness that we will shut our club.'

Bernard Sumner, speaking in *NME* said: 'The Haçienda closing down for six months was an inevitable drain on the finances of both Factory and New Order. But we had to try and stop the violence. We all felt that if we didn't shut The Haçienda, somebody was going to get killed and we had to show the gangs that it was either all or nothing.

The 'Gunchester' tag acquired by Manchester during the late 1980s and early 1990s actually has less to do with clubland than the decision by some of the younger gangs to change their focus away from making money and towards maiming and killing each other over a series of relatively low-scale disagreements. Previously, they hurt their own, so the issue was classed by the media and observers as 'containable'. When those perceived as being outside the gangs became involved, it became a national headline grabber.

For example, when schoolboy Benji Stanley was blasted with a shotgun in a takeaway in January 1993, the whole country sat up and took notice. He was 14 and an apparent victim of mistaken identity. I was a news reporter at the time of 'Gunchester'. I covered many of the gang shootings, stuck my microphone into the faces of grieving girlfriends and relatives and I attended Benji Stanley's funeral. This event – I use that phrase purposely – with Benji's white coffin as the centre piece, rubbed the nation's noses into the reality of what was happening in the city. Up came the politicians and down came the police – hard.

To be fair, the police had plenty of other things to occupy their time, for this was a city under siege. While the gangs tore territorial lumps off each other in and around the city's clubs, the IRA used Manchester as the chief theatre for its mainland terror campaign. Fire bombs were tucked into clothing stores in the Arndale Centre in 1991. Twin rush hour bombs were detonated at either end of Deansgate in 1993. In an especially callous move, the first – behind the former Kendals department store – was detonated slightly earlier than the second, which was close to the former site of Pips disco. As the bloodied office workers ran away from the scene up the busy thoroughfare, they rushed straight into the path of the second blast, which cut the legs from under them. Nearby Warrington got two devices. One – attached to the back of a gasometer – miraculously failed to detonate. Another took the lives of two young boys, Jonathan Ball and Tim Parry. They were aged 3 and 10. Thanks to its intersecting motorway system providing easy access to Ireland-bound ports of Liverpool, Heysham and Holyhead, Manchester and its surrounding towns became deeply dangerous places to be.

Meanwhile, after the six month closure had ended, the atmosphere improved at The Haçienda, but as usual advantage was taken and a void was filled. 'Salford rose like a great big fucking bird,' wrote Tony Wilson in his *24 Hour Party People* memoir. 'From the flames of rubbish burning on the Ordsall estate. A great big fucking bird with wild, staring eyes and a beak that would peck your fucking head off if you dared to return its stare.' Or put another way, the problem continued, it just changed the direction it was coming from. In 1992, Salford was the scene of a series of riots that tripped across the city like a carefully arranged set of tumbling dominoes. The Ordsall estate was home to the worst of the violence. Government buildings were set on fire, including housing and careers' offices, police vehicles came under attack, a police station was firebombed and a masked gang lured officers to one estate by setting off an intruder alarm, then lay in wait before mounting a full scale ambush. It was a show of strength designed to warn off police from targetting the gangs – officers had gone in hard onto the Salford estates and the gangs didn't like it.

Ironically, a key factor in trouble eventually ebbing away from The Haçienda was the very culture that The Haçienda itself created. The futuristic city promised all those years ago finally arrived and Manchester became awash with glass, chrome and groovy bars. Trouble didn't disappear, it became diluted across a new system of outlets and venues.

Around this time, an unexpected regular began to be seen at The Haçienda: Bernard Sumner of top dance rock duo Electronic. 'Towards the early-to-mid-1990s, it became corporate,' says Elliot Eastwick. 'They [New Order] knew that money was getting drained here and there. When he came in, we had to look after him. When Bernard came in, he usually had another celebrity friend with him. He was with Matt Johnson from The The or he was with Johnny Marr or he was with [comedians] Vic Reeves and Bob Mortimer. There was a time when they were shooting a series up here and they were in every night with Bernard – even on a Wednesday, there they'd be. Bob Mortimer was the only person who came up to the bar and asked what bitter we had. This was Acid House, people were buying brandy and coke, Lucozade or water. And he'd come up and ask, "What bitter have you got?" All that time spent sorting the tubes in the cellar out, someone finally asked for Boddingtons! They'd drink an awful lot those three!

The main thing I remember about Bernard, was just how much he fucking drank. Polishing bottle after bottle of Pernod off. It'd be ... Bernard's here, put two bottles to one side. In the end, I put a giant bucket of ice with two bottles of Pernod with it and some cartons of orange juice.'

Estranged from his former New Order colleagues, Bernard had become Mr Manchester, with the two venues he had a stake in, The Haçienda and Dry being the obvious places to call home. 'In all that time,' said Peter Hook in Q about the New Order "split", 'I only saw him once – in Dry – and he was so off his fucking face it scared me.'

'He was kind of like a lost kid when he was pissed,' says Eastwick ...

Bernard Sumner: 'Give me a break! I needed to get something out of the club – what was I supposed to do? Watch everyone else get pissed?'

' ... if I was Bernard Sumner in a club I'd think, *most people are looking at me, they know I'm from New Order, this is my club, so I'll keep out of the way.* But he'd be falling into the wall. I do remember thinking, he just not as cool as I thought he was, he's just a bit of a normal pisshead sort of guy.

He's a little bit shy, reasonably quiet … at that time the club was losing shit loads of money … and the band was making shit loads of money. There was a big iron staff lift that would go down into the cellar to the toilets near the dressing rooms. It needed a member of staff to operate it with a handle. That lift got used an awful lot when Bernard was in, put it like that.'

In June 15, 1996, the biggest possible signal that change in Manchester was about to come went off just oustide Marks & Spencers on Corporation Street. The 'billion pound bomb' planted by the IRA changed the city forever. It's still impossible to get a politician to admit it, but the blast allowed a transformation to occur in Manchester that would never have happened otherwise.

> Bernard Sumner: 'The general consensus is that the bomb was
> good for Manchester, architecturally speaking – cheers, IRA!'

That devastating piece of urban clearance was the best thing that happened to the city since … well, since The Haçienda. It led to an urban design and vibe that finally caught up with what New Order, Rob Gretton, Tony Wilson and Factory-land had in mind when The Haçienda first opened in 1982. A cool and groovy boho Manchester that walked the walk – but not across the sticky-floored grimness of the past.

The bomb was another excuse to have it large and there was an upsurge in The Haçienda's fortunes. But despite this Indian Summer of packed houses, the inevitable came in June 1997: all concerned agreed – especially the accountants – that The Haçienda must be closed. 'I was DJ-ing the last night, the last person to play the last record … not knowingly,' says Elliot Eastwick today. In *24 Hour Party People*, Tony Wilson was on the mike saying "raid the offices" and quoting Communist poetry and God knows what. Wilson was nowhere near the club on the last night. He knew it was going to be the last night. I turned up on the night, the club had just got busy again after a really lean period, Paul Cons had gone back in as the promoter, it was selling out again. I was just DJ-ing – I'd been sacked long before for nicking drinks while I was working on the bar. But they let me in as a DJ. I remember thinking, "This is great, I've finally done it, it's taken me however many years to get to this point. I'm the main guy playing the main room and it's sold out and everyone's come for the music. This is where I wanted to be. This is fucking great … this is my big gig." Played the last record. Remember ringing Paul Cons [the next day], his phone was off. Rang the office answerphone. Off. *This is fucking weird.*

This went on for a couple of days. Then I rang Rob Gretton – phone off. Everybody's phone's off. I went to the corner shop and they had a *Manchester Evening News* billboard outside and it said, "Haçienda Closes For Good." It's like finding out you've been sacked on a billboard outside a shop. I remember looking down at it and thinking ... *You fucking cunts*. But I don't know who the fucking cunts actually were.'

Leroy Richardson: 'A select few were told – none of the staff knew whatsoever. They had been advised there was this ... there was a possibility of re-opening. That was said. Nobody except directors and management knew. They couldn't tell the staff and I was asked not to let anyone know. I understood completely why. Elliot didn't know, nobody knew who worked there. It was purely management and directors.'

'There was none of them there,' continues Eastwick. 'Leroy wasn't there, Paul Cons, Gretton, Hooky, Bernard ... it was a big Saturday night. We were told they had the meeting on the Monday after the Saturday night, they sat down with Bernard, Hooky, the accountant and everyone ... and the accountant said, "We're fucked, this is it, we've actually gone underwater now." But they'd known it was coming. They all knew it would be the last night of the Haçienda. They didn't want to do a big 'Last Night of The Haçienda' party because it was just too heartbreaking for them all. Not one of them could face being there, it was too upsetting.'

Sitting at the kitchen table of his home in south Manchester, I ask Eastwick the inevitable question. Given that he had no idea that he had played the last record ever at The Haçienda ... which record did he play? After all, he had no prior knowledge of what was going to happen, so therefore no opportunity to exploit the situation to the hilt and play a cute, telling, knowing, apposite track that would sum up the whole sad, sad situation.

The end of The Haçienda and the closure of the Mancunian Dream.

'It was a remix of the Sneaker Pimps,' he says. "Post-Modern Sleaze' the song was called. Ironic really.'

CONFUSION ELEVEN:
A FUNNY OLD STATE AT ROB'S FUNERAL

A strange thing had happened on the way to that third Electronic album: New Order had reformed. On Thursday, July 16, 1998, New Order walked onto the stage of Manchester's Apollo Theatre, a rattling, aged venue whose only plus point is a floor that slopes towards the stage, allowing just about anyone and everyone a decent view. The first song they played was 'Regret'. 'All the animosity had burnt out of us, basically,' said Sumner. 'We'd been on tour so much together that we all quite frankly got on each others' nerves. Plus, we had really severe business pressures which aggravated the situation. I guess four years of thinking that we were never going to play together again kind of cleared the air. Extremely cleared the air. We get on better now than we ever did.' They also played 'Love Will Tear Us Apart'.

The music world of 1998 was a very different cove to the one that existed in 1980, when that song was originally released and Joy Division ended and New Order began. The girl/boy groups were king in the British charts as All Saints and B*Witched mopped up the pop gravy from the table being vacated by the disintegrating Spice Girls, while Boyzone did the same trick after Take That had left the building in 1996. Britain's national station Radio 1 had embraced the pop ideal to put clear water between itself and Radio 2, who would soon provide a home for the likes of New Order, but within five years, Radio 1 would change tack, jettisoning pop in favour of indie cool, filling the airwaves with young bands who sounded largely like New Order. Oasis – the last in the line of lauded, dominant and seemingly unassailable Manchester bands that had stretched uninterrupted from Joy Division through The Smiths and The Stone Roses – had crashed and burned with their bloated opus *Be Here Now*. The Haçienda was gone and Manchester had begun rebuilding and reinventing itself after the devastating IRA bomb had wiped the slate clean.

Since they last performed together at the Reading Festival in 1993, a variety of words and phrases had been used to describe what New Order were doing: 'hiatus' ... 'sabbatical' ... anything except 'split'. Now a tentative schedule of shows was being lined up – including a return to Reading – and even talk of going into the studio. 'We're getting on very well,' reported Peter Hook at the time. 'It's the first time in years that we've actually enjoyed each other's company, and I'm very pleased about it indeed. I'm looking forward to it and it's not been very often I've been able to say that.'

New Order made it to the end of the year and a ramshackle Pernod-fired post-Christmas show at their home city's MEN Arena and a show at London's Alexandra Palace. A few Joy Division songs were placed in the set, including 'Isolation' and 'Heart And Soul'.

It was a busy period for Bernard. Electronic had just released a single, The Other Two had one due in two weeks' time and Monaco – Peter Hook's follow up to Revenge – were gigging, but these other projects were largely put out to pasture. New Order became the priority again for all concerned. Johnny Marr was realistic about the turn of events. 'My only regret is that Electronic didn't put out more records,' he said in 2003. 'I'm glad that we called it a day in a cool way … I think it was really right that New Order got back together when they did before it became too late.' Everything was in place – nothing could overshadow the return of New Order. Surely?

On the morning of Saturday, May 15, 1999, Rob Gretton was found dead at his home in Chorlton, south Manchester. He was 46 and died of thyroid and heart problems. At his funeral at St Anthony's Church in Woodhouse Park, Wythenshawe, Gretton was described as the 'gentle giant' of the Manchester music scene. Johnny Marr, Tony Wilson and Mike Pickering were among the mourners.

Terry Mason, Gretton's former right-hand man and Bernard's schoolmate from the Salford Grammar days was also in attendance. Funerals are often the place were hatchets are buried and old scores and problems are forgotten. Sadly, that wasn't to be the case here. There would be no hearty hugs and backslaps for Terry and his old friends.

> Bernard Sumner: *'Not true – I tried to be friendly with him,*
> *but he wasn't interested.'*

'By then, I was in a different world from them,' says Terry. 'By that time, I'd gone to college. Barney was in a funny old state at Rob's funeral, he was with ['World In Motion' collaborator] Keith Allen more than anyone else. They [New Order] seem to to think I'm after money. These are my mates who I grew up with and are no longer there. I don't want their money.'

Also showing their respects to Gretton was New Order roadie and technician Michael Eastwood, the man who said he would have happily cut his arm off for Gretton. For Eastwood, the day somehow managed to turn into a typical Situationist prank. 'When they were down at Southern Cemetery doing the actual burial, it *pissed* down,' he says. 'Proper fucking heavy duty Mancunian rain. There was thousands of pounds worth of suits getting ruined and I remember standing there thinking, *he's done this!* The perfect Rob joke. Stand round his grave being all morose ... and then piss on them. Fantastic.'

Bernard Sumner: 'There was one funny thing about Rob's funeral. Lesley, Rob's girlfriend, was told by the cemetery that they had the perfect resting place for him, right next to Matt Busby. Rob was a mad City fan ... the last thing he said to me was, "I've got to go to a funeral at the weekend, I hate funerals, I always cry." Sad.'

In 2004, a memorial gig for Gretton was held in aid of the charity Manchester Kids at the city's Ritz nightclub. The Ritz venue is a throwback to the kind of Manchester clubs prevalent in the late 1970s, where Rafters and Pips ruled the nocturnal roost, with its sticky floors, blowsy punters and strict dress codes. A typically chaotic affair, Bernard sang a version of 'Bizarre Love Triangle' with Doves, formerly dance act Sub Sub, who'd transformed into a heart-on-the sleeve rock act. There was no appearance by New Order, but Peter Hook did play Joy Division's 'Heart And Soul' with Factory stalwarts A Certain Ratio. He also paid a moving tribute from the stage to other members of the Factory family who, like Gretton, were no longer with us – Ian Curtis and Martin Hannett – before predicting that Tony Wilson would be next. The event was, of course, given a catalogue number: FAC511.

In 1999, Bernard was asked by Q what his abiding memory of Rob Gretton would be: 'Rob used to say to everyone, "What are you doing?" "Well, nothing Rob, nothing." "What should you be doing? Skin up!" I'll remember those words.'

Manchester's music scene would be a quieter place without Rob Gretton. He'd hoped for a New Order reunion and finally saw it happen. There was no question that they wouldn't continue without him. New Order's place in the scheme of things was becoming apparent. They were elder statesmen who'd fought the law, occasionally allowing the law the impression that it'd won. There were accolades like Q's 'Inspiration Award' – Bernard dedicated the honour to Curtis and Rob Gretton – and a new generation of dancemeisters who looked to New Order in the same way that they had previously looked to Kraftwerk. The Chemical Brothers – the dance act that, along with The Prodigy, had been decreed by the indie scene as acceptable to like – were a good example: their track 'Out Of Control' features a vocal from Bernard.

'He's a total hero to us,' said The Chemical's Tom Rowlands on www.dancesite.com. 'New Order are a band we both love. We sent him a tape and he liked it. We spoke to him, got on okay, he came down and put in a lot of work on it. He's always been writing lyrics and melodies as against just rhythms, and that's a particular skill that he has. We probably wouldn't have phoned up Bernard Summer for our first record, that's probably one of those things that comes out of having confidence and success – the fact that we believed we wouldn't be over-powered by someone who's so strong. He's an inspiring person because he loves making music – he was there until 8a.m.'

The first fresh New Order offering of this phase is a track called 'Brutal', tucked away almost unnoticed during the soundtrack of *The Beach,* a film vehicle for Leonardo DiCaprio, which was directed by Danny Boyle of *Trainspotting* fame. Shortly after the film's release, Boyle was linked to a new project, a movie biography of Ian Curtis.

While these medium-sized flurries of activity were being generated, a quieter yet greater change took place: Gillian Gilbert stepped down from the band. The daughter she'd had with Stephen Morris – Grace – suffered from cystic fibrosis and something had to give. 'When something like that happens, you put your family first really,' said Morris at the time. 'It was a difficult decision to make but that's what we decided. It's going to be strange, but we didn't really have very much choice in the matter and it's kind of like, when nature strikes, you've just got to go with it. It had to be one of us really and it ended up being Gillian.' Gilbert's place was initially taken by Billy Corgan of Smashing Pumpkins and then by Phil Cunningham, Electronic's touring guitarist, also of Marion. Cunningham's youthful face – framed by a rash of copper-coloured hair – was gradually introduced to band photographs. New Order was now a 50-50 split between Cheshire and Salford.

Live, New Order became a much more relaxed proposition, with increased between-song banter and a notably more relaxed atmosphere. There was also a new and regular addition to the on-stage set-up: an autocue. Bernard Sumner may have been derided for his lyrics in the past, but at least now he would be word perfect.

'Bernard is an absolute perfectionist,' says former New Order technician Michael Eastwood. 'He's not that 'good' a vocalist and I think he's knows it. So being a perfectionist he gets nervous ... I think nowadays he's got to a point where I don't think he gives a toss. He just gets up and enjoys himself now.' 'I used to get very worried and think that I had to deliver and be a frontman,' said Sumner in *Q*. 'Now I just enjoy it as a party where there's music playing and I'm dancing along to it.'

There was clearly no rush to get in the studio – but a fresh New Order album was finally released in 2001. What *Get Ready* lacks in tunes, bleeps and beats, it makes up for in fuzzy, garage band energy. It's almost as if the other New Order – the American MC5/Stooges supergroup – has slipped in while the band are out at lunch and slammed a few three chord wonders down. It would be an ideal return, if it were possible, to claim that the album is great from start to finish. Actually, it's great at the start *and* the finish. If the idea was to out-rock the young rockers of the day, then it succeeds. Indeed, the video to the opening track, 'Crystal', brought the point home by having a band of snake-hipped young things playing and lip-synching along to the song – New Order themselves were nowhere to be seen. The video is now a Youtube favourite, largely thanks to its argument settling properties, the perennial question being: did The Killers really get their name from an imaginary band in a New Order video? The stand-ins for 'Crystal' are indeed called The Killers. The song itself is an old-fashioned New Order strummer, quite at home if it had been lifted from side one of *Brotherhood*. It hit the spot with record buyers too and returned New Order to the UK Top Ten. It ticks all the right non-dance New Order boxes and bodes well for the rest of the album. But '60 Miles An Hour' largely repeats the process and 'Turn My Way' uses the trilling voice of Smashing Pumpkins' Billy Corgan as a diversion from some of Sumner's rummest lyrics to date. 'Vicious Streak' sees the foot taken off the accelerator and allows a few bleeps in as the pace goes down, but still feels like two sketches spliced together rather than a whole song. 'Primitive Notion' is Joy Division – no question about it. 'Rock The Shack' is another lyrical lowpoint – always beware of any song that uses the word 'Timbuktu' – and Primal Scream's Bobby Gillespie is on hand to make Sumner's vocal seem beefy in comparison. Only on the way out do we get something of real worth: 'Run Wild' is lightly played, sweetly sung and even has a tinkle of melodica for old time's sake. It is a lovely track.

Bernard Sumner: 'It's about my daughter.'

Reviews for the album were oddly positive; there seemed to be an overiding pleasure in having New Order back that smoothed the edges of potentially abrasive reviews. 'There are few bands that have the natural panache to mix the intuitively brilliant and the heroically clueless quite like New Order,' declared *NME*. 'Still, in the throes of that first teenage love affair that miraculously lasted forever, Bernard Sumner's lyrics are still blessed with a naive – and totally punk rock – wonder. It's that sense of idiot joy which colours the whole of *Get Ready*. Being in New Order never sounded like half as much fun as it does here.'

Q magazine was also keen: 'New Order have made better records than this, but not many with such an emotional charge and the expansive noise to carry it off. *Get Ready* shows that there's a way to be 45-years-old without dissolving into empty indolence; that you can keep your hunger and even rediscover it when you thought it had gone.' These are fair reviews made up of kind words, but put *Get Ready* alongside the final Electronic album just two years earlier and there's no comparison. Or as *Mojo* magazine harshly put it: 'Much of *Get Ready* is less a call to arms than the sound of an old man wheezing out of a creaky armchair.'

Essentially though, New Order's return had worked to good effect, but even Sumner admitted that even with the best will in the world, the hunger of the early days was no longer there. 'As you get older and you get successful,' he said on the band's return, 'you tend to get the things in life that you really want – you might not get everything – but you get your nice house, your nice girlfriend. All the things you ever want really. I've got nothing to lose now. I've done what I wanted to do. If I lost the ability to get music across to people, it wouldn't be the end of the world. I've got kids – it shows you that if everything in your world crumbles, you've still got kids.'

New Order's return had been expertly handled. There was a worldwide schedule of gigs to fulfill and a rash of younger bands ready and willing to shake them by the hand and pay cultural homage. These bands, like the music press, recognised an immensely appealing character trait in Bernard and New Order: extreme perseverance.

'We'd all been through so much together,' said Sumner. 'We'd been through the death of Ian Curtis. Various very strenuous things. The death of our producer. Extreme business and gang-related problems in Manchester. We'd been through all of this and we hadn't survived at the end of it. Bit sad really. So it's good not to give up, it's a good thing.'

Post-punk survivor and godfather of dance, Bernard Sumner had seen some strange days and even stranger nights. He'd come a long way from his Grandma's parlour at 11 Alfred Street. You couldn't make it up.

As it happened though, a team of film makers were about to do just that.

Bernard Sumner had always tried to keep his life determinedly low-key. Now they were going to put him in the movies.

CONFUSION TWELVE
– 'BERNARD, IT'S A FUCKING FILM SET'

Since the 1980s, Bernard Sumner's music has been a staple for film makers looking to spread a little alienated angst on screen. The films' titles say it all, to one extent or another: *Donny Darko* ('Love Will Tear Us Apart'), *American Psycho* ('True Faith') *Trainspotting* ('Temptation') and *Pretty In Pink* ('Thieves Like Us', 'Shellshock') are all prime examples. All outsider movies, to varying degrees. And, unusually for a man of his age – unusually for a man that's *alive* – he's been portrayed twice on screen: in *24 Hour Party People* (2001) and *Control* (2007).

'He's not a scandalous person,' according to John Simm on www.partypeoplemovie.com, who portrays Bernard in *24 Hour Party People*. 'I've talked to a lot of people who know him, and they all say that he's a really nice guy. He's just a really personal, quiet kind of guy, from the interviews that I have seen of him, and from what I've known as a kid, from New Order. That's all I can go off really.'

Sumner's former mentor Tony Wilson has a different take. 'Bernard is the exasperating, deeply annoying, *knowing* one,' he told me. 'Let's use the word 'knowing'. I hate Bernard because I like being very clever and I'm always right. Except Bernard's always more right than me. And that really pisses me off.'

24 Hour Party People tells the story of the rise, fall and rise again of Manchester punk and club culture through the eyes of Tony Wilson: Salford lad (though his family moved fairly sharpish to the Stockport village of Marple) and 'serious fucking journalist and Cambridge graduate' as he describes himself in the film. Wilson is played by North Manchester actor and comic Steve Coogan. From the rise of punk to the fall of The Haçienda, Coogan/Wilson is our guide to this series of vignettes based around the creation of Factory, the discovery of Joy Division, the death of Ian Curtis and the explosion of dance, drug and gun culture in Manchester. Coogan uses his gifts as an impressionist to reflect and lampoon Wilson; every pout, every strangulated vowel, every dropped name is present and correct. It's Coogan's film, no question.

As Bernard Sumner, Leeds-born John Simm brings a musical background to the table – he used to play in a club duo with his father called Us2. A graduate of Blackpool Drama College, he moved to the London Drama Centre and formed a band – Magic Alex – that toured with the scallydelic Echo And The Bunnymen in the 1990s. The band's moniker must surely have appealed to the Bunnymen – it's the nickname of The Beatles' electrician. Simm's wife Kate MacGowan also appears in *24 Hour Party People*, as Tony Wilson's partner Yvette Livesey. He bears a striking resemblance to Sumner.

For director Michael Winterbottom, it was the mix of musical ability and look that got Simm the part. 'You just want to cast the people that are right for the part. It's incredibly subjective and it's no more complicated than that really. You look around for people, and when you find someone you like, you cast them. Obviously, in this case, there were some musical requirements, some of the people are supposed to be in bands, so if they could play an instrument, that was good. You obviously don't want to have four people on stage who look so different to the originals that they're just completely distracting, looking like a different band, but at the same time you wouldn't really cast anything to be just look-a-likes because you want them to be able to perform.'

We first see Simm in the Lesser Free Trade Hall with Peter Hook [Ralf Little] and Rob Gretton [Paddy Considine] watching the Sex Pistols on June 4, 1976. The fact that the pair didn't actually meet Gretton until 1978 is clearly the difference between a documentary and a feature film. There's no sign of Terry Mason, John Berry, 'Crazy' Mike or Sue Barlow either.

Simm's Bernard Sumner is the good guy of the piece, the voice of reason and the peacemaker. We see his concern over how the band's name – which he endorses, though sees the funny side of – attracts Nazi sieg-heilers to their gigs. It's Simm's Sumner that shows an immediate response to Curtis [Sean Harris], as he experiences an epileptic fit during a recreation of the Bury Town Hall gig that ended in a riot. And it's Simm's character that explodes with rage at Peter Hook for stealing Curtis' cigarettes as he fits helplessly on the dressing room floor. This scene *enraged* the real-life Hook ... not least because he doesn't smoke.

Bernard Sumner: 'It was Steve who took Ian's cigs, Hooky had his wallet!'

Jokes aside, Sumner himself admits he's not the easiest person for an actor to get a handle on. 'I sometimes feel that the me that gets out of bed in the morning is a different person to the me that goes to bed at night,' he told *Observer Music Monthly*. 'I am certainly a different person now to the one I was in Joy Division. I also don't like people to know what I am thinking, so I hide quite a lot but I do think John Simm did an excellent portrayal of the bits that were showing.' But not everyone was quite so impressed by Simm in the film. Bernard's Electronic collaborator Johnny Marr – who was offered one of the many cameos in the film, but declined – felt the portrayal was too 1980s, missing the actual timezones the film was set in. 'I thought the guy playing Bernard Sumner was a bit lazy in his research,' he told *Magnet*. 'It doesn't take much to dye your hair black to be in Joy Division. Put a tie on, you know? Bernard in Joy Division is actually Bernard doing 'The Perfect Kiss' in New Order from 1985 in terms of the way he looks. In the movie, when it was supposed to be Joy Division, it was actually Bernard five years hence. Bernard didn't discover peroxide and long trousers until at least 1984.

The film makers caused quite a stir when they shot key scenes on location in Manchester. They were even able to film inside the real Lesser Free Trade Hall, just before 90 per cent of it was knocked down to be made into a hotel. But there was one location that was no longer available for filming: The Haçienda. The Haçienda was no more and had eventually been knocked down. Peter Hook did the honours, starting the demolition on Granada's regional TV news show – the same show that Joy Division made their debut on in 1978. The apartments built on the site are now called ... The Haçienda.

As the real thing had gone, a new Haçienda had to be built for the film – in a warehouse in the Ancoats district, just outside Manchester city centre. It would finally provide Bernard and everyone involved with the 'Last Night Party' that they were denied in 1997. 'Rob Gretton said if we knew it was going to go, we could have had a big blast,' says Leroy Richardson. 'Which ultimately the filming turned out to be.'

The Haçienda recreation was also the first time that actor John Simm had actually met Bernard Sumner. 'I don't know what I was expecting, really,' said Simm on set. 'He was kind of how I was expecting him to be. I would like to have met him under different circumstances than him walking into The Haçienda for the first time since it was knocked down, 'cos he was a bit freaked out by it. But he seemed really nice and happy that I was playing him. I said, "I hope I do you justice."'

Towards the end of the film, we see the re-imagining of the last night of The Haçienda, with Wilson scanning the club and seeing Bernard Sumner and all the key players having the time of their lives, including Martin Hannett [Andy Serkis] and Ian Curtis. 'Ladies and gentleman,' announces Steve Coogan from the DJ booth. 'The hour is upon us. I'd like you to leave in a disorderly fashion.' Coogan's Wilson then invites the crowd to loot the offices of computer gear and musical equipment and use it wisely. Again, it's a film, not a documentary.

'Everybody saw the filming as the closing party that we never had,' says former Haçienda manager Leroy Richardson. 'And a final thank you to New Order, Factory and Rob Gretton in particular. It was fantastic – apart from stopping for the filming – the people involved having to do something again. It was weird because a tune would come on and it'd be, "Hold on! Stop! We need to do that again." That never happened at The Haçienda! That was a shock when I saw 'Rob' there [actor Paddy Considine] because he had the mannerisms down to a tee.'

'Bernard came up to me and asked me to get him a Pernod. I said, "Bernard, it's a fucking film set, I'm not working!" It's good to see it was a celebration of The Haçienda. It's a shame the set wasn't left there so we could have done something with it.

The filmakers approach to research seemed to some a little scattergun and, despite his credentials, Richardson and many other key players weren't even asked to help. 'I'm the longest serving employee – not just of The Haçienda but of Factory Records – and then there's Ange Matthews who was in there at the best of it. We were never spoken to concerning the filming. We were never asked anything at all. I didn't know who the director was, there no input like this [being interviewed for this book]. If it hadn't have been for Tony Wilson, I wouldn't have even got an invite to the screening of it. When they were doing the filming, I turned up and they [former Haçienda employees] let me drive me car up to where the film set was ... someone [from the film company] said, "Who's he? What's he doing?" They said, 'He's the one who ran The Haçienda and he's fucking coming in.'

One person who chose not to go to the filming was DJ Elliot Eastwick, who played the final record on the *real* last night of The Haçienda. 'I just remember thinking, *I don't want to go to a pretend version of the club that's full of cunts.* The next day everyone said, "You should have gone" ... that it was the most amazing, freaky night."

'It was great,' confirms Leroy Richardson. 'When I walked in, there were so many people there. It was emotional, but not sad emotional. They'd done a really good job. It was the reaction of people outside afterwards ... they were saying, "Is this going to be every week?" Let it go, it's gone, that's the last you're going to see of it. A lot of people were saying, "Let's get the set and make a club." No, it's gone, that's it. I still get people saying, "What do you think of those apartments [on the site of The Haçienda building]?" Well, at least *something's* there. I'm glad The Haçienda's gone. It shouldn't be left there as a monument. It's more about people's experiences ... and you're never going to forget them, are you?'

'I went to the premiere in Manchester,' said Elliot Eastwick. 'I'd heard they'd been a bit bendy with the truth. I remember watching the film, a load of us who'd worked there were all sat in the same row. Wilson doing the big speech, and me getting nudged from both sides and going "Fuck–ing–HELL!" God, I wish it *had* been like that, it was great, instead of me thinking ... *it's factually incorrect* ... I thought it was great. It gave me an insight into what it *could* have been like, instead of just an okay night.'

Shot on digital cameras, *24 Hour Party People* is a bold, maddening, flawed and funny film. Given the subject matter, that's exactly as it should be. There are enough cameos – Howard Devoto cleaning the toilets, Mark E Smith queuing politely outside a club – to give it much-needed Manchester credibilty, and Coogan manages to sneak at least one physical or verbal laugh out of most of his scenes. The one thing that lets it down is the poor staging of the music performance scenes. There seems no attempt to make Simm and the rest of the actors sound remotely like they're playing live. Given that John Simm's ability to actually play was a major part in his casting, this is an odd technical decision.

Sumner himself was part-baffled, part-amused by the film: 'When you first see it, and you see a story that you've seen first-hand, it's a bit disorientating, seeing someone play you. I was gobsmacked when I left the film theatre. It's very weird. Every scene that you watch you think *it's not quite right*, but I think the film's pretty good, in the end. It's a funny film, which I'm glad about. I lot of people take us very, very seriously, and we're not like that as people.'

Tony Wilson had considerable reservations about the film prior to release, due to historical innacuracies and borderline legal concerns in the script. He now believes *24 Hour Party People* is 'a great rock and roll movie ... by chance. Not by chance. It was the genius of Winterbottom and [writer] Frank Cottrill-Boyce ... quite stunning.'

'I watched *24 Hour Party People*,' says actor James Anthony Pearson. 'I didn't really like it very much. It was really long. I watched it because I thought I ought to.' James is the second actor to bring Bernard to the big screen; he plays the part in 2007's *Control*. Perhaps unfairly, I asked Pearson what he thought of John Simm in *24 Hour Party People*. 'I thought he looked really old,' he replied. 'He looked like he was mid-30s.' Born in Rochdale, Greater Manchester, then raised in Bradford and Aberdeenshire, playing Bernard is a big break for Pearson. It's the first time the youthful-looking 25-year-old has actually played an adult.

'When I heard they wanted me to read for Bernard, he's the oldest in the band so I thought I don't have a chance of getting that. I didn't know much about Joy Division at all. But I can see the resemblance. The shirt I wanted to wear for the audition wasn't washed and I ended up wearing this really drab shirt that wasn't ironed which turned out to be perfect, just the kind of thing Bernard would have worn, really understated.'

'In the film, you first meet Bernard when he's with Hooky and they're at the Lesser Free Trade Hall. Tony Wilson's at the bar and Ian comes wandering over. He's dead quiet. They were there to see a gig and at the end of the gig, Ian asks if he could be in the band. Immediately after that, you see them when they were playing their first gig as Warsaw with [punk poet] John Cooper Clarke ... the real, actual John Cooper Clarke makes a cameo. He was fantastic.'

Shot in black and white on location in Macclesfield and Nottingham, *Control* is based on Deborah Curtis' book, *Touching From A Distance* and is directed by Dutch photographer Anton Corbijn. Anton was responsible for many of the washed out, imposing music press pictures of Joy Division – and especially of Ian Curtis – that froze the band's image forever in many people's minds as aloof – dare we say doomed – outsiders.

James Anthony Pearson, who plays Bernard in Anton Corbijn's movie, Control.

'The decision to film in black and white is important,' producer Orian Williams told *The Staffordshire Sentinel*. 'When people read about the band for the first time, everything was in black and white – the photographs, the *NME*.' Williams, whose first film, *Shadow Of The Vampire*, was nominated for two Oscars, had been trying to get *Control* made since 1997. 'It has been difficult, but I'm sure it will open up a lot of people, who weren't born when the music was made, to who Ian Curtis was and the music of Joy Division.'

'When I was 24,' said Corbijn at a press conference to launch the film, '*NME* was like the Bible in Holland and Paul Morley's writing about events a lot and I was thinking of leaving Holland anyway and Joy Division records made the decision quicker. So I moved in October 1979 to England to be close to where the news came from and actually within two weeks I'd managed to photograph Joy Division. Now I've been here 25 years. So I'm kind of circling round to be able to make a movie about good times for me and about Ian Curtis.'

Curtis is played by 25-year-old Sam Riley from Leeds, a musician who had a bit part in *24 Hour Party People* – a part that was left on the cutting room floor. Names as high-profile as Jude Law were mentioned in connection with the role, which Riley didn't exactly go begging for. 'I initially went auditioning for the drummer,' Riley revealed in the *Yorkshire Evening Post*. 'But then they asked me back. I left without much hope. But I guess I didn't do too bad. I didn't believe it to begin with, because I know there were a couple of major Hollywood actors interested, but it was obviously a pretty amazing present. They asked me not to tell anyone because they didn't want it leaking on to the internet.' Matt Greenhalgh, *Control*'s writer, was aware from the start that the film was a big risk, particularly when it comes to satisfying members of the Manchester scene – they're noted for their disdain of anything seemingly inauthentic. 'Ian [Curtis] is, for want of a better word, a god in this city,' Greenhalgh told journalists at the press conference. 'And to be actually undertaking to do a bio on him is probably every young Mancunian pop person's dream ... there's a lot of people to please, a lot of people that know that scene inside out, Tony Wilson, a few in New Order and obviously Deborah [Curtis].'

'It's very exciting after all these years,' Deborah Curtis told the same news conference. 'The film thing's been going on for a long time. There was a time when I thought that it was better not to do it at all – but we've found the right people now.'

'The film is very much about Ian Curtis and it's very much Ian's story,' says James Anthony Pearson. 'I felt really close to Sam [Riley] who plays

Ian in the film. That's because of the script. The impression I got was that Bernard and Ian were really, really close and it was a special relationship and quite unspoken. I think they both admired each other without having to talk about it. I think it's the honest Bernard. He's very dry in the film. There's lots of one liners. He's almost like a naughty schoolboy. We had two weeks of rehearsals before filming began. We all got together as a band. I was really intimidated because I couldn't play guitar at all, I felt like the weakest link from that point of view. By the end of the two weeks, we felt like an actual band.'

When I put it to Pearson that Bernard Sumner doesn't bear the burden of being the world's greatest guitarist, he gives an answer that's fantastically devoid of PR polish. 'That made the whole thing so much better! Listening to some of their early live stuff, you can hear so many mistakes that they all made, especially Bernard. And the way he plays guitar, the way he stands. I thought ... punk rock band ... jumping all over the stage. But then to see the way Bernard played [in Joy Division] standing dead still, eyes fixed on his fingers, that made the whole thing loads easier. He wasn't approaching it from a knowledgeable point of view. He was just playing what he thought sounded cool. That's what gave them a real edge.'

The Dutchman Corbijn ensured he maintained control by sinking his own money into the film; he says he's given his all to make the film happen. 'This is something that requires 110 per cent of me,' he told Dutch television news in 2006. 'Your breathing ... everything ... is just about filming. It's fantastic music. A lot of musicians' bands these days have been enormously inspired by Joy Division.' 'Anton was so calm and he was so in control on the set,' says Pearson. 'He spent his own money on the film. He never blew his top once, it meant that no one else had the right to do that.'

Unfortunately, one person did blow his top at Corbijn – Peter Hook. 'I'm pissed about the movie right now because Anton Corbijn seems to be getting too much control, precisely,' bassist Peter Hook opined towards the end of 2006. 'I would have preferred that he showed more respect for us. That's what he should do ... Anton is too passionate about the movie, but I think he should have a wider view. At the beginning, he would say, "Come everyone, to help," but now he closed the doors and sent everyone to piss off. We're supposed to [record the film's soundtrack] but the problem is that he's telling us what to do. If we don't tell him how to direct, why is he telling us how to make music? Bernard and Steve seem to be okay about it, but it bothers me a lot.'

Bernard Sumner: 'Ever heard of a film with three directors?'

Luckily, Peter Hook and the rest of the band were in a better frame of mind when Pearson and the other key members of the cast went to meet them in the early stages of production. 'We all went to a New Order gig in Liverpool. It was a great day out. Samantha Morton [Deborah Curtis] was there and Sam and all the band and Anton. We went to meet them [New Order] beforehand and watched the gig and went to meet them [again] afterwards, it was really cool.

It was the first time I'd seen them on stage and they were fantastic. It was the first week of rehearsals and everyone was just really finding their feet. I can remember walking into their little room. I was really aware that I looked about 12-years-old. Terrified of saying something completely uncool. Bernard gave me a glass of wine and said, 'Oh, are you old enough to drink, then?' What was really weird about it was, it's Anton's film. My whole connection to Joy Division and New Order is through the film. That's what I'm doing ... I'm an actor. I really realised when I was there that Bernard and Hooky and Steve Morris probably didn't care that much about the film. Why would they? It's quite weird someone doing a film about an ex-band member who killed himself and you're a supporting actor in it. It was great to be there and I did feel very welcome but, at the same time, I did feel a bit like an outsider. I felt a bit like a *model*. I'm not quite sure what I felt about it. It was great but it was just quite a bizarre experience. He was very nice after the gig because I saw him [Bernard] alone and chatted with him, he was really lovely. He just said, "Just do your own thing and don't feel any pressure about having to do anything in a particular way – just do your own thing and that's fine." Which I thought was quite ... noble.'

Early on in production, a rival Curtis film put together by Double A Films in New York was on the horizon. Tony Wilson was brought in as a co-producer alongside Deborah Curtis. 'My job on *Control* was to see off the rebel movie and make sure the film got made,' says Wilson. 'And I did my bit. If another two people buy, or are open to, wonderful music like Joy Division, then it's worth it.'

James Anthony Pearson: 'This film and *24 Hour Party People* are totally poles apart. Anton just didn't want much talking. It was all quite one-liney. Hand on heart, I think it's absolutely fantastic. From my experience on set – my first feature film – everyone said how we've been spoiled.'

One key gig was recreated – the Bury performance that ended in a near-riot. Members of a kick-boxing club in Hanley, Staffordshire were used as bouncers and the band of actors played the concert for real.

'I felt so proud that we played the music live in the film,' says Pearson. 'Because the music has such a huge following. It was a really great feeling. They used quite a lot of Joy Division fans as extras and it was really scary. Sam Riley threw up before we played the first 'gig' because he was so terrified. There was one guy in the 'audience' who had a tattoo of Ian Curtis on his chest. I'm not prepared, I've not really thought about negative opinions from die-hard fans.'

In the film, Curtis is the local 'weirdo', disenfranchised from his family and mocked by the local kids – it's always nice to hear someone referred to as a 'knob cheese' in contemporary cinema. The environment of *Control* is the washed out, monochrome world of 35 years ago, bypassed by those promises of a futuristic existence given by *Tomorrow's World*. This is the *real* 1970s; you can practically smell the Spangles sweets, taste the frothy Cresta pop and hear the crunching gears of the Chopper bikes in every scene. Some sequences are taken directly from Deborah Curtis' book – including one of Ian cowering in fear of her when she simply says 'boo' to him on the stairs of their home. Morton's Deborah Curtis is every inch the 'wallflower' described by Terry Mason, while Annik Honoré [Alexandra Maria Lara] is portrayed as an über rock chick, genetically programmed to beguile. James Anthony Pearson's Bernard is a slightly camp, tittering figure, watching proceedings from a mischeivious distance, even accusing Curtis of being a 'drama queen' when he has an epileptic fit. The casting of relative unknowns – Morton is the most famous face by a long stretch – works in the film's favour, even if Sam Riley's Curtis looks oddly like Dee Dee Ramone.

After a delay in its release, *Control* was finally unveiled at the Cannes Film Festival in May 2007 (it opened up the 'Director's Fortnight' section of the competition), where it was awarded the honour of 'Best European Film' (Europa Cinemas prize), CICAE Art and Essai Prize for 'Best Film' and the Regards Jeunes prize for 'Best First Or Second Feature'.

All the hassle and heartache seems to have been worthwhile. As James Anthony Pearson says, Joy Division's music means a great deal to many people – from Peter Hook to the guy on the film set with the Ian Curtis tattoo – and emotions can run high. Although *24 Hour Party People* and *Control* are feature films – not documentaries – it's important to get things right. Detail can drive the picky Manchester scenesters to distraction. In terms of *Control*'s recreation of the Bury riot gig – during which violence was memorably dismissed by Bernard Sumner as being so very *temporary* – additional information was required. As part of preparations for the sequence, a researcher was despatched to interview key players in the drama

– including Crispy Ambulance's Alan Hempsall. If you recall, Hempsall was one of three singers who deputised for Curtis that night as he stood in the wings, fresh from his hospital bed after a botched suicide attempt.

The researcher despatched by the film-makers to Hempsall's home in Chorlton was Natalie Curtis, Ian's daughter. Detail, you see. Very important.

CONFUSION THIRTEEN: A YOUNG MAN'S BUSINESS

'It's shit getting old,' Bernard Sumner told readers of Q in 2005, in response to the magazine's cheeky 'Cash For Questions' section. 'There's nothing good to say about it really.'

As he approached his fiftieth year, Bernard Sumner would have good reason to be somewhat perplexed. The flush of goodwill that went in his direction after New Order reformed was about to ease off and the band were apparently entering that awkward stage that many of the most influential artists reach. A stage that most of their contemporaries had approached and dealt with in differing ways already. It's the stage where the public prefers the *idea* of what you do over what you actually *are*. You'll get the admiring nods of approval and your legacy will be safe, but when it comes to the front line of the record store or the ticket office, then the very bands you've inspired and influenced will often take precedence.

'It's very difficult when you get older in a young man's business,' nods Tony Wilson, in full sage mode when the question is put to him. 'How do you keep going? Their [New Order's] way of keeping going is they keep thinking they're writing new songs ... or keep thinking they're doing something useful. Do you do what Phil Oakey [Human League] does and become a tribute band ... to yourself? New Order don't because they play new songs.'

Sumner's place in music history – and that of the bands he has played with – was by now assured. There's a slew of accolades to prove it. There's the *NME* 'God-Like Genuis Award', the German 'Lifetime Dance Music Award' and the respect of younger acts like The Killers. Both Joy Division, New Order and – to a less visible extent Electronic – have become touchstones for many bands in the UK and the US. 'I can see our influence in a lot of other bands around at the moment,' offered Sumner in the *Observer Music Monthly*. 'The Killers, Interpol, Death in Vegas. Franz Ferdinand look just like Joy Division ... the thin bastards.' Alongside the music, there was the other easy reference point for any up–and–coming act that New Order provided: that of the uncompromising outsiders, seemingly happy to cut their own noses off, even if it meant spiting their own faces.

'A career,' pointed out Stephen Morris nearly twenty years previously in *Zig Zag*, 'is forward planning. [With us] there isn't any forward planning. We don't do what we think is successful. We do what we want to do.'

Most of their contemporaries had either fallen by the wayside or succumbed to the kind of 'Tribute-itus' described by Tony Wilson. There are exceptions: Echo And The Bunnymen, though essentially running at 50 per cent strength with only Ian McCulloch and Will Sergeant remaining, were still releasing new material and touring the world ('No pensions in this game, La,' McCulloch pointed out to me in 2002); The Cure, though nowhere near as productive, still mirrored New Order in terms of credibilty as they had previously done musically; and then there's U2, still using every trick in the book – bombast, politics, irony, disco, you name it – to stay on top of the game.

Bernard, Peter and Stephen were now legends – to prove it, Joy Division were given a Q 'Legend' award in 2005. The gong was promptly handed over to Ian Curtis' daughter Natalie by Peter Hook. 'Don't tell Bernard,' Hook told a reporter who collared him at the ceremony. 'He'll go fucking mad if we don't go back with an award. There'll be a fucking witch hunt for it.'

Hook claims the reason Sumner didn't attend the ceremony was because of the two star review the magazine had given to New Order's album released the same year, *Waiting For The Siren's Call*. 'He thinks Q are a bunch of two-faced cunts after the review they gave us,' added Hook, just in case anyone had any doubts on the issue.

That album is a superior piece of work, better than many magazines gave the band credit for. Slicker from the outset than *Get Ready,* and starting with the mid-tempo stummer 'Who's Joe?' – 'Hey Joe' is the lyric used, perhaps it was pointed out that title was already taken – this album is traditional 'disco in one ear, rock in the other' New Order. Is that any bad thing? No one else does it, after all. 'Hey Now What You Doing?' maintains the same vibe as the opener but boasts a very Marion-esque note-bending riff and a sweetly sung chorus. There's more than a touch of Johnny Marr here – again, no bad touch to have. The title track is a neat, electrochugger and the upbeat 'Krafty' finally acknowledges the ever-present influence of the German dance pioneers, with its synth washes and pulsing bass. The reggae-fied 'I Told You So' may make Ace Of Bass sound like Burning Spear, but it's still a neat pop song. 'Dracula's Castle' is far better than its name would suggest – imagine bringing that title into the rehearsal room – and 'Jetstream' has Ana Matronic of the Scissor Sisters providing a touch of camp, vocal glamour and a breathy voiceover. 'Guilt Is

A Useless Emotion' is a prime invitation for dancing with a killer chorus – you'd love to slosh around the dancefloor of Pips spilling your pint to this one. Only 'Working Overtime' sounds out of place – like a Morrissey b-side – but it's the last track and easily dispensed with.

Like the content, the reviews were mixed but generally pretty strong. 'It's a remarkably coherent, consistent record,' said *Uncut* magazine. 'This may seem like faint praise for a band who once veered so flukily between the divine and asinine. But if nothing here is quite touched by the hand of God, then maybe it's all the more engagingly human.'

Rolling Stone was also on board: 'Bernard Sumner still sings and strums with his boyish air of distractable pique, and he writes some of the most genius crap lyrics around. His secret is his sincerity, the way he whoops and yelps through blood-curdling poetry that a more clever singer would shame himself trying to play straight.'

Tellingly – bordering on worryingly – Sumner admitted the album was a compromise, the very compromise the band had been struggling with for over twenty years. 'The last album was guitar-heavy,' he told *NME*, 'simply because we felt that we'd left that instrument alone for a long time and we thought that was what the general trend was and what people wanted to hear. But when we started doing live gigs, we found that people got off on the more dance-oriented and synth stuff just as much. This album really splits into two halves. It's a mixture of two, because that's what New Order fans like.' There was a time when Bernard Sumner would have done what he wanted to do, rather than what the research indicated he ought to do. This tip-toe approach did not escape the notice of some reviewers. The aforementioned Q magazine described *Waiting For The Siren's Call* as, 'a patchy affair,' and *Mojo* went even further: 'There's little real sense of progression here ... and at times New Order sound dreary and ordinary.'

Bernard Sumner, it would appear, couldn't win.

Perhaps pleasure can be taken in different ways if the great reviews – seemingly guaranteed in the past – aren't always forthcoming. Rock's elder statesmen can often be found doing good works. Bernard Sumner is no different, but has done his good works in his own way. In November 2005, New Order returned to Salford to play a gig at Oakwood High School in Eccles, apparently to mark the school's recent success after a Government inspection. The band performed an hour-long set with Peter Hook giving the kids an earful by shouting 'Fuck Off!' from the stage – he got a big cheer from the kids nonetheless! On the day though, headteacher Janis Trisca seemed to be in forgiving mood: 'It was absolutely fantastic,' she said. 'It was a real rock concert. We still can't believe they came, and they are so nice. They worked really hard to make it something special for our children. This is something the children will never forget. It makes them feel important. No rock band this big had to do this – they are amazing.'

Sumner was grabbed by a reporter from the local paper as he and the rest of New Order posed for pictures with pupils. Some of the kids are in wheelchairs, as Oakwood is a special needs school. 'There is an innocence to these children,' he said. 'I didn't know how they would react to our music. I didn't expect them to all get into it. We did this to give these kids some self-esteem. It is not just a special school, it is a very special school.' At no stage did Sumner make any reference to his own mother's special needs. The reporter, the teachers and the kids are left in the dark about the real reason that Bernard Sumner is so entranced by the pupils of Oakwood.

The band were also to be found involved in 'John Peel Day' on October 13. When the revered Radio 1 DJ had died a year earlier, there was a nationwide level of shock; it was generally accepted that the genially bumbling, music obsessive would go on forever, championing so much left of centre music that some of it was bound to filter through, if nothing else possibly purely on a law of averages. To mark his passing, a gig was put on at London's Queen Elizabeth Hall. Peel favourites The Fall, Misty In Roots and Super Furry Animals were on hand, along with New Order. Bernard told the audience they would have gotten 'nowhere' without Peel's patronage, as they launched into a set made up entirely of Joy Division songs: 'Transmission', 'She's Lost Control', 'Love Will Tear Us Apart', 'Atmosphere', 'Shadowplay' and the first song the band ever played together, '3 1 G'. 'We thought [Peel] would have liked it that way,' Hook told *NME* backstage. 'We've been flirting with it for ages, talking about doing a Joy Division set, because we thought the contrast would be nice, and I just decided for this to do it. But it's worked, it sounds good and it's interesting. We're playing two songs tonight we've not played for 25 years.'

January 2006 saw Bernard and the band top of the table at 'Manchester Versus Cancer'. The gig came about after ex-Smith Andy Rourke's manager had the twin blow of having his father and sister both diagnosed with cancer. The initial idea of a low-key fund-raiser featuring The Charlatans quickly grew and grew into a huge show at the *Manchester Evening News* Arena. When The Charlatans were forced to pull out, New Order stepped in. 'We realised straight away,' says gig co-organiser Tom Smetham, 'that with New Order being such a huge Mancunian export, and the whole idea being Manchester versus cancer, it just seemed to be perfect.' New Order decided they would again be performing a set consisting entirely of Joy Division songs. 'That was their idea – a great idea,' says Smetham. 'At the time, the posters said New Order, so apologies to anyone who turned up thinking that they were going to get New Order. I didn't know they were going to play a purely Joy Division set until perhaps a week before the concert. They played '24 Hours' for the first time since Ian Curtis' death. They broke a bit of history for us.

Bernard had a cold. He'd been quite ill all week. When he turned up, he sounded so bunged up I was surprised ... he sounded pretty bad. He said he was a 'coldaholic', constantly ill. But their sound on the night was terrific. I thought it was an absolutely immense performance. Nobody complained about the lack of New Order songs. Because of the show and what it was about, there wasn't that much ego knocking around. They've been together so long, they don't seem to notice each other are even there.'

During an evening of considerable ramshackle charm, Johnny Marr even managed to bury the musical hatchet with his former bandmate Andy Rourke after the legal action the pair where embroiled in during the 1990s. Rourke was introduced as someone 'he'd first played with in school in 1978.'

When New Order/Joy Division finished their headline set, there was an *en masse* rendition of Happy Mondays' 'Wrote For Luck', featuring New Order, Johnny Marr, Doves, Badly Drawn Boy and some customised lyrics by Shaun Ryder: 'Bernard, Bernard where have you been? I know you're after my botty ...'

More than £100,000 was raised for Manchester's Christie Hospital and other cancer charities by the gig, and the '......Versus Cancer' concept is now on the way to becoming an annual affair. The second 'Versus' gig in 2007 largely repeated the winning formula of the first, held at the *Manchester Evening News* Arena and organised by the same team as before; it was righteously ramshackle too, with some of the more refreshed artists being practically lifted on stage. It had Manchester luminaries like Noel Gallagher and Peter Hook and it all ended in a mass singalong of the Stone Roses' 'I Am The Resurrection'. The only thing missing was Bernard Sumner. Rather bizarrely, many of the acts were to be seen enthusiastically pulling on a ciggie while on stage, studiously ignoring the exercise's point.

After the 2006 'Versus' show, New Order played festival and arena shows in the UK and the continent, including an unusual show at Blackpool's ornate Empress Ballroom. Elsewhere on the tour, support slots had been given to the likes of The Fall-ish Gabrielle's Wish and Phil Cunningham protégés The Shores, whose handsome brand of U2-lite is as easy on the ear as it is on the eye. In Blackpool, the gig was given to Bernard's contemporaries Section 25, the band who had provided Bernard with a bolthole when Ian Curtis committed suicide in 1980. Section 25 had been through the wars themselves. Centred on brothers Larry and Vin Cassidy, the band had been overlooked in favour of more easy-going acts and in the midst of a return in 2000, were hit by a series of traumas, including guitarist Ian Butterworth sustaining serious head injuries and a diagnosis of cancer for Larry's wife and musical collaborator, Jenny Cassidy. Sadly, Jenny died in 2004. Soldiering on, they took the decision to ask New Order if they could have the Blackpool support slot in October 2006.

'It came about because I'd heard about the gig when it was advertised on the radio,' says Section 25 drummer Vin Cassidy. 'We'd promoted Joy Division's Blackpool gigs early on. We promoted their last one before Ian topped himself. I thought, we've always been involved with them, now we're active again, why not? We asked and they said yes. It was important to us. It's been therapeutic for me. I was completely fucked up with drugs towards the end of the band. To get back involved with music is quite a big step for me. I'm twelve years clean and sober. Quite scary.'

With family and friends there as their own 'support', Section 25 took to the stage of the cavernous Empress Ballroom and played a loop-heavy set of electronica. 'The best part for me was seeing Bernard,' says Vin. 'I'd always got on well with Bernard. I was more nervous about seeing him than playing. He was very gracious, he made a point of coming to our dressing room, having a chat for half an hour. He didn't have to do that. He's always been alright with us.'

2007 was a key year for Bernard, for New Order and for Joy Division. 2006 had been the year of punk – easy history means that thirtieth anniversaries are very difficult to pass up. Britain's *Mojo* magazine had already declared 2007 'The Year of Joy Division' on its January front cover and even the *Sunday Times* 'Style' section had put the word on the street that the Joy Division 'look' – skinny ties and 'serious' side-parted hair – was *the* thing for boys to be seen in this season. Everything seemed to have been carefully put in place for maximum impact and benefit: there was the movie *Control* to be premiered at the Berlin Film Festival in February, a series of repackaged re-releases timed to retail at specific points, then a documentary chronicling the life and times of Joy Division, written by journalist and author Jon Savage. A lot of time and money had been spent making sure that this particular piece of easy history did not go by unnoticed or unmarked.

Thirty years after Warsaw became Joy Division, Bernard Sumner continued to fulfill his role as leader of New Order. It's his band and he calls the shots.

Peter Hook sometimes feigns scenarios wherby he lives in fear of his old schoolmate. They live quite close to each other – the Salford half of New Order have seen the light and now live in Cheshire – but geography aside, they share so much history that it's always been hard to imagine them apart. 'We went to school together,' Hook said of Sumner in *Q*. 'We saw the Sex Pistols together. You can't just walk away from things like that.' Off the record though, Peter Hook can be quite harsh about Bernard Sumner. You may recall, one interviewee checked with Hook to see if it was okay to co-operate with me on this book. 'It's fine,' Hook told them. 'Bernard'll never read it – he can't fuckin' read.'

Despite hard times and harsh words – or maybe even because of them – the three remaining members of Joy Division, who became New Order because they didn't quite seem to know what else to do ... continued. Maybe it's a healthy dose of what Haçienda designer Ben Kelly would call *inside/outside tension* that binds things together. Militarian Stephen Morris – a collector of tanks no less – is rumoured to have the gun turret of one of his collection permanently pointed at Bernard's house.

After finishing this latest slew of UK dates, New Order headed for South America and promptly split up.

Apparently.

During an interview with Buenos Airies newspaper *Pagina 12,* Peter Hook seemed to effectively announce the end of the band. 'We've been together for 29 years, I don't believe another year would be of importance, truthfully. We still hate each other. It's a question of love-hate.' Hook's feelings were seemingly backed up by Stephen Morris: 'This is a strange time to be New Order ... it was good a couple of years ago when everyone was saying we were "Godlike Geniuses" and the fans recognized the band. In a certain sense, there are now many New Orders around and we're the old guys in the neighborhood. I could say there won't be New Order for a couple of years, but ... we're bad at planning things, so let's see what happens.'

The interview set the internet buzzing and the comments were picked up by entertainment news outlets around the world. It was claimed that something had been lost in translation – aligned to the band's ultra dry sense of humour and tendency to wind up journalists – and that New Order had no plans to call it a day. 'It's the first I've heard of it,' drummer Stephen Morris told the *Manchester Evening News* when he and the rest of the band returned to Britain. 'We've got an album to finish and a movie coming out this year.'

But maybe a different perspective can be found from the front row of that Buenos Aires gig. Adriana Leoni was at the Club Ciadid concert, a big deal for local music fans. 'The show was absolutely amazing, well organized ... perfect. Full of emotion. It was the first time New Order have played in Argentina and you could see how happy Bernard and Hooky were.' From her vantage point at the front, Adriana did notice one thing that was odd. Since the band had reformed, Peter Hook had taken to scrawling messages on his speaker cabinets – 'Salford Rules' was a particular favourite. At the Club Ciudad, Hook had these words written on his amp: 'The End'. 'If that show was the last,' says Leoni, 'I would feel very proud ... but on the other hand, very sad too.'

After the issue had seemingly been smoothed out, Peter Hook then unravelled all the good PR work. While appearing at a literary festival in Wales in March 2007, Hook did a question-and-answer session onstage with 'World In Motion' collaborator Keith Allen. While talking about his planned book on The Haçienda, he took Allen and the small audience at the Laugharne event by surprise by apparently saying that he and Bernard would no longer be working together and that it would appear to be the end of New Order. Even the slickest of PR types would struggle to claim this was lost in translation. In May, Hook did it again. During an interview with Clint Boon on XFM, Hook made it clear that New Order was finished and laid the blame at Bernard Sumner's door: 'Bernard went off for a break with Electronic, but that was different. But it's like the boy who cried wolf this time.'

As usual, the shutters came down and no comment was forthcoming, other than one suggestion from the New Order camp that Hook was just 'messing about.' The fan sites were largely supportive of Hook's heart on the sleeve attitude; many were angered by Bernard Sumner's silence. But as we have learned, if Sumner does not want to talk about something, he doesn't talk about it. That's very much not the case with Peter Hook. 'Because it was me saying it, it was out at last,' Hook later said on his MySpace site, which had opened up for business just a week earlier. 'I'm relieved, [I] really hated carrying on as normal with an awful secret. So, let's move on shall we?' Hardly the words of a man messing about; rather those of a musician calling time on more than thirty years of friendship and collaboration with a heavy heart.

Bernard Sumner: 'After thirty years of being in a group together, I would have thought Hooky would have approached Steve and me directly before going to the press. That's why we made no comment because he didn't tell us. There is more to

*this than meets the eye, Hooky has had some problems and to protect his privacy
I can't go into that. But to put a line under it, Steve and I are still in New Order,
even if we don't ever make another record, we ain't left.'*

'I'm okay with him [Sumner] ... I can only talk about myself,' Hook told
a Brazilian website after dropping the bombshell. 'I felt it was time to stop.
I don't know if the others agree, I've never talked about it with them.
We're in touch with each other through the management. It was a really
tough decision for me, I'm still in mourning. Maybe the others can go on
as New Order.' Now that really is messing about.

A 'hibernation' period seems to have come again for New Order – a
series of shrugs and non-committal words along very similar lines to 1993,
when they went their separate ways ... without officially telling anyone.
'Hiatus' will probably be mentioned at some stage – so will talk of 'taking a
break from each other.' Maybe even 'sabbatical'. Whichever way you slice
it, other than their work on the soundtrack of *Control*, it seems likely that it
will be a long time until you hear from New Order again.

'The rest of the world probably thought that New Order had split
sometime at the end of the 1980s/early 1990s,' says Terry Mason, former
Stiff Kitten, ex-road crew chief and a keen Sumner observer since those
Salford schooldays of the 1960s. 'It's only the band and their management
and record companies that have been in denial. Perhaps if they did actually
admit to splitting up – after all there's nothing to prevent them reforming –
it would actually give them the personal freedom to really go out into the
world and totally commit to other projects, rather than having New Order
hanging about them as their 'day jobs'.'

Which leaves us with the question, what next for Bernard Sumner?

Tony Wilson says the reason that he was so attracted to Bernard and Joy
Division when he first saw them perform at Rafter's disco in Manchester in
1978, was that he believed that they were not on stage because they wanted
to be, but because, 'they had no fucking choice.' Today, Wilson believes
that it's right for Sumner to end his role as a performer, the role that
Wilson himself had a hand in Bernard taking on; he should be using his
talents in ways other than on stage touring the world with New Order.
'Put someone in a room and get them to listen to 'Blue Monday',' says
Wilson today, 'and they'll say "Fine, he is a great producer." And maybe in
the latter part of his career, he'll think, *That'll be nice*. He doesn't have to do
it [touring] anymore.'

'I only hope he can start enjoying his life,' offers Terry Mason. 'Every
photo I've seen of him for the past couple of decades has had him looking

like he's just come from a lemon eating competition. There's no point in saying he should do whatever he wants – he's already done that for the past twenty-odd years, and that doesn't seem to have made him happy. He should turn off his phone, put an 'Out of Office' response on his email, and just get on his boat and do nothing. Once he's well and truly bored with that – and knowing Barney that could take a while – he can then do something else. If he does decide he wants to do something musically, the technology is all there whereby he can do what he wants without leaving the house, he can run it as a cottage industry ... shunning record labels and commercial constraints.'

In fact, by early summer 2007, Bernard Sumner did move on and announced a new musical collaboration. May of that year saw the first performance of *Shimmer,* a collaboration between Bernard and the *So Many Words* theatre group. It took place at The Studio Theatre in Salford's Lowry Centre. *So Many Words* is made up of members of Oakwood Youth Club – part of the school Bernard visited in 2005. The members of the company all have learning difficulties. The visit to Oakwood two years earlier had a lasting effect on Sumner – more than the pupils and staff at the school will ever know.

CONFUSION FOURTEEN: BARNEY'S ANGELS

'The thing is David,' said New Order's firm but charming manager Rebecca Boulton during a meeting at her home in Chorlton, south Manchester, 'will anyone actually learn what Bernard's like from reading this book?'

Well, yes, I think they will, actually. Mainly because we knew so little about him before. Up until now, he's been a cypher in the city of Manchester and within the world of music. A famous man, a vital player in a key story …yet a mystery. As we now know, although Salford would claim him as their own, Bernard Sumner was actually born in Manchester.

Typical – Salford does the work, Manchester gets the credit. But it's Manchester – and its unique desire to punch far above its cultural weight – that is the only place that could have provided the backdrop to our story of *Confusion*.

I've lived in Manchester for 80 per cent of my life. I've seen it get blown up – twice – and I've seen it expand and excel as a result. I've worked in it and been beaten up in it – often at the same time. I've gotten drunk in it and I've dried out in it. So unsurprisingly, I – like so many others who've had similar Mancunian experiences – have an opinion on the place. So here goes: Manchester's residents are pop culture hungry like no other city; so much so that if true stories are short on the ground, they'll go for the legend instead. Mancunians love nothing better than a good *myth*.

Bernard Sumner has provided many of those for us over the last half a century, mainly thanks to the cloak of silence and secrecy that has been stoically maintained around him throughout that time. Here's a man who'd been in the public eye for thirty years, yet we knew only the sparsest of details about him – a key pop culture figure whose origins, life and times have been a blank. From his family background to events at the Lesser Free Trade Hall; from the death of Ian Curtis to the anonymous success of New Order; from The Haçienda to his representations on the cinema screen – all the stuff of myth. We may not have known a great deal about him – until now that is – but Sumner himself appears very self-contained on the subject: 'I know what I am – I'm my own person. I know exactly what I'm like. And I'm my own worst critic. I know what my faults are and I know what my good points are.'

So, what might these points be?

Where are the markers that might help us make sense of Bernard Sumner?

The first key point is obviously his background. The Lower Broughton of his youth has all but gone. The sci-fi promises of a better future never came; it's one of the few areas of Greater Manchester that has seriously declined in the last thirty years. When Sumner lived in Alfred Street, Lower Broughton was bustling and busy with 12,000 people proud to call themselves residents. Today, only 2,000 people live in Lower Broughton. The reason for the rapid population decline is simple: no one wants to live there. The area has been battered by crime, health problems and unemployment. Not my words – that's the assessment of Salford City Council. As Manchester boomed after the bomb in 1996 and whole sections of Salford became *des res* with the redevelopment of the docklands, Lower Broughton, tucked in a bend of the River Irwell, was forgotten about. It now rubs up along Salford University and provides the amazingly diverse students who study there some tales of living in 'The 'Hood' for when they return to the Home Counties.

But help for the area, however late it may be, is now at hand. A plan to spend £500 million on Lower Broughton is being rolled out – three and a half thousand new houses are central to the new look area, along with shops and leisure facilities – even a new primary school. The billboards are going up as I write.

They've even got a catchy name for it: *New* Broughton. The adverts are promising *superbia* lifestyles for those who buy into the scheme. It's very different from Bernard's days spent dodging in and out of the bomb shelters with the Grimshaws.

Bernard Sumner's done alright for himself.

But plenty of working-class lads from tasty areas have made good. The pop charts and football pitches of Britain are full of them. What makes Sumner stand out is the unique household that he grew up in, the way disability played such an overriding part in his young life and the fact that he's *never* mentioned it. Bernard Sumner was raised in a two-up, two-down house shared with a disabled mother, a disabled adoptive father and his grandparents. In thirty years in the public eye, he's never even hinted at the true nature of his upbringing. Look at the 'celebrities' of today and the tell-all culture that they've created. Barely a stubbed toe passes by without being accompanied by a hefty article about 'my pain' by the toe's owner. It's the modern disease to use misfortune to one's own advantage. Not an accusation that could ever be levelled at Bernard Sumner.

The abiding image for me from this whole story is that of Bernard and New Order playing at Oakwood School in Salford in 2005, doing an hour-long set and posing for pictures with the kids at the special needs facility. Anyone else would surely have been tempted to publicly show empathy with the pupils through their own experiences – or at least lean over to a member of staff and say, 'D'ya know, my mum and my step-dad were both disabled.' It would have made a perfect headline to the story. 'NEW ORDER STAR'S SECRET HEARTACHE'.

Not Bernard Sumner.

His way seems to have been to do things very much on the quiet. From helping other bands get a leg up the ladder, to sanctioning cash to Terry Mason in his hour of need, to giving a hefty support slot to Section 25, to playing a gig for disabled kids without letting on about the way disability has played such a dramatic part in his own life; everything is done very much on the quiet.

The next point is his extraordinary reserve of perseverance. The benchmarks for rock 'n' roll misfortune tend to be Def Leppard and The Charlatans, two bands always referred to when examples are needed of things going very badly wrong. The Charlatans, led by Salford-born Tim Burgess, managed a bass player with a nervous breakdown, the loss of their guitarist, the jailing and eventual death of keyboard player Rob Collins and a hefty dose of financial problems. Sheffield's Def Leppard – formed at almost exactly the same as Warsaw – had to sack founding member Pete Willis, managed to continue after drummer Rick Allen lost an arm in a road smash and guitarist Steve Allen died. Both carried on, wearing their war wounds with pride.

Bernard Sumner's obstacles outstrip them all. A uniquely difficult and different childhood; persevering through the suicide of a friend and fellow band member to take on a role he clearly neither wanted nor relished; divorce from his teenage sweetheart; financial mismanagement on a grand scale with fortunes won and lost; propping open the doors of a vastly unpopular club until the world catches up and it becomes one of the most popular; attracting, then defying Manchester's ganglords who saw the club as a prize for the taking; a very public grapple with depression that's served up as entertainment on television; the deaths of his mentor/producer Martin Hannett and that of mentor/manager Rob Gretton; the collapse of the record label that launched him; the closure of the prized club that helped define a generation; the disintegration of the band he had steered through to even greater success and the loss of teenage friendships as a result of those pressures; then in 2007, the serious illness of another key mentor, Tony Wilson; and finally, the end of the road for his relationship with Peter Hook. An astonishing catalogue of events that would test the mettle of anyone: Bernard Sumner versus the world.

Musically, what Sumner wanted to do was stand at the back and play the synthesiser, but history didn't allow it. It's little wonder he was reluctant to take over from Ian Curtis after the singer's death in 1980; it was surely rock music's most thankless task.

The grimness of events that led to Curtis' death is apparent from the coroner's report; the unpleasant aspects of Curtis's character are clear from Deborah Curtis' accounts and those of Terry Mason. But Sumner has always been Ian Curtis' biggest champion, self-deprecating about his own skills compared to his predecessor's and keen from the early days onwards to avoid deifying the singer, when all around were clambering to do just that. 'He was not a weird guy,' Sumner said in 1981, when he finally broke his silence about Curtis' death in *Melody Maker*. 'He was a normal person like anyone else, that was the thing about it, but a very emotional person, and some people can show their emotions, but he didn't show his – except on rare occasions in his lyrics.'

When Ian Curtis committed suicide, Sumner seems to have done everything in his power to try to avoid taking his place – from asking the likes of Crispy Ambulances's Alan Hempsall if he fancied the job, to hiding behind the courage provided by licorice-flavoured French spirits. He clearly never hungered for centre-stage.

'Life toughens you up,' stated Sumner in *Select* in 1993. 'It teaches you that sometimes to sort people out, you have to be a twat. Business-wise, if you're nice all the time, people view that as a weakness. I think you've got to be a bit of a twat to be a lead singer really. I've grown to fit the job.'

He's also needed to grow a broad set of shoulders and a medium-to-thick covering of skin, to survive the last thirty years in the public eye. Sumner's been critically mauled for everything from his singing and guitar playing to his song-writing and lyrics. Even Tony Wilson – and he's a Cambridge fucking graduate lest we forget – finds it difficult sometimes to grasp what Sumner is getting at with his seemingly simple, sing-song lyrics.

'It's a kind of nonsense poetry,' says Wilson, of Sumner's way with words. 'It's Bernard's natural poetic voice, which works a treat. Peter Saville [New Order sleeve designer] wouldn't agree with that. We have rows about it all the time. Peter will quote verbatim a modern New Order lyric and quoted flat they can sound utterly, utterly appalling. Then I will quote something like, "Pretending not to see his gun, I said, Let's go out and have some fun," (from 'The Perfect Kiss') which is an extraordinary lyric about AIDS.

Three years afterwards, I discover what it's about. It's a song about AIDS.' It's generally accepted that, when it comes to lyrics, he's no Ian Curtis. The first person who accepts this appears to be Bernard Sumner.

As a live performer, Bernard can – by his own admission – be inconsistent. The early gigs were Pernod-fuelled affairs, a habit that seems to have lasted some time. 'That's the thing with New Order,' says former Haçienda DJ Eastwick. 'They never had anyone reigning them in, which has contributed to their reputation of being a really hit-and-miss live band. 'Cos they never had anyone saying, "That gig was fucking *appalling*." It almost became their thing: "We're going to see New Order ... will it be the good one or the bad one?" They never had someone from the record company or a manager after the big gig going, "Look, you can't fucking do that, telling the audience they're a bunch of cunts during the gig." They had Rob Gretton, who was effectively like a member of the band who probably encouraged them ... then they'd go back to the label [Factory] and there's Tony Wilson. "Errr, Bernard told the audience they were cunts! ... "Brilliant, the best news I've had all day!"'

Added to this has been Sumner's desire to try out new, raw ideas and material live, sometimes before they're actually ready. 'We always know how we want them [songs] to sound,' said Sumner in *The Face*, confirming that the desire to drag material on stage as soon as possible has been standard practice almost from the start of New Order's career. 'The way we write a song is usually to start off by improvising stuff in the rehearsal room. Then we take it out live. Sometimes you haven't got any lyrics so you just make up some garbage. Then you listen to the live tapes, write some more words and go back and rehearse some more. By the time we record it, we pretty well know how it should be.' Fearless, some might say – dangerous, others might counter.

'I've got a lot of bootlegs and you can hear versions of early songs,' says Eastwick. 'There's a version of 'Perfect Kiss' that's called 'I've Got A Cock Like The M1'. He's obviously written the first half of the first verse, got a drumbeat and the songs like [singing], 'I've got a cock like the M1, Da Da Da, whoo!' He's rehearsing on stage.' 'His cock *is* as big as the M1,' adds Peter Hook helpfully in Q. 'He's got services on it. There's a Kentucky Fried Chicken and a Costa Coffee.'

Bernard's relationship with Peter Hook is as vital to our story as it is confusing. Childhood friends who appear to drive each other mad. The loud one and the quiet one. The sociable bass player and the withdrawn singer. To Bernard, it was a relief when New Order 'split' in 1993 – to Hook it was a tragedy. I asked Tony Wilson what the main difference between the two is: 'Hooky is really annoying, but doesn't realise he's being annoying. Bernard is annoying and is fully aware of the fact.'

When the idea of New Order reforming was mooted, Hook offered this, also to Q: 'Pottsy [David Potts of Hook's Monaco band] was telling me, "You'll only ever really be happy with Bernard, give it another go." It was like a mistress telling you to give the wife another go.' But it's unusual to see Sumner and Hook together off-stage. If a PR job needs doing, it tends to be Stephen Morris and Hook who are despatched to play the card on TV and radio shows. Both can deal out blokey good humour to order, with Hook as the maverick, grumpy Disco Dad and Morris as the quietly anarchic, sarcastic uncle. Sumner is usually otherwise engaged. Terry Mason is adamant that New Order was always Bernard's group, but the singer and bass player have often been at odds, from those very first rehearsals at 11 Alfred Street to the messy debacle of Hook announcing New Order's demise in 2007. According to New Order guitarist Phil Cunningham, the pairing can still be as volatile as it ever was. He recounts an incident during a gig at Glasgow's Barrowlands, during a tour to promote 2001's *Get Ready* album, that started over a decision to drop 'Blue Monday' – and escalated. 'It really kicked off backstage with Hooky and Bernard,' says Cunningham. 'They had a real 'Oasis' moment. Champagne bottles through mirrors and stuff. By the time the argument had died down, it was, "Alright, I'll go and do it." But by that time, of course, the place was empty because everyone had left. It must have been twenty minutes later.'

Bernard Sumner: '[The argument] was about on-stage volume. I have tinnitus.'

Lyricist, performer, song-writer and bottle chucker – there's one more role: Sumner's guise as a producer is perhaps the most overlooked one of his career. His obsessive attention to detail has cost him dear, but some associates believe it's his most unrecognised and under-used skill. 'I imagine that if he's not too bored and too rich he will produce something,' says Tony Wilson. 'Hannett was one of the greatest producers in history ... but so is Bernard Sumner. But nobody knows that.'

Bernard Sumner now lives some miles away from the streets of Lower Broughton, in north Cheshire. This area is favoured by the business classes and top end footballers; local shopkeepers shed a tear when David and Victoria Beckham moved out a few years ago. Resident Bernard Sumner is now a father of four. His other passion though, is the sea.

'I do own a boat and go on holiday on boats,' he confirmed in *Observer Music Monthly*. 'I like the sea, always have. I don't really know why – I suppose it's wild and somewhat dangerous, and when you sleep on a boat it feels like the earth is breathing. In my job, I've stayed in plenty of hotels and I'm always with other people, so the boat is the opposite of all that. I wouldn't write a song about that though, as no one would be able to relate to it, and it would be a bit corny.'

'Yes, Barney as the yachtsman,' says Tony Wilson, genuinely perplexed why a lad from Lower Broughton, spitting distance from the River Irwell, should feel the call of the ocean. 'The fact that the rest of the group would allow him to sail them ... they go a *long way* out to sea. From LA, they'll go south of the Mexican border. Very strange.'

Tony Wilson finishes his white wine, thanks me for lunch and get's ready to untether his unruly dog. A few days later he will be in hospital, having a kidney removed after a diagnosis of cancer. I've interviewed Wilson on half a dozen occasions and it's not easy to get a word in edgeways when he's in full flow. It's even harder to stop him in his tracks; I managed it with one final question. 'Is Bernard Sumner your friend?'

'... Yes. Yes,' he blinks, puzzled at first. 'He's someone you've shared thirty years work with ... shared dreams and visions with. I'd do anything for Bernard,' says Tony Wilson. 'And I think he'd do anything for me as well. Last December I turned on the [local] Christmas lights for him, because he was away in Wales picking a yacht up.'

> *Bernard Sumner: 'Sailing is my antedote to the hedonistic days of The Haçienda – you've gotta do something on a Saturday night.'*

Yachts – a recurring theme. Perhaps the building that became The Haçienda caught his eye for very different reasons than those of his colleagues at Factory Records. It was, after all, a yacht showroom, incongruously sited in the centre of Manchester. Now it'll cost you a quarter of million pounds to buy a two bedroom apartment on the site of The Haçienda. But don't try to find these backdrops to our story; most of them, like The Haçienda, are long gone. The Lesser Free Trade Hall is now a top flight hotel; Pips is part of a smart shopping square; the last night of The Electric Circus is a distant memory; Rafters, the scene of Joy Division's angry breakthrough gig in 1978 remains – it's now called The Music Box and caters for the young metal and dance crowds.

Had it not been for Bernard Sumner, Manchester's dance crowd – and its equivalent in cities across the world – might be spending Saturday nights in very different ways. Whether he realised he was providing it or not, at the time, the financial wedge that he and New Order laid on to hold open the doors or The Haçienda may well be the most culturally important thing that he's ever been involved in. Had he and the rest of the band realised just how hefty a wedge that would turn out to be, they might have baulked at the task. Maybe it was for the best that they were largely in the dark about it. 'As businessmen, we're shite,' confirms Sumner. 'Give me a tenner and I'll turn it into minus ten grand in half an hour.' Peter Hook is currently working on his own book, specifically about what went right and what went wrong with The Haçienda.

Money and its ebb and flow has been a constant theme through our story. Whatever the rights and wrongs of how the cash got there, the fact that New Order's money allowed The Haçienda to ride out the lean years – and they were *very* lean – meant that the gap was bridged between the goth years and the dance explosion. The drugs and the technology finally caught up with The Haçienda – had it closed in the mid-1980s, would the planets have lined up anyway in a different city? Very unlikely. If you have a problem with that, just remember that rock and dance were in different worlds at the time – they rarely, if ever, came together. Unless, of course, you'd just been to the toilet in Pip's nightspot in Manchester – stand in the right place and you got disco in one ear and punk in the other, remember. If nothing else, translating that experience into an internationally influential series of records with Joy Division, Electronic and New Order provided a key series of pointers for the ecstasy generation; it simply wouldn't have happened without Bernard Sumner. But please don't be fooled into believing the myth that The Haçienda was no good before the dance years kicked in. It was great. I was there along with many other stalwarts, it's just that very few other people agreed with us.

Though globally influential, Bernard and New Order were never universally successful. Those who've been involved claim that this is the band's own fault, particularly in America. 'They killed the fanbase,' says former friend and road chief Terry Mason. 'U2 figured it out years ago. To do well in this business, all you have to do is show your face in America, minimum every two years, because they have a two-year college cycle. Not rocket science. I'd see people that would tell me what ludicrous things had been happening. They [New Order] wouldn't speak to each other for years. I was told that Barney would see Steve and Gillian walking down Market Street [Manchester's pedestrianised shopping area] and crossed over to the other side to avoid them …

Bernard Sumner: 'Not true, I just did not see them.'

'... They'd stopped doing things, they had years where they didn't see each other, an offer would come in and they'd have a meeting. The opportunities were there and were ignored or turned down. The things that they turned down and what they could have led to ...'

Businesswise though, attitudes did change as time went by. A version of 'Blue Monday' with orange juice-endorsing lyrics was shelved in the Rob Gretton years, for fear of it shredding the band's carefully engineered credibility; the song was recently to be heard on an advert for Mars bars.

The gang wars of the Gunchester years that seeped from the city's outlying areas and in through the doors of The Haçienda have now also been absorbed into the Great Manchester Myth. The shootings and machete attacks have become the stuff of legend and the cyclical nature of youth culture means the same issues plague the city's streets today; back then, they sold tee-shirts celebrating that famous Strangeways siege, yet in 2007 you can buy 'Gunchester' shirts and even fake bullet-proof vests. The problems Bernard Sumner had to face are largely still there.

Then there's the N word. *Nazi*. It's an enormous insult wherever you're from. Bernard grew up in an area still physically scarred by the bombing raids of the Second World War, in a household where Grandad John's war memorabilia took pride of place in the back room of 11 Alfred Street, a street that still had those bomb shelters when Sumner was a child. Bernard and Peter Hook would scour the scouting shops close to Manchester's Piccadilly train station, looking for Germanic clothing for shock value. There's his agreement to change the band's name from Warsaw to Joy Division and the umlaut encrusted sleeve of their first EP – a Bernard Albrecht design, no less. Not to mention the discarded opportunity to put things right when the name, New Order, was chosen. There's no evidence to suggest that Sumner is anything in fact but apolitical – as conclusively confirmed by Terry Mason – so the least he can be accused of is naivety. Unlike many sections of Greater Manchester, Salford was not a culturally or racially diverse area in the 1960s and 1970s – compared to many places, it still isn't today. Is it possible to be genuinely blind to the offence that could be caused by your actions, if race hadn't played a major role in your life so far? Maybe. Ill-chosen? More than likely. Nazi? No.

A noted perfectionist but with a poor work ethic, perhaps?

Apolitical yet dogged by accusations of Nazism.

The man who does good deeds on the quiet yet freezes out those who cross him.

Sometimes desperately short of money yet uncompromising, even if cash is there on a plate. *Confusing.*

Bernard Sumner: 'I haven't got a poor work ethic, I work fucking hard.
I just don't like long tours – I like to see my family and,
after what happened to my parental family, is that a crime?'

Bernard Sumner has had a considerable journey and by no means all of it has been a smooth ride. So when things aren't going quite your way, it's always good to know that someone out there loves you. Joy Division and New Order are the kind of bands that the internet could have been designed for, steeped as they are in conspiracy, controversy and continuing obsessive interest; each website seemingly has the inside track on what it all means. Theories are expounded upon, muscles of fan authenticity are flexed and the tiniest glint of weakness is pounced upon and kicked to bits. There is, however, one exception. As we've kept to the less travelled route so far on our story of *Confusion*, let's stick with it as we reach the end; for a very different take on Bernard Sumner and his place in the grand scheme of things, give yourself a treat and head for *Barneysangels.com*.

Established in 2006 by 26-year-old Ohio teacher Jennifer Vaughn, *Barney's Angels* is a blessed relief from the hard-core earnestness found elsewhere on the net: it's the self-styled home of 'girlie chat' about Bernard Sumner and – to very much a lesser extent – New Order, Electronic and Joy Division. They discuss Bernard's hair, his legs, his smile, his nipples and sometimes even his music. It works – as Tony Wilson might say – on several levels. '*Barney's Angels* is indeed an "I Heart Barney" site,' says Jennifer, loud and proud. 'That's its primary intention. But I want *Barney's Angels* to be a place where people have the option to talk about anything they want [to] concerning the band. *Barney's Angels* offers visitors the chance to discuss topics concerning Bernard Sumner that would be off-limits at other sites, so that is what the members and visitors take advantage of. The majority of the members are women of all ages and from around the world. We have members who are teenagers, members who are in their forties and fifties, and every age in between. I love the fact that these diverse people from every inch of the globe can converge and share a single passion with one another. Most of all, the members are intelligent, witty and enjoy having a good time. The primary reason people visit *Barney's Angels* is because they are allowed to discuss topics about Bernard Sumner and New Order that are either ridiculed or simply not permitted at other New Order websites. We seldom delve into anything too serious or bizarre, but discussing Bernard Sumner's best haircut is not appreciated everywhere like it is at *Barney's Angels*! On a selfish note, I just enjoy being able to communicate with other New Order fans. I live in the Midwest of America so I am not exactly surrounded by others who share my interest in Bernard Sumner and New Order.'

Perhaps Jennifer and her fellow Angels have hit upon something here. It may even be something that just about everyone else – myself included – has so far missed by a nautical mile. Maybe it's not about whether he's a great singer or not, if he's as good a frontman as Ian Curtis or if he's a blinding guitarist, a canny businessman or a fool who's been parted from his money too easily? Is he a great lyricist or actually a technically brilliant producer masquerading as a musician? What if none of that's important? Perhaps it's all very simple and Jennifer Vaughn and her fellow Angels – they have tee shirts, mouse mats and everything – actually have a better grasp on this than anyone.

Maybe some people just 'Heart' Bernard Sumner.

And there's nothing confusing about that.

LIVE TRANSMISSION – OUTRO

'New Or-DAH ... New Or-DAH ... New Or-DAH,' chant the waccy-baccied crowd. Steam is rising from the bullet heads of the faithful and its moistening the gold leaf of the rococo ceiling high above the stage of the Empress Ballroom, Blackpool.

'This next song is very beautiful,' says Bernard Sumner. 'It's also our last song tonight. It's called 'Love Will Tear Us Apart'.

A man in his fifties from Lower Broughton, Salford transports the room to another time. It will be one of the last times that New Order perform in Britain.

Joy Division's breakthrough song, previously sung by Ian Curtis, throbs around the gigantic space. Its woefully sad tale of passion withered by aching familiarity is offset by the shimmering glamour of the Eurobeat pulse that accompanies it.

Bold, sharp colours and angles framed by apparently bleak and forbidding backdrops – it's never an easy look to pull off.

Cast of *Confusion* – A Catch-Up

Here are those who have played a part in this tale of *Confusion*. Who are they and – where appropriate – where are they now? (Alphabetically listed to avoid ... confusion):

Keith Allen
The confrontational comedian is now on teatime TV as the Sheriff of Nottingham in the BBC's Robin Hood *series. Has tried further football anthems with Fat Les and once considered suing Skinner and Baddiel for loss of earnings after they re-released that other England footy anthem, 'Three Lions'.*

Ron Asheton
The man who first thought that New Order would be a good name for a band is now back with a reformed Stooges.

Tim Ashworth
Expert on Salford history – works at the Local History Library, part of Salford Museum near the city's university.

Tom Atencio
New Order's former North American business manager is co-producer of 2007's Joy Division *documentary.*

Susan Barlow
Bernard's former wife now works for Salford Council. She declined – politely mind – to be interviewed for this book, but she did manage to clear up one point for me. Was she really at that Sex Pistols' gig at the Lesser Free Trade Hall on June 4, 1976? 'As far as The Gig That Changed The World is concerned,' she told me, 'I Swear I Was There!'

Karl Bartos
The former Kraftwerk man and collaborator on Electronic's 'Prozac' album is still making music, DJ-ing and also teaches Auditory Media Design at the Berlin University of the Arts.

John Berry
The lad from Salford Technical High School now works at United Utilities in Warrington. 'Good coin,' he says, approvingly. Through the interviews for this book, he is now back in touch with his old schoolmate, Terry Mason.

Rebecca Boulton
New Order co-manager and current go-between for Bernard and Peter Hook.

John Brierley
The former owner of Cargo Studios in Rochdale has returned to his original profession – he's now a cameraman with Sky TV.

Ian Brown
The teenage Joy Division fan and Stone Roses singer is now a solo artist with varying degrees of success but unswerving levels of self-belief.

Steve Burke
Ranch barman and co-creator of Shy Talk fanzine. Lives in Moss Side and works at Manchester Airport. When I asked why his fanzine was called Shy Talk he told me, 'It was my dad's idea. It works on two levels … Shy Talk or Shite Talk.'

Larry Cassidy
Now playing live and recording with Section 25 again.

Vin Cassidy
Back behind the drums with Section 25 with brother Larry.

Paul Cons
The former Haçienda promoter now lives in London, but has a club in Manchester … called South. He is a founder of The House of Homosexual Culture, a series of events that explore gay and lesbian ideas.

Kevin Cummins
The former member of The Negatives is now a noted rock photographer.

Phil Cunningham
The New Order guitarist is a producer of acts like The Shores and has returned as guitarist with the reformed Marion, the delicate Macclesfield band that managed to swerve major – and surely deserved – success in the 1990s.

Deborah Curtis
Widow of Ian Curtis is co-producer of the Control film alongside Tony Wilson, for whom she had some harsh words in her book Touching From A Distance.

Ian Curtis
Died in 1980. Listening to the few remaining audio recordings of Curtis today, it's amazing how old he sounds for a man in his early twenties; like a contented pensioner in a pub.

Natalie Curtis
Ian and Deborah's daughter, now a photographer working in Manchester.

'Crazy' Mike
Went with Bernard, Peter Hook, Terry Mason and John Berry to see the Sex Pistols in Manchester in 1976. Didn't like it. Now a fireman.

Sarah Dalton
The former Haçienda crimper – known as "The Vision" – is married to Bernard Sumner.

Andrew Davis
The young fan with a camera at New Order's Trinity Hall gig in Bristol is a dry stone waller on Prince Charles' estate in Bath. 'You see him about quite a lot,' he says of the future King. 'He's alright.'

Howard Devoto
The organiser of the Sex Pistols gig at the Lesser Free Trade Hall in 1976 and the first ever post-punk has recorded an album with Pete Shelley under the name Buzzkunst and worked as a photo archivist.

Steve Diggle
Now maintains a solo recording and gigging career alongside his responsibilities in Buzzcocks.

Elliot Eastwick
The DJ who played the last record on the last night of The Haçienda. Still DJs and works on art projects and installations. Also does music therapy for kids with learning difficulties. 'You do stuff like recording the sounds their bodies make, multi-tracking it and making an electronic rhythmic track out of a little yawn or a creak or a heart beat. Brilliant fun.'

Andrew Eastwood
The Joy Division fan who became a roadie and programming technician with New Order and Electronic now works in IT and is a font of knowledge on all things Factory.

Gillian Gilbert
Lives on the outskirts of Macclesfield with Stephen Morris and Grace.

Iain Grey
The early musical collaborator of Ian Curtis and Morrissey is still involved in music, playing on the cabaret circuit.

Rob Gretton
The late former Manchester Airport worker, DJ and manager is still a revered figure in the Manchester music scene; many of his notes and artefacts are being collated and preserved for future exhibition.

Martin Hannett
The Joy Division and New Order producer died in 1991. In 24 Hour Party People, he was played by Andy Serkis, the actor responsible for two other striking screen characters, King Kong and Gollum.

Alan Hempsall
Works in publishing and has toured with a reformed Crispy Ambulance. I told him that, of the people I'd interviewed so far about Bernard Sumner, no one had exactly gushed about him. 'I'll gush,' said Hempsall. 'He's a sweetie.'

Chris Hewitt
The Cargo Studios landlord and Haçienda soundman has lived his life for rock music and now runs Ozit-Morpheus Records. I asked how I should describe him for this part of the book: 'Describe me as PA/music shop, recording studio and record label owner, festival mogul or impresario.'

Paolo Hewitt
Hewitt spent ten years in the music press and was the only person to write a sensible review of Closer. *He's the author of* The Looked After Kid: Memoirs from a Children's Home.

Annik Honoré
After a long period of silence, Ian Curtis' lover has assisted in the making of the film Control, *taking about her time with the singer before he died.*

Peter Hook
The tireless bassist can be found regularly playing DJ sets around the world. He's also working with Freebass with fellow four stringers Mani [Stone Roses] and Andy Rourke [The Smiths]. 'I know Bernard better than anyone,' he told me. 'Apart from Bernard, obviously.'

Oliver James
The TV psychologist behind Bernard's Prozac experiment can now be seen helping viewers on ITV1's This Morning *programme.*

Mike Joyce
The former drummer with The Smiths is currently playing with Vinny Peculiar and presents a show on Manchester radio station The Revolution.

Ben Kelly
Runs BKD (Ben Kelly Design) from offices in London. Kelly's design for The Haçienda still takes pride of place on the company's website.

Frank 'Foo Foo' Lamarr
Clubland drag artiste and owner of Manchester venues The Palace and The Ranch. When Frank died in 2003, it was the lead story on Granada News.

Adriana Leoni
The woman in the front row of the last New Order show in Buenos Aires is a teacher by day. 'I teach Maths in a secondary school,' she says. 'The aim of my life is to have fun, go dancing and listen to music.'

John Lydon
The Artist Formerly Known as Johnny Rotten has reformed the Sex Pistols twice since they split in 1978. Now a TV presenter with wildlife shows being a particular speciality.

Steve Maguire
Saw Joy Division aged 14 at The Electric Circus. 'I'm a taxi driver in Stockport now. I listen to music regularly, but nothing can compare to the sound of Joy Division. It was the best time of my life.'

Johnny Marr

The former Smith and one half of Electronic still continues his apparent quest to play alongside every musician on the planet. His latest collboboration is as guitarist with American band Modest Mouse, who hit the US number 1 spot in 2007.

Terry Mason

After a career in IT Marketing, Terry was between jobs when we spoke for the purposes of this book. 'I always wanted to put fighter pilot on my passport under occupation,' he says. 'No one ever questions it, do they?'

Malcolm McLaren

The former manager of the Sex Pistols lives in Paris and is still working on his much-delayed and highly anticipated autobiography.

Joan Miller

Now aged 79, the organiser of the 1st Leigh Youth Festival has lived in Spain for the last twenty years. 'The best bit of the festival for us was Tony Wilson tapping politely on our portakabin door. "Joan, can I please have a word?" – "Piss off Tony, you're full of shit!" was our chorus in reply. "Okay, I'll try again later." "Oh, come in and have a brew for Christ's sake!"'

Morrissey

The Smiths singer – sat a few rows back from Bernard and friends at the Lesser Free Trade Hall in 1976 – is now a solo artist with varying levels of success. He and his fellow Smiths are expected to be inducted into the Rock And Roll Hall of Fame in 2009.

Geoff Moore

The director of Granada Reports, So It Goes *and* What's On *now runs his own production company. He remembers the rows with Tony Wilson in the 1970s. 'Sometimes he'd get his own way, for example, about The Clash ... who I thought were crap. He was right. When was I right? XTC. Mink de Ville. Siouxsie And The Banshees.'*

Paul Morley

The NME writer and member of The Negatives is now an author and TV pundit.

Steve and Stuart Murray
The irrepressible Murray brothers still play as Fast Cars and are disproportionately popular in Japan. 'Power pop?' says Steve, 'We practically invented it.'

Stephen Morris
The Joy Division and New Order drummer is now an avid collector of military vehicles.

James Anthony Pearson
The young actor went straight from the set of the Control *movie — where he played Bernard Sumner — to* Pinocchio *in Edinburgh. Where he played Pinocchio.*

Leroy Richardson
The former Haçienda manager now runs the One Central Street club in Manchester — his former job can still cause problems to this day. 'I was advised not to apply for the licence myself for my club because of my connections with The Haçienda. There's still that edge.'

Gonnie Rietveld
Quando Quango's Gonnie is now Dr Hillegonda Rietveld, Reader in Dance Culture at London South Bank University. She is, if you will, a House Doctor. Oh, please yourselves ...

Shaun Ryder
Slimmed down and currently in 'it's great when you're straight' mode, Ryder is back playing under the Happy Mondays' banner and recently had his appalling teeth sorted out on Granada Reports.

Jon Savage
The journalist and author recently released an account of youth culture called Teenage *and has scripted the 2007* Joy Division *documentary.*

John Simm
The actor who played Bernard Sumner in 24 Hour Party People *has since found mainstream television success in 1970s cop pastiche* Life On Mars. *The police headquarters seen in the series is actually in Stockport, a mere spitting distance from the site of Strawberry Studios.*

Tom Smetham
As well as being an organiser of the 'Versus Cancer' charity gigs, Smetham also makes the radio version of TV show The Tube.

Mark E Smith
He stills holds down his position in The Fall. Which is more than can be said for anyone else who's been in the band.

Pete Shelley
Toured the world with Buzzcocks on the thirtieth anniversary of their performance at the Lesser Free Trade Hall.

Chris Taylor
Bernard's former colleague at Stop Frame and Cosgrove Hall has spent more than 35 years in animation – and when resting between jobs pursues his love of calligraphy at home in the Peak District.

Jennifer Vaughn
The Ohio school teacher runs the 'I Heart Barney' site. 'I think men are shy about visiting Barney's Angels, it is a decidedly feminine site but all are welcome,' she says. 'Maybe I should look into purchasing www.gilliansangels.coom for the men?'

Andy Wake
The teenage follower of Joy Division now runs an events management company with his wife, a former podium dancer at The Haçienda. 'When Ian Curtis died I was just a kid and it was a real shock,' he says. 'Everyone played their Joy Division records and that's where the myth started.'

Paul Welsh
The former editor of Manchester fanzine Penetration *now works in IT. 'I remember in the 1960s, seeing old Teddy Boys in drape coats, brothel creepers and DAs looking about sixty years old and thinking how sad they looked. I think those images created my dislike for nostalgia.'*

Tony Wilson
Now known as Anthony Wilson – but is still called Tony by everyone he meets. Presenter on BBC Radio Manchester, XFM Manchester and Channel M. By the time you read this, he will hopefully be back to full strength doing what he does best – annoying people.

Michael Winterbottom
The prolific director of 24 Hour Party People *is still making populist art house movies, including* A Cock And Bull Story *with Steve Coogan and the music and pop shot opus* 9 Songs.

And finally ...

Bernard Sumner
Finally married Sarah – aka 'The Vision' – in July 2007. Bernard finished his contribution to this book a few days after the wedding ... and then went away sailing.

REFERENCES

I have included all my original interviews conducted for this book, their locations and dates, plus vital or associated books, key websites and information sources for additional quotes.

Tim Ashworth interview – Salford Local History Library, October 2006.
John Berry interview – Manchester city centre, October 2006.
Steve Burke interview – Sainsbury's cafe, Hazel Grove, Stockport, November 2006.
Larry Cassidy interview – Preston, Lancashire, February 2007.
Vin Cassidy interview – Blackpool, April 2007.
Paul Cons interview – Urbis, Manchester, November 2006.
Howard Devoto interview – London, March 2001
Steve Diggle interview – Spice of Life, London, January 2006.
Elliot Eastwick interview – Chorlton, Manchester, November 2006.
Michael Eastwood interview – Didsbury, manchester April 2007.
Alan Hempsall interview – Chorlton, Manchester, October 2006.
Chris Hewitt interview – Northwich, Cheshire, November 2006.
Paolo Hewitt interview – London, February 2007.
Mike Joyce interview – Granada Television, Manchester, May 2002.
Adriana Leoni interview – Buenos Aires, May 2007
Joan Miller interview – Spain, March 2007.
Peter Hook interview – Granada Television, Manchester, May 2001.
Terry Mason interview – Salford, December 2006 and January 2007.
Geoff Moore interview – Granada Television, Manchester, October 2006.
Steve and Stuart Murray interview – Stockport, December 2006
James Anthony Pearson interview – Edinburgh, December 2006.
Leroy Richardson interview – 1 Central Street, Manchester, December 2006.
Hillegonda Rietveld interview – London, December 2006.
Pete Shelley, interview – London, March 2001.
Tom Smetham interview – Chinatown, Manchester, March 2007.
Chris Taylor interview – High Peak, Derbyshire, January 2007.
Jennifer Vaughn interview – Columus, Ohio, January 2007.
Andrew Wake interview – Bury, Greater Manchester, October 2006.
Anthony Wilson interview – *Choice* restaurant Manchester (mini fish and chips, black pudding in batter) December 2006.
Paul Welsh interview – Timperley, south Manchester, November 2006.

The following books, websites and sources are either invaluable references or simply very entertaining.

Touching From a Distance, Deborah Curtis – Faber and Faber 1995.
Gang War, Peter Walsh – Milo Books 2005.
Johnny Marr, The Smiths & the Art of Gun-Slinging, Richard Carman – Independent Music Press, 2006.
Manchester England - Dave Haslam -Fourth Estate 1999

www.cerysmaticfactory.info
Website for all things Factory Records which also produces Scream City, an 'old school' Manchester fanzine.

www.joydiv.com
Joy Division Central – enormous yet growing site featuring detailed band information. Includes details of every gig Warsaw and Joy Division ever played.

www.niagara.edu/neworder
Maintained by Torbjöörn Ivarsson, created by Richard P. Kernin and Dennis Remmer. User-friendly resource that thankfully has no "na na na-na-na" forum attached to it.

www.neworderonline.com
Officially sanctioned site. Packed with detail and an ever changing roster of photos. Includes a comprehensive "na na na-na-na" forum.

www.barneysangels.com
A site for 'girlie chat' about Bernard. Works, as they say, on several layers. Genius.

www.salford.gov.uk
Salford census information, electoral rolls, pub history (no such pub as The Black Swan, actually) and street maps via the Salford Local History Museum.

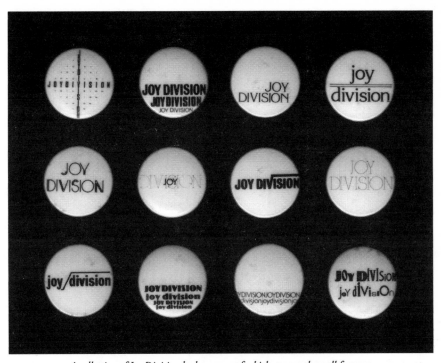

*A collection of Joy Division badges, some of which are worth small fortunes.
Sumner's bands have always provoked obsessive and fiercely loyal followings.*

Discography

UK releases with key b sides/additional tracks/compilations/collaborations.

Joy Division

A Factory Sample
Digital/Glass – Fac2 –1978

SINGLES

An Ideal For Living
Warsaw / No Love Lost / Leaders Of Men / Failures – Enigma PSS 139 1978
Transmission / Novelty – Fac13 1979
Love Will Tear Us Apart / These Days
– Fac23 1980 (1983/1995 reissue/remix)
Atmosphere / The Only Mistake – Fac213 1988

ALBUMS

Unknown Pleasures
FACT 10 1979
*Disorder / Day Of The Lords / Candidate / Insight / New Dawn Fades
/ She's Lost Control / Shadowplay / Wilderness / Interzone
/ I Remember Nothing*

Closer
FACT 25 1980
*Atrocity Exhibition / Isolation / Passover / Colony / A Means To An End
/ Heart & Soul / Twenty Four Hours / The Eternal / Decades*

Still
FACT 40 1981
*Exercise One / Ice Age / The Sound Of Music / Glass / The Only Mistake
/ Walked In Line / The Kill / Something Must Break / Dead Souls / Sister Ray
/ Ceremony / Shadowplay / Means To An End / Passover / New Dawn Fades
/Transmission/Disorder/Isolation/Decades/Digital*

Substance 1987
FACT 200 (Compilation)
*Warsaw / Leaders Of Men / Digital / Autosuggestion / Transmission
/ She's Lost Control / Incubation / Dead Souls / Atmosphere
/ Love Will Tear Us Apart / No Love Lost / Failures / Glass
/ From Safety To Where / Novelty / Komakino / These Days*

Permanent
London 828 624 1995
*Love Will Tear Us Apart / Transmission / She's Lost Control / Shadowplay
/ Day Of The Lords / Isolation / Passover / Heart And Soul
/ Twenty Four Hours / These Days / Novelty / Dead Souls / The Only Mistake
/ Something Must Break / Atmosphere / Love Will Tear Us Apart*

Heart And Soul – London 1997
81 Track box set of outtakes and alternative material from *Unknown
Pleasures* and *Closer* plus rarities and live tracks.

Martin Hannett Personal Mixes
Interstate 10797 2007
Alternative versions, studio chat and synth noodling. Looks like a bootleg
but it's an official release on Interstate.

Live Albums (Official)

Preston 28 February 1980
NMC FAC.D 2.60 1999

Les Bains Douches 18 December 1979
NMC FAC.D 2.61 2001
(These two albums are also available together under the heading *Fractured*)

Live at Leigh Rock Festival 1979
Interstate 2006
*Disorder / Leaders of Men / Colony / Insight / Digital / Dead Souls
/ Shadowplay / She's Lost Control / Transmission/Interzone*
Two disc set also features *OMD / A Certain Ratio / Teardrop Explodes*

Peel Sessions/BBC

1986 Exercise One / Insight / She's Lost Control / Transmission
SFPS 013 Strange Fruit

1987 Love Will Tear Us Apart / Twenty Four Hours / Colony
/ Sound Of Music
SFPS 033 Strange Fruit

1990 – Exercise One / Insight / She's Lost Control / Transmission
/ Love Will Tear Us Apart / Twenty Four Hours / Colony / Sound Of Music

Complete BBC Recordings 1993

Exercise One / Insight / She's Lost Control / Transmission
/ Love Will Tear Us Apart / Twenty Four Hours / Colony / Sound Of Music
/ Transmission / She's Lost Control / Interview (Richard Skinner interviews Ian
Curtis and Stephen Morris)

Before And After 1995
As above plus New Order BBC tracks:
Touched By The Hand Of God / Temptation / True Faith / Your Silent Face
/ Every Second Counts / Bizarre Love Triangle / The Perfect Kiss
/ Age Of Consent / Sister Ray

New Order

SINGLES

Ceremony / In A Lonely Place Fac33 1981
Procession / Everything's Gone Green Fac 53 1981(Everything's Gone Green also released as a single on Factory Benelux)
Temptation / Hurt Fac 63 1982
Blue Monday / The Beach Fac73 1983
Confusion Fac93 1983
Thieves Like Us / Lonesome Tonight Fac103 1984
Perfect Kiss / The Kiss of Death Fac123 1985
Sub-culture Fac133 1985
Shellshock / Thieves Like Us (instrumental) Fac143 1986
State of the Nation / Shame of the Nation Fac153 1986
Bizarre Love Triangle Fac163 1986
True Faith /1963 Fac183 1987
Touched by the Hand of God / Touched by the Hand of Dub Fac193 1987
Blue Monday 1988 Fac73R 1988
Find Time / Don't Do It Fac223 1988
Round & Round / Best & Marsh Fac263 1989
Run 2/MTO Fac273 1989
World in Motion Fac293 1990 (ENGLANDneworder)
Regret NUOCD1 1993
Ruined in a Day NUOCD2 1993
World (The Price of Love) NUOCD3 1993
Spooky NUOCD4 1993
True Faith '94 NUOCD5 1994
Nineteen63 NUOCD6 1995
Blue Monday '95 NUOCD7 1995
Video 586 Tone7 1997
Crystal NUOCD8 2001
60 Miles an Hour NUOCD9 2001
Someone Like You NUOX10 2001
Here to Stay NUOCD11 2002
Confusion 2002 WACT002 2002
Krafty NUOCD13 2005
Jetstream NUOCD14 2005
Waiting for the Sirens' Call NUO15 2005
Guilt is a Useless Emotion Warner Bros (US) 2005

ALBUMS

Movement
FACT 50 1981
Dreams Never End / Truth / Senses / Chosen Time / I.C.B. / The Him / Doubts Even Here / Denial

Power, Corruption and Lies
FACT 75 1983
Age of Consent / We All Stand / The Village / 586 / Your Silent Face / Ultraviolence / Ecstasy / Leave Me Alone

Low-life
FACT 100 1985
Love Vigilantes / The Perfect Kiss / This Time of Night / Sunrise / Elegia / Sooner Than You Think / Sub-culture / Face Up

Brotherhood
FACT 150 1986
Paradise / Weirdo / As It Is When It Was / Broken Promise / Way of Life / Bizarre Love Triangle / All Day Long / Angel Dust / Every Little Counts / State of the Nation

Substance 1987
FACT 200 1987
Ceremony [re-recorded version from FAC 33T] / Everything's Gone Green / Temptation / Blue Monday / Confusion / Thieves Like Us / Perfect Kiss / Sub-culture / Shellshock / State of the Nation / Bizarre Love Triangle / True Faith

Technique
FACT 275 1989
Fine Time / All the Way / Love Less / Round & Round / Guilty Partner / Run / Mr. Disco / Vanishing Point / Dream Attack

Peel Sessions
Strange Fruit Records SFR LP 110
Truth / Senses / I.C.B. / Dreams Never End / Turn the Heater On / We All Stand / Too Late / 5-8-6

Republic
London / Centredate 828413 1993
*Regret / World / Ruined in a Day / Spooky / Everyone Everywhere
/ Young Offender / Liar / Chemical / Times Change / Special / Avalanche*

? – (The Best Of) New Order
London Records 828580 1994
*True Faith-94 / Bizarre Love Triangle-94 / 1963-94 / Regret / Fine Time
/ The Perfect Kiss / Shellshock / Thieves Like Us / Vanishing Point / Run 2 +
/ Round & Round-94 / World (The Price Of Love) / Ruined in a Day
/ Touched by the Hand of God / Blue Monday 1988 / World in Motion*

? – (The Rest Of) New Order
London Records 828661 1995
*World / Blue Monday / True Faith / Confusion / Touched by the Hand of God
/ Bizarre Love Triangle / Everything's Gone Green / Ruined In A Day / Regret
/ Temptation / Age Of Consent / Spooky*

Get Ready
London Records 89621 2001
*Crystal / 60 Miles an Hour / Turn My Way / Vicious Streak / Primitive Notion
/ Slow Jam / Rock the Shack / Someone Like You / Close Range / Run Wild*

International (Import)
Warner 0927492262 2002
*Ceremony / Blue Monday / Confusion / Thieves Like Us / Perfect Kiss
/ Shellshock / Bizarre Love Triangle [Extended Dance Mix] / True Faith
/ Touched by the Hand of God [Original 12"] / Round and Round / Regret
/ Crystal / 60 Miles an Hour / Here to Stay / True Faith (Video)
/ Perfect Kiss (Video) / Blue Monday (Video–Live)*

Retro
WEA / London Records 49499 2002
60 track four disc box set including remixes and live tracks

In Session
Strange Fruit SFRSCD128 2004
True Faith [John Peel Sessions 1998] / Isolation [John Peel Sessions 1998]
/ Touched by the Hand of God [John Peel Sessions 1998]
/ Atmosphere [John Peel Sessions 1998]
/ Paradise [John Peel Sessions 1998]
/ Slow Jam [BBC Evening Sessions 2001]
/ Your Silent Face [BBC Evening Sessions 2001]
/ Close Range [BBC Evening Sessions 2001]
/ Rock the Shack [BBC Evening Sessions 2001]
/ Transmission [video from John Peel Sessions 2002]

Waiting For The Sirens' Call
London / Warner Music 2202 2005
Who's Joe? / Hey Now What You Doing / Waiting for the Sirens' Call / Krafty
/ I Told You So / Morning Night and Day / Dracula's Castle / Jetstream
/ Guilt is a Useless Emotion / Turn / Working Overtime

Singles

London Records 2690 2005
Ceremony / Procession / Everything's Gone Green / Temptation / Blue Monday
/ Confusion / Thieves Like Us / Perfect Kiss / Subculture / Shellshock
/ State Of The Nation / Bizarre Love Triangle / True Faith / 1963
/ Touched by the Hand of God / Blue Monday / Fine Time
/ Round And Round / Run 2 / World In Motion / Regret / Ruined in a Day
/ World (Price Of Love) / Spooky / Crystal / 60 Miles An Hour / Here To Stay
/ Krafty / Jetstream / Waiting For The Sirens' Call / Turn

Electronic

SINGLES

Getting Away With It / *Lucky Bag* – Fac257 1989
Get the Message / *Free Will* – Fac287 1991
Feel Every Beat / *Lean To The Inside* / *Second To None* – Fac328 1991
Disappointed / *Idiot Country Two* – Parlophone 1992
Forbidden City / *Imitation of Life* / *A New Religion* – Parlophone 1996
For You / *All That I Need* / *I Feel Alright* – Parlophone 1996
Second Nature / *Turning Point* / *Feel Every Beat* – Parlophone 1997
Vivid / *Haze* / *Prodigal Son* – Parlophone 1999
Late at Night / *Warning Sign* / *Make It Happen* – Parlophone 1999
(Withdrawn)

ALBUMS

Electronic
FACT 290 1991
Idiot Country / *Reality* / *Tighten Up* / *The Patience Of A Saint* / *Gangster* / *Soviet* / *Get The Message* / *Try All You Want* / *Some Distant Memory* / *Feel Every Beat*

Raise the Pressure
Parlophone 1996
Forbidden City / *For You* / *Dark Angel* / *One Day* / *Until The End Of Time* / *Second Nature* / *If You've Got Love* / *Out Of My League* / *Interlude* / *Freefall* / *Visit Me* / *How Long* / *Time Can Tell*

Twisted Tenderness
Parlophone 1999
Make It Happen / *Haze* / *Vivid* / *Breakdown* / *Can't Find My Way Home* / *Twisted Tenderness* / *Like No Other* / *Late At Night* / *Prodigal Son* / *When She's Gone* / *Flicker*

Get the Message: The Best Of
Parlophone 2006
Forbidden City / Getting Away With It / Get The Message / Feel Every Beat / Disappointed / Vivid / Second Nature / All That I Need / Prodigal Son / For You / Imitation Of Life / Out Of My League / Like No Other / Twisted Tenderness / Late at Night.

Further collaborations

Singles / EP's

Section 25 – *The Beast*
Fac66 1982
Produced by Section 25, Jon Hurst and Bernard Sumner

Section 25 – *Back to Wonder*
Fac68 1983
BeMusic production + Bernard Sumner guitar

Section 25 – *Looking From a Hilltop*
Fac108 1984
Bernard Sumner / Donald Johnson remix

Shark Disco – *You Hurt Me*
Fac111 1984
Produced by Bernard Sumner

Paul Haig – *The Only Truth*
Crepuscule TWI 390 1984
Bernard Sumner guitar

Quando Quango – *Atom Rock / Triangle*
FAC 102 1984 / 85 Produced / Programming by Bernard Sumner

Section 25 – *Crazy Wisdom*
FBN 045 1985
Produced by Bernard Sumner

Happy Mondays – *Freaky Dancin'*
FAC 142 – 1986
Produced by Bernard Sumner

Section 25 – *Bad News Week*
Fac157 1987
Re-mix by Bernard Sumner

A Certain Ratio – *Won't Stop Loving You*
A&M ACRCD 540 1990
Bernard Sumner re-mix

The Beat Club – *Security*
CD ROB 01 1991
Features Bernard Sumner vocal

A Certain Ratio – *Shack Up*
Creation Records SCR 659374 2 1994
Produced by Bernard Sumner and Johnny Marr

Sub Sub – *This Time I'm Not Wrong*
Rob's Records ROB 53 1997
Features Bernard Sumner vocal

Chemical Brothers – *Out of Control*
Freestyle Dust CHEMSD10 1999
Co-written / Vocal by Bernard Sumner

Albums

Section 25 – *From the Hip*
FACT 90 – 1984
Produced by Bernard Sumner

Banderas – *Ripe*
FFRR 828 247-2 1991
Guitars / vocals Bernard Sumner

Primal Scream – *XTRMNTR*
Creation CRE239 – 2000
Features Bernard Sumner on guitar

Gwen Stefani – *Love, Angel, Music, Baby*
Polydor 2103177 – 2004
Track The Real Thing features Bernard Sumner and Peter Hook

BeMusic / Further Collaborations

Cool As Ice:
The Be Music Productions LTM 2377
52nd Street – *Can't Afford (To Let You Go)*
/ **Section 25** – *Looking From A Hilltop*
/ **Marcel King** – *Reach For Love*
/ **Quando Quango** – *Love Tempo*
/ **52nd Street** – *Cool As Ice*
/ **Paul Haig** – *The Only Truth*
/ **Quando Quango** – *Atom Rock*
/ **Thick Pigeon** – *Babcock + Wilcox*
/ **Nyam Nyam** – *Fate*
/ **Hate Life** – *Tell Me*
/ **Section 25** – *Beating Heart*
/ **BeMusic** – *Theme*

Twice As Nice
BeMusic / DoJo / Kamins / Arthur Baker Productions LTM 2398
52nd Street – *Express*
/ *Cheyne* – *Call Me Mr. Telephone*
/ *Quando Quango* – *Low Rider (400 Blows Remix)*
/ *Anna Domino* – *Summer (Arthur Baker Remix)*
/ *52nd Street* – *Look Into My Eyes*
/ *Quando Quango* – *Genius (Pt.2)*
/ *Marcel King* – *Keep On Dancing*
/ *Shark Vegas* – *You Hurt Me*
/ *New Order* – *Video 586 (Edit)*
/ *Section 25* – *Sakura*
/ *Thick Pigeon* – *Jess + Bart (Remix)*
/ *RFATP* – *Motherland*
/ *52nd Street* – *Cool As Ice (Jellybean Mix)*

Thanks to
Joy Division Central

New Order Discography Maintained by Torbjöörn Ivarsson.
Created by Richard P. Kernin and Dennis Remmer.

ALSO
AVAILABLE

FROM

INDEPENDENT MUSIC PRESS

Also available from Independent Music Press

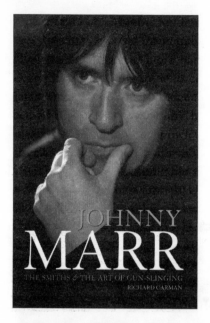

JOHNNY MARR: THE SMITHS & THE ART OF GUN-SLINGING
by Richard Carman

The Smiths were the best British band since The Beatles. Their shimmering, muscular, guitar-driven pop remains the barometer for everyone who looks back at the 1980s with affection. In a decade that arguably produced more poor pop music than any other since the 1950s, The Smiths shone like a beacon and inspired a generation of indie guitar bands, and their influence continues undiminished to this day. After The Smiths, Marr continued to inject beautiful, sophisticated guitar into some of the best music of the period: The Pretenders, Kirsty McColl, Billy Bragg, The The and Talking Heads all benefited from his incendiary input. More recently with his band Johnny Marr & The Healers,Johnny remains as influential and important as ever. This is the first full-length biography of Johnny Marr, looking beyond world of The Smiths and into the solo career of Britain's most influential guitar player of the last two decades – a tale coloured by exclusive interviews with people such as key Smiths insider Grant Showbiz, Billy Bragg and David Byrne. A must-read for anyone who cares about The Smiths as well as great rock or pop.

ISBN 0 9549704 8 9 208 Pages Paperback, 8pp b/w pics £12.99 World Rights

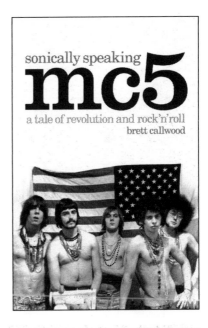

MC5: SONICALLY SPEAKING – A TALE OF PUNK ROCK AND REVOLUTION
by Brett Callwood

The first in-depth biography of the group, Sonically Speaking charts the career of this most seminal of bands, as well as unravelling what became of the members after the break up of the MC5. For this definitive book, author Brett Callwood travelled to Detroit and Los Angeles to track down and interview the three surviving founder members of the MC5 in-depth. He also spoke at length with other key players in this remarkable tale, such as former manager John Sinclair, artist Gary Grimshaw, former White Panther Pun Plamondon, Leni Sinclair, Jackson Smith – the son that MC5's Fred had with Patti Smith – and Russ Gibb, manager of the legendary Grandee Ballroom, among others.

ISBN 0 9552822-2-5 224 Pages Paperback, 12 b/w pics £12.99 World Rights

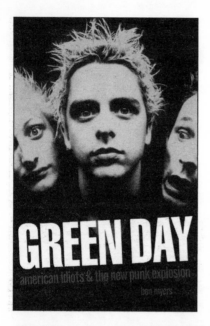

GREEN DAY: AMERICAN IDIOTS AND THE NEW PUNK EXPLOSION
by Ben Myers

The world's first and only full biography of Green Day. Self-confessed latch-key kids from small blue-collar Californian towns, Green Day have gone on to sell 50 million albums and single-handedly redefine the punk and rock genre for an entire generation. Inspired by both the energy of British punk bands as well as cult American groups, Green Day gigged relentlessly across the US underground before eventually signing to Warners and releasing their 1994 major label debut *Dookie*, which was a 10-million-selling worldwide hit album. With the arrival of Green Day, suddenly music was dumb, fun, upbeat and colourful again. Many now credit the band with saving rock from the hands of a hundred grunge-lite acts. In 2004 Green Day reached a career pinnacle with the concept album *American Idiot*, a sophisticated commentary on modern life - not least their dissatisfaction with their president. Myers is an authority on punk and hardcore and in this unauthorised book charts the band members' difficult childhoods and their rise to success, speaking to key members of the punk underground and music industry figures along the way.

ISBN 0 9539942 9 5 208 Pages Paperback, 8pp b/w pics £12.99 World Rights

I SWEAR I WAS THERE: THE GIG THAT CHANGED THE WORLD
by David Nolan

On June 4, 1976, four young men took the stage of a tiny upstairs hall in Manchester for a gig that, quite literally, *changed the world*. In front of a handful of people they played one of the most important live sets of all time. Alongside Woodstock and Live Aid, the Sex Pistols performance at the Lesser Free Trade Hall has been named by critics as one of the most pivotal performances in music history … not necessarily because of the quality of the music – but because of the effect the music had on the audience.

Members of Joy Division and New Order, the Smiths, the Fall and Buzzcocks were there that night as well as Tony Wilson. The truth behind that gig – plus the Pistols repeat performance six weeks later and their first ever TV appearance – has been shrouded in mystery for thirty years. Until now, everyone's been happy to print the legend. For the first time, here's the truth. Featuring previously unpublished photos and interviews with key players and audience members.

ISBN 0 9549704 9 7 208 Pages Paperback, 40 b/w pics £12.99 World Rights

Visit our website at *www.impbooks.com*
for more information on our full list of titles, including books on:

Bruce Dickinson, Slash, Damon Albarn,
MC5, Dave Grohl, Muse, The Streets,
Green Day, Ian Hunter, Mick Ronson,
David Bowie, The Killers, My Chemical Romance,
System Of A Down, The Prodigy and many more.